Guide to

BIRDS

of the Kruger National Park

Warwick Tarboton
& Peter Ryan

Published by Struik Nature
(an imprint of Penguin Random House
South Africa (Pty) Ltd)
Reg. No. 1953/000441/07

The Estuaries No. 4, Oxbow Crescent,
Century Avenue, Century City, 7441
PO Box 1144, Cape Town, 8000 South Africa

Visit **www.struiknature.co.za** and join the
Struik Nature Club for updates, news, events
and special offers.

First published in 2016

10 9 8 7 6 5 4

Print: 978 1 77584 449 5
ePUB: 978 1 77584 450 1
ePDF: 978 1 77584 451 8

MIX
Paper | Supporting
responsible forestry
FSC
www.fsc.org   FSC® C144853

Publisher: Pippa Parker
Managing editor: Helen de Villiers
Project manager: Roelien Theron
Editor: Joy Clack
Designer: Gillian Black
Cartographers: Michèle Tarboton,
Liezel Bohdanowicz (enhancement of
Kruger site map)

Reproduction by Michèle Tarboton and
Hirt & Carter Cape (Pty) Ltd
Printed and bound in China by RR Donnelley

Front cover: Saddle-billed storks
(male and female)
Back cover: (top to bottom) African
Jacana, Rattling Cisticola, Black-headed
Oriole, Bateleur, Woodland Kingfisher,
Southern Ground Hornbills
Spine: Crested Barbet
Title page: African Barred Owlet
Contents page: (left to right) Lappet-
faced, White-backed and Cape vultures

ACKNOWLEDGEMENTS

This book has benefited greatly from ideas, information and, especially, photographs provided
by friends and associates and we greatly appreciate their assistance. In particular we thank
David Allan, Garth Batchelor, Martin Benadie, André Botha, Patrick Cardwell, John Carlyon,
Hugh Chittenden, Derek Engelbrecht, Johann Grobbelaar, Joe Grosel, Trevor Hardaker, Joseph
Heymans, Peter and Bruce Lawson, Duncan McKenzie, Ivan Motlik, Richard Peek, Pieter and
Christine Roussouw, Philip Tarboton, Les Underhill, Ian Whyte and Nic Zimbatis.
    The information gathered by people who contributed bird atlas data to the 'Turning
Kruger Green' project has been invaluable, as has the Animal Demography Unit's willingness
to share these and other data collected during the course of the second South African
Bird Atlas Project (SABAP2). In this regard, Duncan McKenzie's contribution in particular
is acknowledged.
    We thank Pippa Parker and the staff at Struik Nature who contributed to the smooth
running of the book's production and, above all, Michèle Tarboton is thanked for the
hundreds of hours spent at the computer preparing the distribution maps and fine-tuning
the images that appear in the book.

CONTENTS

INTRODUCTION

The Kruger National Park offers a birding experience that is, in the opinion of many, unsurpassed anywhere in the world. Its sheer size is a major contributing factor to this, as is its accessibility and infrastructure of rest camps, bush camps, hiking trails, hides and lookout points. Another factor is its great road network, which enables a visitor to explore large parts of its two-million-hectare expanse with relative ease and in safety and comfort. One can easily spend weeks or months in the park crisscrossing it from north to south and east to west, staying in new places, covering new ground and encountering something different every day.

Part of the park's attraction for the birder is the diversity of landscapes across this great stretch of country that is essentially unmodified by man. There are open plains, undulating country dotted with granite inselbergs, much-dissected rock-strewn hills, deep cliff-lined gorges, large perennial rivers, small seasonal streams, pans and dams, and the ephemeral floodplains along the Limpopo and Luvuvhu rivers. These landscapes are cloaked with an equally diverse range of plant communities, from tall riparian forest and the widespread marula-knob thorn savannas to semi-arid mopane scrubland. Then there is the added diversity brought on by the changing seasons, from the heat in summer to the mildness in winter, the consequences of an unpredictable rainfall that brings with it both harrowing droughts and ruinous floods, and the effect of fires that briefly create extensive areas devoid of groundcover.

Intimately linked to all this, of course, is the diversity of birds recorded in the park. Particular vegetation types support suites of bird species specific to them. Summer brings a host of migrants, some from tropical Africa, others from the Palearctic. Winter brings forest species down from the Drakensberg escarpment. Floods that intermittently fill the temporary pans attract a variety of unusual tropical waterbirds, while droughts see a range of arid-country refugees, such as the Lark-like Bunting, pouring in from the Kalahari.

THE PARK'S AVIFAUNA
By our assessment, about 275 bird species are year-round residents in the park, another 80 are regular visitors and 20 more visit less regularly. Then there is an ever-growing list of vagrants, species recorded now and then, mostly well outside of their normal

Wetlands in the park, such as this one in the vicinity of Lower Sabie, vary greatly with rainfall, seasonally and across years.

ranges. Most of these 140 vagrants are listed at the end of the book, with a few included and illustrated in the main text. By adding these totals together, the bird list for the park currently stands at 518 species. Given the size of the park and its proximity to the escarpment forests, the highveld grasslands and the coastal plain, there is no end to new species, mostly vagrants from these biomes, that will possibly be added over time. One of the pleasures of birding in the park is finding and adding such birds to the list.

While the predatory cats – lion, leopard and cheetah especially – are a major draw-card for the more than 1.5 million people who visit the park each year, it is the incomparable assemblage of predatory birds that draws birders. Sixty-seven raptor species have been recorded in the park, among them 10 breeding eagle species, five resident vultures, six species of sparrowhawk and goshawk, bat hawks, cuckoo-hawks, harrier-hawks, falcons and kestrels, plus 10 owl species and at least a dozen migrant species from the Palearctic.

Many of the large eagles and vultures here were once common and widespread across the savanna regions of South Africa, but have long since disappeared as a result of deleterious land-use practices and a number of them are red-listed. Five of the park's vultures are ranked as 'Critically Endangered' or 'Endangered', the Martial Eagle is 'Vulnerable' and the Bateleur is 'Near-threatened'. Seeing such species in South Africa outside the park is an unusual event, yet within minutes of crossing into the park the chances are good that a Bateleur will sweep by overhead or that a circling kettle of high-soaring vultures will be spotted.

Waterbirds provide another great attraction – not the concentrations of tens of thousands of waterfowl that can be seen on some wetlands in the world, but a diverse and interesting assortment of river-living species complemented, in the years of high rainfall, by a large influx of tropical species, from Dwarf Bittern and Striped Crake to Black Coucal and African Openbill, that come to breed on the ephemeral pans and vleis. More than a hundred waterbird species have been recorded in the park and about half of these, mostly river-living species, are resident. They include, for example, healthy populations of Goliath Heron, Saddle-billed Stork, African Fish Eagle and White-crowned Lapwing, and small numbers of African Finfoot and White-backed Night Heron.

All but a few of the park's terrestrial birds – these numbering about 40 species – are resident. They range from the very large and conspicuous (Common Ostrich, Southern Ground Hornbill, Kori Bustard) to gamebirds, lapwings and coursers, sandgrouse, larks and pipits. Some species in this group, the ground hornbill being a prime example, are sedentary, living year-round in well-defined, long-established territories; others, especially coursers, lapwings and pipits, are nomadic, moving about locally in response to the effects of fires and grazing pressure on the groundcover.

Kori Bustard males display like this at communal leks at the start of the breeding season.

The White-crowned Lapwing's carpal spur projects prominently from the bend of the wing.

Female Magpie Shrikes may be distinguished from males by the white patches on their flanks.

In White-fronted Bee-eaters the sexes are alike and males and females mate for life.

A large proportion of the smaller bird species found in the park (passerines and near-passerines) are insectivorous. Some of these are very conspicuous, rollers, bee-eaters, Magpie Shrikes and Fork-tailed Drongos, for example, while others are more skulking, such as chats, thrushes, warblers, bushshrikes and others. It is in the ranks of these insectivores that most of the migratory species are to be found, and it is with them that the contrast between birding in the park in summer and in winter is most noticeable. The arrival of tens of thousands of migrant birds in the park at the start of summer, and their departure five or six months later, is one of the largely unwitnessed wonders in the bird calendar. Many of them come south from the tropics to the park to breed, returning here under cover of darkness yet unerringly homing in on the previous year's nesting area. Others come to spend their off-season in the park and examples of these are the flocks of European Bee-eaters and Barn Swallows one sees in summer, ranging widely in response to changing insect availability.

An inventory of the park's more significant avifauna would be incomplete without a mention of the Red-billed Quelea. This gregarious, sparrow-sized seed-eating bird comes and goes in the park, as it does across southern Africa, in numbers that almost defy belief. In high-rainfall summers when a massive yield of grass seed is produced, queleas arrive in the park in vast numbers – 33.5 million birds was the estimate in one summer.

They rapidly establish huge breeding colonies that cover dozens of hectares in which every tree is filled with nests. Breeding takes a month to complete, after which the birds disperse and eventually disappear until the next big seed-crop. The nesting colonies are quickly discovered by predators, which pack in to take advantage of the easy pickings – eagles, vultures, hawks, storks, snakes, monitor lizards, even leopards and lions come to the feast. Such predators take their toll inside the park, whereas elsewhere in southern Africa quelea colonies are destroyed wherever they are found on account of their impact on the crops of small-grain farmers.

GEOLOGY, CLIMATE AND BIRDLIFE

In broad terms, the park's underlying geology is divided along a north–south axis into Archaean granite/gneiss/schists in the western half of the park and Karoo basalt in the eastern half. The Archaean rocks in the west give rise to coarse-grained, sandy soils with a low clay content, whereas in the east the soils derived from the basalt have a high clay content and are nutrient-rich.

Topographically the two sides of the park also differ. The western side is mainly undulating country with granite inselbergs in places and is much dissected by drainage lines, whereas the eastern side, underlain by the basalt, consists mostly of open plains against the eastern backdrop of the Lebombo Mountains. The granites are well wooded, but grass cover is often sparse and sour. Here, south of the Olifants River, *Combretum*

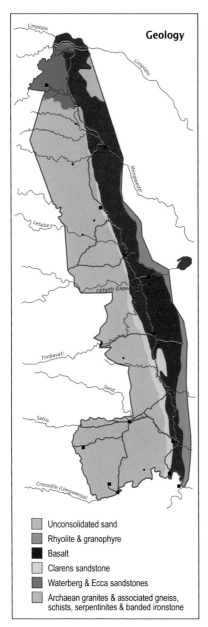

Geology

- Unconsolidated sand
- Rhyolite & granophyre
- Basalt
- Clarens sandstone
- Waterberg & Ecca sandstones
- Archaean granites & associated gneiss, schists, serpentinites & banded ironstone

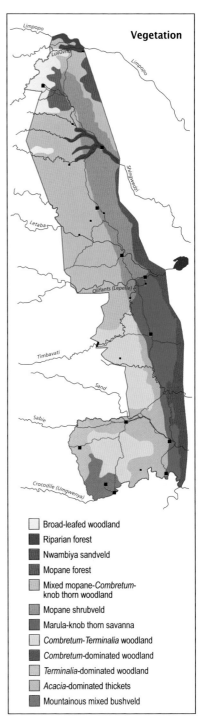

Vegetation

- Broad-leafed woodland
- Riparian forest
- Nwambiya sandveld
- Mopane forest
- Mixed mopane-*Combretum*-knob thorn woodland
- Mopane shrubveld
- Marula-knob thorn savanna
- *Combretum-Terminalia* woodland
- *Combretum*-dominated woodland
- *Terminalia*-dominated woodland
- *Acacia*-dominated thickets
- Mountainous mixed bushveld

species dominate the woodland whereas north of this it is dominated by mopane. The basaltic soils along the eastern side support a dense grass cover, but tree cover is often sparser, dominated by marula and knob thorn south of the Olifants River and by mopane shrubland north of it. Distribution maps of many of the bird species reflect this dichotomy: a number of the smaller, insectivorous, tree-living birds, for example, are more common and sometimes exclusively restricted to the granites, whereas many plains-living or open-grassland species such as Secretarybird, bustards, migratory harriers and Black Coucal are confined to the eastern side of the park.

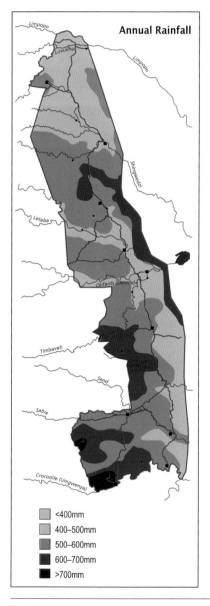

Other geological formations become apparent at a finer resolution. Along the granite/basalt divide running north–south is a discontinuous outcrop of Karoo-age sandstone, at its widest south of the Olifants River. It supports a distinctive thicket community dominated by *Acacia* species and this thicket extends out westwards along the drainage lines of the Sabie and Crocodile rivers. The Lebombos, a ridge of high ground along the eastern boundary, are made up of weather-resistant, Karoo-age rhyolite and granophyre and the soils here are shallow and stony. In the far north, around Punda Maria, Waterberg and Ecca sandstones outcrop extensively and the soils derived from these are fine-grained sand that are low in nutrients. The broad-leafed woodland ('sandveld') here is distinctive with many unusual plant species represented and several unusual birds too. West of Punda Maria along the Mozambique border is a second distinctive sandveld community known as the Nwambiya sandveld that grows on recent wind-blown sands.

Etched across this geologically diverse landscape are the rivers that drain off the escarpment west of the park and, at intervals across the park, traverse it from west to east. They have scoured out valleys into the underlying geology and have filled these in places with wide expanses of nutrient-rich alluvial soils that support tall, dense, evergreen woodland/forest. These riparian belts provide corridors for the seasonal movements of forest-living birds between the forested escarpment to the west and the coastal plain to the east, and they give lowland forest-associated species (Trumpeter Hornbill, for example) access to the park from the east.

The park's bird fauna has been further increased by the presence of cliff-lined gorges where the rivers have cut through resistant rocks, the best examples being along the Luvuvhu River ('Lanner Gorge') and through the rhyolite where the Olifants River has cut through the Lebombos. Some rivers, especially the Limpopo and Luvuvhu, have developed floodplains with cut-off oxbow lakes along their margins, these filling and drying in response to river flow, bringing with them influxes of tropical waterbirds when they fill.

The park receives its rainfall in summer, mainly between October and March, but how much rain falls varies tremendously, both regionally across the park and from year to year. The highest rainfall area in the park is the southwest, with Berg-en-Dal rest camp averaging 805mm per annum. This declines northwards, Olifants rest camp receiving, on average, 459mm per annum and Shingwedzi rest camp 427mm per annum. The Limpopo River valley receives the least rainfall, Pafuri Gate averaging 359mm per annum. The rainfall is seldom consistent from year to year, though, with El Niño-driven oscillations resulting in cycles, each lasting about 10 years, of above-average and then below-average rain years. Above-average rain years result in dams, river floodplains and seasonal pans filling and attracting many waterbirds not otherwise present in the park. In below-average rain years, especially in the drier north, the park is visited by numerous dry-country bird species. The distribution maps for many of the park's birds reveal that they favour either the wetter southern half of the park (Burchell's Starling, Red-chested and Black cuckoos, for example) or the drier northern half (Dusky Lark, Namaqua Dove, for example).

BIRDING IN THE PARK

For the most part, birding in the park is done from a vehicle and this, of course, has pros and cons. The vehicle acts as a hide and so enables one to get closer to birds than would be the case if you were on foot, and for photographers the vehicle's door provides support for a large lens. It can be frustrating, though, being confined to a vehicle when there is a tantalising call coming from a thicket just out of range, or not being able to explore fully an interesting place on foot.

Those who want to walk in the bush can sign up for one of the organised trails in which prearranged groups accompany on foot a field guide and armed guard. There are also many picnic sites, lookout points and hides where one can get out of a vehicle, and time spent at these can be very rewarding. The rest camps themselves offer good birding opportunities too, and camps such as Skukuza, Lower Sabie, Letaba and Shingwedzi, which look out across rivers, provide birding opportunities as good as those to be had when out driving. Organised night drives are arranged at all the larger camps and these provide a great opportunity to see nocturnal species, especially owls, nightjars and coursers.

There is some birding interest to be had in the park in every month of the year but, overall, birding is more productive in summer than in winter. This is partly because there is more water about, fruit and seed production is at its peak, many migrant species are present, and breeding for most species is in full swing, so song, displaying and nesting-related activities are observable everywhere. On the other hand, in winter the climate is milder and more pleasant, there is less foliage and so visibility is better, and most of the larger raptors breed at this time.

All parts of the park provide birding opportunities. However, as the species

The bird hide at Lake Panic near Skukuza rest camp is one of many such hides in the park.

distribution maps show, many species are restricted to one or other section of the park and if they are being sought, then their areas need to be visited. For birders, the far north has special appeal as a dozen or more tropical species occur here that cannot be seen elsewhere in the park.

Several ongoing bird research projects are being undertaken in the park and the researchers involved in these always welcome information from the public, especially relating to the positions of wing-tagged, colour-ringed or tattooed birds. For example, there are ongoing projects on the Martial Eagle, Southern Ground Hornbill and all the vulture species in the park and many of these birds wear coloured rings or wing tags that allow them to be individually identified. Where such individuals can be identified (and preferably photographed) and their position accurately recorded, the information should be forwarded to the researcher involved.

The male Southern Ground Hornbill can be identified by its all-red throat.

ABOUT THIS BOOK

DISTRIBUTION MAPS

The distribution maps for each species are courtesy of the University of Cape Town's Animal Demography Unit and the Second Southern African Bird Atlas Project (SABAP2). As part of this programme, a concerted effort was made to collect distribution data for birds in the park, this being known as the 'Turning Kruger Green' (TKG) project (green being a measure of atlas coverage), and it has contributed in no small measure to the exceptional coverage achieved in the park.

Each dot on a map marks a 'pentad' in which the species was recorded at least once. A 'pentad' (5 minutes longitude x 5 minutes latitude) measures about 8km x 9km and covers an area of about 70km². The park is covered by 283 pentads. Small dots indicate a low recording rate and large dots a high recording rate in each pentad.

Different colour tones are used to indicate resident species and visitors. Green dots are used for resident species and red dots for visitors. The maps also show the distribution of species beyond the park's boundary, so as to include coverage of the adjacent, privately owned conservation sections in the west and non-conservation territories

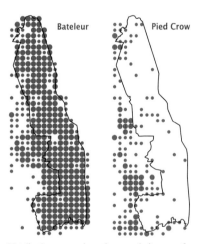

Distribution maps show the recorded range of resident species (green dots) and non-resident species (red dots) in the park.

in the southwest, where there are extensive urbanised areas and areas under intense agriculture. The spread of dots on the maps thus provides a quick overview of the species' relative abundance and distribution in and alongside the park.

Comparing distributions inside and outside the park sometimes reveals startling contrasts. See, for example, the maps for Pied Crow (p134) (common outside the park, rare inside), or Bateleur (p48) and Crested Francolin (p58) (common inside, rare outside).

A constraint with a mapping project of this nature is that not all species are equally detectable, and when making comparisons between maps of different species this must be taken into account. The map of a common, easily detectable species such as a Lilac-breasted Roller (p110), for example, indicates that it is uniformly abundant throughout the park, whereas a less easily detectable species which numerically may be more abundant than a roller, Square-tailed Nightjar (p96), for example, has a map that suggests the opposite is the case.

SPECIES ACCOUNTS

The English and Afrikaans bird names used in this book are those adopted by BirdLife South Africa. The scientific names, in the few instances where they differ from those used by BirdLife, follow the most recent World Bird List of the International Ornithological Congress. The list is available at **www.worldbirdnames.org**.

The family sequence applied in this book largely follows that used in the fourth edition of *Sasol Birds of Southern Africa*, this being the sequence that is familiar to most birders in the region.

The average length and average weight of each species come from measurements given in the seventh edition of *Roberts' Birds of Southern Africa*, but in a few instances where the sample size was small this was supplemented with bird-ringing data.

We list all the bird species that have been reliably reported in the park in recent decades, but vagrants and very rarely recorded species are listed at the back, separate from the more frequently recorded species for which distribution maps and more comprehensive species accounts are provided.

The species accounts provide an up-to-date record of the status and preferred range and habitat of each species. These accounts give the bird's average length, weight and, in larger species that soar, average wingspan. Following this is a brief outline of the bird's diagnostic features and, if the sexes differ, how they

In the species accounts, photographs of rarer species, such as the Jackal Buzzard shown here, are included alongside images of more common, similar-looking species (for example, Steppe Buzzard) to aid identification.

are distinguished. Brief identification pointers are provided where a species can be confused with others in the park; and distinctive call-notes are described for species that are often undetectable except from their calls, or where their calls distinguish them from other similar-looking species. Where it is known, the estimated size of the population in the park is given.

'Resident' species occur year-round in the park; 'visitors' may occur seasonally (for example, in summer or winter) or erratically, in response to rainfall-linked events. A bird's relative abundance in the park is denoted by the terms 'very common', 'common', 'fairly common', 'uncommon', 'scarce' or 'rare'. Vagrants and rarely recorded species (i.e. those unlikely to be encountered by visitors to the park) are not given this treatment, although, in some instances, they are mentioned in the text of a more common, similar-looking species.

ABBREVIATIONS USED

(♂) – male	(♀) – female
ad – adult	sub-ad – sub-adult
imm – immature	juv – juvenile
br – breeding	
non-br – non-breeding	

OSTRICH, SECRETARYBIRD AND GROUND HORNBILL

These tree large, charismatic and terrestrial birds, all in small families, are confined to Africa. Most Ostriches in South Africa are derived from domesticated stock; only those in the Kruger and Kgalagadi parks are remnants of wild populations. The Secretarybird is an extraordinary long-legged terrestrial raptor that looks for prey as it walks over open ground, as do Southern Ground Hornbills. Both species are red-listed as Vulnerable, with numbers decreasing due to bush encroachment and infrastructure impacts (electrocution, fence and powerline collisions).

COMMON OSTRICH
Struthio camelus

♂**2.4m,** ♀**1.8m,** ♂**128kg,** ♀**100kg** The world's largest, heaviest and fastest-running bird, and the continent's only flightless terrestrial bird. Ad male larger, black with white wings and tail; female and juv smaller with brown body and dirty white wings and tail. The park's population numbers about 450 birds, which may be encountered anywhere, although most common in open country on basaltic soils in the eastern half of the park. Gregarious; lives in small groups year-round. Multiple females lay eggs in the same nest but only the alpha female and male incubate (female by day, male by night). The female can recognise her own eggs from their pore pattern and ensures they remain in the centre of the clutch where they are less likely to be predated. Ostriches are capable of running at 70km/h in short bursts, and can sustain 50km/h for up to 30 minutes. VOLSTRUIS

SECRETARYBIRD
Sagittarius serpentarius

1.38m, 4.0kg A huge, long-legged raptor, usually encountered walking steadily through open country. Scarce breeding resident throughout the park. Pairs remain together year-round and occupy large (50–100km²) territories; juvs wander widely. Typically walks at 2–3km/h, looking down to search for grasshoppers and other insects, rodents, snakes and lizards. Small prey are swallowed whole; snakes and rodents are trampled before being swallowed. Atlassing data indicate that numbers in the park declined dramatically between 1990 and 2010, probably due to bush encroachment, linked at least in part to increased levels of atmospheric carbon dioxide. SEKRETARISVOËL

SOUTHERN GROUND HORNBILL
Bucorvus leadbeateri

1.1m, ♂**4.2kg,** ♀**3.3kg** Large, black turkey-like birds with white primary feathers visible in flight. Male has all-red facial skin; female facial skin is red with blue below the bill; juv and imm facial skin is dull yellow. Takes 6–8 years to reach sexual maturity. Commonly encountered resident; lives in family groups year-round, typically numbering 3–5 (rarely 2–11) birds. Methodically walks the veld looking for insects, reptiles, small mammals and birds. Groups roost together at night in tall trees. Each group occupies a large territory (approx. 100km²; smaller when breeding) from which other groups are excluded; one of the characteristic sounds at dawn is these birds' deep rhythmic booming call, 'hudu hudu hududu', audible from 3km away. Only the alpha pair in each group breeds, laying two eggs in a hole in a large tree. Other group members assist with food provisioning and nest defence but, at most, only one young is reared per year. Reproductive rate is very low, with no breeding attempted in some years. Lack of suitable nest cavities may limit the population; artificial nests erected in adjacent reserves have greatly improved chick production. Some second-hatched chicks are collected to bolster a captive population used for reintroductions elsewhere in its former range. The park is a critical stronghold for this vulnerable species. BROMVOËL

Common Ostrich ♂

Common Ostrich ♀

Secretarybird

Secretarybird

Southern Ground Hornbill ♂ and ♀   Southern Ground Hornbill imm and ♀

GREBES, CORMORANTS AND DARTERS

These three waterbird families spend much of their time diving for food, using their feet for propulsion. Grebes are the closest relatives of flamingos; only three species occur in sub-Saharan Africa, of which the Little Grebe is the smallest. Cormorants and darters are closely related families that are unusual among waterbirds in not having fully waterproof feathers. This reduces their buoyancy, making it easier to dive, but also their insulation, which means they cannot remain in the water for long and have to warm up between feeding bouts. Cormorants have sharply hooked bills for grasping slippery prey, whereas darters have sharp, dagger-like bills with fine, backward-pointing serrations that are used to spear their prey.

LITTLE GREBE
Tachybaptus ruficollis

20cm, 146g Small size, rufous head and rounded, fluffy appearance distinguish it from ducks and other waterbirds. Head rufous when breeding, dull buff at other times. Gape spot white in ad; bill yellowish in juv. Found singly, in pairs or in small groups on dams and pans, seldom on rivers; very rarely seen on land. Nomadic, occurring widely but erratically; present in good numbers in years of high rainfall. Breeds on nests of floating vegetation in pans with emergent plants. Feeds on aquatic insects and small fish. Orientates back to sun and raises back feathers to warm passively; sleeks down back feathers before diving. Call is a distinctive, high-pitched trill: 'tr-r-r-r-r-r-r-r-r-r-r-r'. KLEINDOBBERTJIE

WHITE-BREASTED CORMORANT
Phalacrocorax lucidus

90cm, 1.8kg A large, heavy-bodied cormorant. Ad has white chest, juv has white chest and belly; both are much larger than Reed Cormorant, with a shorter tail and longer bill. A rather scarce resident, found mainly along the large perennial rivers and occasionally on larger dams. Occurs singly or in small groups while feeding; roosts communally with other cormorants and herons at night. Breeds colonially in winter after summers of high rainfall; nest a large pile of dead twigs built in a tree or on an island, often with other waterbirds. WITBORSDUIKER

REED CORMORANT
Microcarbo africanus

55cm, 550g A small, slender cormorant with a long tail and short bill. Ad black with pale-centred back feathers; juv much smaller, with off-white underparts and a shorter bill and longer tail than White-breasted Cormorant. Common resident on perennial rivers and dams. Found singly or in groups; flocks often commute to and from communal roosts at dusk and dawn. Hunts fish and frogs by diving underwater, emerging every 20–30 sec before diving again. Groups sometimes hunt together, herding fish schools into the shallows; often attended by other fish-eating birds (Little Egret, Pied Kingfisher, Hamerkop). Shares breeding sites with darters, herons and ibises. RIETDUIKER

AFRICAN DARTER
Anhinga rufa

90cm, 1.5kg Resembles a cormorant with a very long, slender neck and long, corrugated tail; juv is paler buff brown. Fairly common but localised resident on dams and large rivers. Solitary when foraging but joins other waterbirds at communal roosts. Soars well. Commonly called Snake-bird because it swims with its body submerged and just the head and neck exposed. Saturated plumage allows it to hang motionless underwater. Catches fish and frogs by shooting out its long neck and impaling them with its bill, bringing them to the surface where they are thrown into the air and then swallowed head first. After fishing, warms up with wings spread and back facing the sun. Shares breeding sites with cormorants, herons and ibises. SLANGHALSVOËL

Little Grebe

Little Grebe non-br

White-breasted Cormorant

White-breasted Cormorant

Reed Cormorant

Reed Cormorant imm

Reed Cormorant

African Darter

African Darter

LARGE HERONS

Herons, egrets and bitterns are a cosmopolitan family of mainly aquatic birds that have long necks, legs and bills. They vary in habits and plumage, and especially size, ranging from the massive Goliath Heron to the pigeon-sized Dwarf Bittern. The names 'heron' and 'egret' have no evolutionary significance; the main division is between the diurnal herons and the stockier, shorter-necked and shorter-billed night-herons and bitterns. Most species breed colonially, often with other waterbirds such as ibises, cormorants and darters, in trees or reedbeds, but some breed singly in dense reeds or trees.

GREY HERON
Ardea cinerea

94cm, 1.5kg The most commonly seen heron in the park. Ad distinguished from similar-sized Black-headed Heron by yellow bill (orange-pink at start of the breeding season), white head and neck and, in flight, all-grey (not black-and-white) underwings; juvs of both species similar with grey bills, distinguished by whitish (not grey) cheeks. Often gives a harsh croaking call when flushed. Found along rivers and on dams and pans. Resident, but individuals move widely in response to changing water conditions. A solitary species except when roosting and breeding; individuals defend feeding sites. Stands patiently in water or walks slowly, rarely swims; even drops onto prey from the air. Feeds almost entirely on aquatic prey, mainly fish and frogs. BLOUREIER

BLACK-HEADED HERON
Ardea melanocephala

92cm, 1.4kg Ad distinguished from similar-sized Grey Heron by black bill, black-and-white head and neck and, in flight, contrasting black-and-white (not plain grey) underwings; juvs of both species similar with grey bills, distinguished by dark grey (not white) cheeks. Rather scarce and nomadic, found mostly in open grassy areas along the margins of the larger rivers. Unusual among herons in that it mainly feeds in terrestrial habitats, stalking its prey in open grass. Feeds on grasshoppers and other insects, also rodents and small reptiles, impaling them with its bill and swallowing them whole. Molerats are a favoured prey; strikes when the molerat brings fresh soil to the surface at molehills. SWARTKOPREIER

GOLIATH HERON
Ardea goliath

1.43m, 4.3kg, wingspan 2–2.3m A rich rufous heron, resembling the much smaller Purple Heron, but has an unmarked rufous face (not black-striped) and dark grey (not yellowish) bill. Common but localised resident, restricted to larger rivers and dams. A solitary species except when breeding; individuals mostly encountered as scattered, spaced widely apart along rivers. Forages by wading slowly and methodically in water up to 0.5m deep, head tilted as it watches for movement. Fish in the size range 300–400g form the bulk of its diet but frogs and other animals are also taken. Pairs nest solitarily in large trees overhanging water. REUSEREIER

PURPLE HERON
Ardea purpurea

85cm, 870g A rich rufous heron that resembles the much larger Goliath Heron, but has black stripes across face and yellowish (not dark grey) bill. Scarce, localised resident, found mostly along the reedbed-fringed sections of the Sabie and Crocodile rivers. Hunts solitarily along water edges with tall emergent vegetation where it is easily overlooked, keeping still when sensing danger. Coloration blends with the reeds. ROOIREIER

Grey Heron

Black-headed Heron

Goliath Heron

Purple Heron

Goliath Heron

Grey Heron

Black-headed Heron

Purple Heron

EGRETS

The names 'egret' and *Egretta* come from the French *aigrette*, which refers to the elaborate nuptial plumes acquired by many species on their backs and/or breasts at the start of the breeding season, and which are fanned during displays. Bill colour and facial skin colour also change at onset of breeding. Egrets and herons have powder down feathers on the breast, which release fine particles to mop grease off their plumage. Preening is assisted by their comb-like toenails.

GREAT EGRET · *Ardea alba*

95cm, 1.1kg A large, heron-sized egret. Breeding ad has black bill and green facial skin; non-breeding birds have yellow bills and faces. Told from smaller Yellow-billed Egret by their longer neck, larger bill (longer than head), all-black legs and gape that extends past the eyes. Occurs widely and fairly commonly, mostly along the larger rivers; nomadic, moving about in response to changing water conditions. Solitary birds are encountered most often, typically seen hunting for fish in shallow water by wading, still hunting or in pursuit. In years of high rainfall, when rivers expand onto adjacent floodplains, this species breeds colonially, especially along the Limpopo River. GROOTWITREIER

YELLOW-BILLED EGRET · *Egretta intermedia*

69cm, 384g Easily mistaken for non-breeding Great Egret; distinguished by smaller size, shorter neck, shorter bill (shorter than head), gape that only extends to below the eyes, and legs that are yellow above the 'knee'. Larger than Western Cattle Egret, with longer bill and legs and all-white plumage. Pre-breeding ad has orange-red bill and upper legs and green facial skin. An uncommon visitor to the park; favours flooded grass rather than open water for foraging. Several birds sometimes hunt in loose association. GEELBEKWITREIER

LITTLE EGRET · *Egretta garzetta*

64cm, 530g Long, slender black bill and black legs with yellow feet are diagnostic. Ad has head plume. Pre-breeding ad has violet facial skin and reddish toes; juv has green-yellow facial skin and bill base. Occurs widely throughout the park on the larger rivers and dams. Single birds are usually encountered, wading briskly in shallow water in pursuit of small fish, sometimes sprinting after an escaping fish, half-opening their wings to maintain balance. Also foot-stirs in muddy water to lure prey closer. When a Reed Cormorant comes into shallow water, they often follow it, hoping for fish the cormorant misses. KLEINWITREIER. **Black Heron** *E. ardesiaca* (Swartreier) is an uncommon visitor; plumage blackish.

WESTERN CATTLE EGRET · *Bulbulcus ibis*

54cm, 360g A small, dry-land egret. Breeding ad has diagnostic buff-coloured filoplumes on crown, chest and back; non-breeding bird is all-white with yellow bill and variably coloured legs. Easily mistaken for larger, longer-billed Yellow-billed Egret. A common, gregarious species, also known as Tick Birds; often associated with grazing animals, which function as beaters for grasshoppers and other insect prey. Although common and abundant wherever there are cattle just outside the park, they are scarce within the park, where they associate mainly with buffalo, elephant, rhino and hippo. Often seen commuting in flocks at dawn and dusk; roosts in trees or reedbeds. A few remain year-round but most disperse northwards in winter. VEEREIER

Great Egret br

Yellow-billed Egret

Little Egret

Western Cattle Egret

SMALL HERONS, NIGHT HERONS AND BITTERNS

Herons, like many other waterbird species, are highly mobile. Among the small herons, only the Green-backed Heron is resident in the park; the others come and go in response to areas flooding and drying out. The small herons and bitterns tend to remain in dense cover and are less obtrusive than the large herons and egrets. As their name suggests, the night herons are mainly active at night; they roost during the day in dense trees, emerging at dusk to hunt.

SQUACCO HERON
Ardeola ralloides

43cm, 248g In flight, the white wings and tail may result in confusion with Western Cattle Egret but unmistakable when seen close up. Occurs widely but sparsely throughout the park, along rivers and on the margins of dams where there are emergent reeds, sedges or grass. Solitary except when breeding. Its scientific name *ralloides* ('like a rail') reflects its furtive nature: it often remains concealed in vegetation and freezes when threatened. Stalks prey – mainly small fish and frogs – by slowly picking its way through flooded vegetation, pausing at intervals. When it detects prey, it very slowly extends its head and neck before lunging forward. RALREIER

GREEN-BACKED HERON (Striated Heron)
Butorides striata

41cm, 215g Easily mistaken for the smaller Dwarf Bittern (p22), especially in flight when diagnostic breast markings are not visible. Common resident; pairs defend territories along most perennial rivers and streams that are fringed by overhanging trees. They are not shy, but are easily overlooked; often only seen once a bird flies off, uttering its characteristic '*chowk*' flight call. Hunts small fish by stealth, remaining in one position close to the water, tensed up with neck extended forwards, ready to strike when prey comes into range. Occasionally uses bait to attract fish, dropping a grasshopper or even just a leaf into the water. GROENRUGREIER

WHITE-BACKED NIGHT HERON
Gorsachius leuconotus

54cm, 450g A compact, nocturnal heron with a rufous neck and white spectacles; juv duller than ad with streaked neck and white spotted wing coverts. Easily overlooked, as it roosts in dense trees overhanging water during the day. Resident; recorded widely but sparsely, mostly along larger perennial rivers; probably more common than the few records suggest. After dark, pairs emerge from their roosts to forage in areas of shallow open water where they fish from rocks, causeways and sandy edges. Breeds singly in dense trees over water. WITRUGNAGREIER

BLACK-CROWNED NIGHT HERON
Nycticorax nycticorax

56cm, 630g A compact, nocturnal heron; ad striking black, grey and white; juv brown with white spots. Recorded widely but sparsely throughout the park, usually along wooded streams and along the verges of larger rivers. Typically roosts in small flocks in dense trees or reedbeds by day, when it is easily overlooked. Circles overhead when disturbed from roosts, occasionally giving a harsh '*haark*' call. Forage at night; at dusk they fly to areas of shallow water where they stalk-hunt fish and frogs. GEWONE NAGREIER

Squacco Heron non-br

Squacco Heron br

Green-backed Heron

Green-backed Heron imm

White-backed Night Heron

Black-crowned Night Heron

Black-crowned Night Heron imm

DWARF BITTERN
Ixobrychus sturmii

30cm, 150g Smaller than Green-backed Heron (p20) with diagnostic breast markings and different habitat. A tropical migrant that visits the park in years of above-average rainfall when seasonal pans and low-lying areas flood. The birds arrive within days of flooding, typically in early January, and quickly pair off; males utter a dog-like bark from flooded trees and bushes to attract a female. Breeding is completed within two months and by late April most birds have disappeared. Eats mainly frogs, which are hunted in flooded grass, mostly at dusk and after dark. DWERGRIETREIER. **Little Bittern** *I. minutus* (Kleinrietreier) is a scarce resident or summer visitor. Skulks in dense reeds; usually only seen in flight, when its pale buff wing coverts, neck and underparts contrast with its green-black crown, back, tail and flight feathers.

HAMERKOP, IBISES AND SPOONBILLS

The Hamerkop is the only member of its family; it is distantly related to pelicans and the Shoebill, and is confined to the Afrotropics, including Madagascar. Ibises and spoonbills are fairly large birds with distinctively shaped bills. They mostly feed in aquatic habitats, although the Hadeda Ibis is a dry-land species. Two aquatic ibises are irregular visitors.

HAMERKOP
Scopus umbretta

56cm, 500g A fairly large, chocolate-brown wading bird with a heavy black bill and shaggy crest. A common resident, found wherever there is surface water, including rivers, dams and pans. Mostly solitary when feeding but up to a dozen may roost together in a tree. Gives a loud yipping call in flight or when displaying. A frog- and fish-hunting specialist; wades slowly in shallow water, sometimes moving its feet to flush prey or raising its wings for balance. Pairs construct a huge, domed nest of plant material in a tree or on a cliff ledge; many disused nests are occupied by genets, owls, geese or other birds. HAMERKOP

HADEDA IBIS
Bostrychia hagedash

76cm, 1.3kg A short-legged, olive green ibis with iridescent wing coverts. Fairly common resident throughout; confiding; frequently forages on rest camp lawns. Although not an aquatic species, it often forages on damp ground near rivers and streams, probing for invertebrates. Gregarious; usually in small groups even when breeding. Well known for its raucous call *'ha, ha, ha-aa'* (hence its name); when several birds call simultaneously the noise can be deafening. Breeds and roosts in trees. HADEDA. **Glossy Ibis** *Plegadis falcinellus* (Glansibis) is smaller, more slender and longer-legged than Hadeda Ibis. **African Sacred Ibis** *Threskiornis aethiopicus* (Skoorsteenveër) is white with black head, neck (adult) and tips to the flight feathers. Both species are uncommon visitors to dams and pans throughout the park.

AFRICAN SPOONBILL
Platalea alba

83cm, 1.6kg A tall, white wading bird with reddish legs, face and spoon-tipped bill; male longer-billed than female. Fairly common nomad on rivers and dams throughout the park; seldom remains in one place for long. Usually forages singly or in small groups in shallow water, especially in pools along the large rivers. Prey is mainly detected by feel; it typically sweeps its partly submerged, slightly opened bill from side to side while moving slowly forward; also actively pursues small fish. Other prey includes aquatic invertebrates and frogs. LEPELAAR

Dwarf Bittern

Hamerkop

Little Bittern ♂

Hadeda Ibis

African Sacred Ibis

Glossy Ibis

African Spoonbill

CICONIA STORKS

Storks are large wading birds with long necks and bills. They can soar well and routinely use thermals to gain height – whether travelling between adjacent wetlands or continents. They are easily recognised by their broad, deeply slotted wings, long legs and long necks, which are extended in flight. Storks are silent birds except at the nest, where mates greet each other with loud bill-clattering. The *Ciconia* storks have dagger-like bills, which are linked to their generalised diets; other stork genera have varied bill shapes, adapted for specific feeding techniques and diets.

WHITE STORK
Ciconia ciconia

1.1m, 3.5kg, wingspan 1.6m A mostly white stork with black flight feathers; told from Yellow-billed Stork (p26) by its red (not yellow) bill, black (not white) tail and mainly terrestrial habits. Common visitor to the park from breeding grounds in central and eastern Europe, arriving in October and departing in March–April, with a few birds remaining throughout winter. Gregarious and nomadic; flocks appear in an area, stay a few days, then move elsewhere. Forages in open grassy areas, mostly on basaltic soils along the eastern side of the park; particularly attracted to recently burnt areas. Diet is varied but usually dominated by grasshoppers in savanna regions. WITOOIEVAAR

BLACK STORK
Ciconia nigra

1.0m, 3kg, wingspan 1.5m A large, mostly black stork with long red bill and legs; in juv legs are greyish-yellow. Resident and local nomad, occurs sparsely throughout the park and is likely to be encountered along any river, dam or pan. A few pairs breed in large stick nests built on cliff ledges in the Luvuvhu and Olifants river gorges, but the park also attracts non-breeding visitors from the interior of South Africa, especially in dry years. Mostly found singly, but small groups may gather where prey is abundant (e.g. in drying pans). Fish and frogs, caught in shallow water, comprise the bulk of their diet. GROOTSWARTOOIEVAAR

ABDIM'S STORK
Ciconia abdimii

76cm, 1.3kg A small, mostly black stork with a white back (visible in flight) and blue-grey bill and legs (not red as in Black Stork). Erratic summer visitor with scattered records throughout the park; breeds in the Sahel. Feeds mainly on grasshoppers and other insects; attracted to recently burnt ground where it sometimes feeds alongside White Storks. Highly nomadic, being present for a few days, then disappearing. Gregarious; invariably in flocks which may number hundreds of birds. KLEINSWARTOOIEVAAR

WOOLLY-NECKED STORK
Ciconia episcopus

84cm, 1.7kg A medium-sized black stork with a distinctive white neck. Tail black, but long, stiff, white undertail coverts extend beyond tail tip, so tail appears white from below. A fairly common resident, found at wetlands throughout the park, including perennial rivers, streams and large dams. Mostly encountered solitarily; typically found wading slowly in shallow water, picking and probing as it goes, in search of aquatic insects, molluscs, crabs, small fish or frogs. Also forages on dry land at times, taking alates at termite emergences; occasionally scavenges carrion. WOLNEKOOIEVAAR

White Stork

Black Stork

Woolly-necked Stork

Abdim's Stork

White Stork

Black Stork

Abdim's Stork

Woolly-necked Stork

OTHER STORKS

The differences in bill shapes in the four stork species here reflect their different diets and foraging techniques. Each of these four storks has 'sister species' in Asia: Painted and Milky storks (Yellow-billed Stork), Asian Openbill (African Openbill), Black-necked Stork (Saddle-billed Stork), and Greater and Lesser adjutants (Marabou Stork).

YELLOW-BILLED STORK
Mycteria ibis

97cm, 1.8kg, wingspan 1.6m A mostly white stork with black flight feathers; told from White Stork (p24) by its long yellow (not red) bill, black (not white) tail, and mainly aquatic habits. Occurs on the larger rivers and dams, usually in small groups. Mainly found in summer, although some individuals remain year-round. Breeds in years of high rainfall, usually alongside cormorants, herons and other storks. Down-curved bill tip is packed with tactile receptors to detect prey underwater; forages for fish and frogs by wading in shallow water with bill submerged and partly open, ready to snap shut whenever prey is encountered. Often raises a wing or stirs a foot, presumably to lure or frighten potential prey. NIMMERSAT

AFRICAN OPENBILL
Anastomus lamelligerus

82cm, 1.0kg The only all-brown stork; bill gap is diagnostic, but poorly developed in juv. Nomadic; numbers vary greatly, with periodic influxes after summers of high rainfall. In favourable years it breeds in small colonies. Feeds in shallow water, especially as pans dry out; uses its peculiar-shaped bill to extract freshwater snails and mussels from their shells. Piles of discarded mollusc shells are a tell-tale sign of the past presence of this species at such sites. OOPBEKOOIEVAAR

SADDLE-BILLED STORK
Ephippiorhynchus senegalensis

1.5m, 6kg, wingspan 2.5m A tall, striking stork; female has yellow eyes; male has dark eyes and a small yellow wattle at the base of the bill. Juv duller. Localised resident, mainly along the larger rivers. Each winter 25–30 pairs breed in the park, building a large stick platform nest on top of a tree, often far from water; birds commute long distances between feeding areas and the nest. Mostly seen in pairs, typically wading in shallow water intently watching for movement. Bill is very long, sharp-tipped and slightly up-curved, designed for spearing large fish; also feeds on frogs, reptiles and small birds and mammals. SAALBEKOOIEVAAR

MARABOU STORK
Leptoptilos crumeniferus

1.5m, ♂7.1kg, ♀5.7kg, wingspan 2.6m A huge, grey-backed stork with a distinctive bare head and pinkish throat wattle. Occurs commonly throughout the park year-round, sometimes in hundreds. Renowned scavenger; competes with vultures at kills, using its massive conical bill to open carcasses. Also an opportunistic forager that eats a range of prey, from termites and nestling queleas to monitor lizards. Small groups often gather on large rivers, fishing, bathing or basking on sandbanks, and at rest camps where they scavenge from refuse disposal sites. Breeds colonially in tall trees; however, breeding has not been recorded in the park to date. MARABOE

Yellow-billed Stork

African Openbill

Saddle-billed Stork ♀

Marabou Stork

Yellow-billed Stork

African Openbill

Saddle-billed Stork

Marabou Stork

GEESE AND DUCKS

Often referred to as waterfowl or wildfowl, geese and ducks are familiar birds, thanks to a centuries-old history of domestication and of being hunted for food or sport, and from the rich folklore with which they are associated. The 173 species are concentrated in the Northern Hemisphere; only 10 species occur regularly in the park. They are designed for living on water, with well-insulated bodies, short, strong legs and webbed toes for paddling. The four species here demonstrate how heterogeneous the family is, from the tiny, colourful Pygmy Goose to the large Spur-winged Goose.

EGYPTIAN GOOSE
Alopochen aegyptiaca

68cm, 2.0kg A large, mainly brown shelduck with white wing coverts that are conspicuous in flight. A common breeding resident, found along the larger rivers, dams and pans. Pairs aggressively exclude others of their kind from their territories, giving loud hissing and honking calls. Breeds on the ground, on cliff ledges or in old Hamerkop, raptor or crow nests, sometimes far from water; ads lead chicks to water shortly after they hatch. Non-breeding birds move about widely throughout southern Africa in response to changing conditions; at times flocks are encountered in the park. Feeds largely on short emergent grass; retreats to water mainly when threatened. KOLGANS

SPUR-WINGED GOOSE
Plectropterus gambensis

98cm, ♂5.1kg, ♀3.6kg A very large, mainly black 'goose' with a red face and bill. Extent of white breast varies among individuals, and tends to be greater in males. Nomadic; a wetland-dependent species recorded year-round but nowhere regularly present. Frequents large dams, pans and river margins, singly or in small groups. Forages on plants, both on dry ground and in shallow water, eating rhizomes and stems of emergent plants, grass and sedges. Largely silent except in flight, when it utters a soft, wheezy '*chi-vi, chi-vi, chi-vi ...*', surprising for a bird of this size. WILDEMAKOU

AFRICAN PYGMY GOOSE
Nettapus auritus

33cm, 262g A tiny, brightly coloured duck; female lacks male's colourfully patterned head. A scarce, erratic visitor in small numbers; occurs mainly in years of high rainfall, on dams and pans that are extensively covered with *Nymphaea* water lilies. Their green, rufous, white and yellow plumage blends well with these plants, making them easy to overlook. Eats mainly plant matter, especially water lily pods, buds and seeds. DWERGGANS. **White-backed Duck** *Thalassornis leuconotus* (Witrugeend) is banded brown and black with a white patch at the base of the bill; occasionally recorded on seasonal pans in years of above-average rainfall.

KNOB-BILLED DUCK
Sarkidiornis melanotos

67cm, ♂1.9kg, ♀1.4kg A fairly large, handsome duck; only the male has the fleshy comb on its bill, and this is only fully developed when breeding. Fledglings have a pale supercilium and can be confused with vagrant Garganey *Anas querquedula* (not yet recorded from the park). Small numbers occur year-round but there is a large influx to emphemeral pans and flooded areas in summers of high rainfall. In these conditions, pairs rapidly form, find nest sites in holes in trees, and breed. Ringing has shown that some birds move between the savannas of southern Africa and the Sahel, north of the equator. KNOBBELEEND

Egyptian Goose

Egyptian Goose

Spur-winged Goose

African Pygmy Goose ♂

African Pygmy Goose ♀

Knob-billed Duck ♂

White-backed Duck

DUCKS AND WHISTLING DUCKS

Most ducks are gregarious, often forming mixed-species flocks. Like many other waterbirds, they are highly mobile, moving large distances to exploit seasonal or ephemeral wetlands, although a few species defend territories year-round. Most ducks and geese (Anatidae) moult all their wing feathers at once, becoming flightless for several weeks. This usually occurs at a large waterbody where they can remain safe from terrestrial predators. Whistling ducks are a separate family, Dendrocygnidae, which don't have a flightless moult. In addition to the species here, four other ducks occasionally visit the park (p204).

AFRICAN BLACK DUCK
Anas sparsa

55cm, 1.1kg A rather plain, blackish-grey duck with white speckles, a purple-blue speculum and orange legs; females slightly duller than males. Resident, mainly along the strongly flowing perennial rivers, especially the Crocodile, Sabie and Luvuvhu. Pairs defend sections of the river from others of their kind, and are typically seen swimming along the margin of the river; also seen in flight, sometimes chasing neighbouring birds. A so-called 'dabbling duck', owing to its behaviour of foraging in shallow water in search of plant seeds and small aquatic insects. SWARTEEND. **Yellow-billed Duck** *A. undulata* (Geelbekeend) has yellow (not blue-grey) bill and green speculum; single birds or small groups occasionally recorded, mostly along the Sabie and Crocodile rivers.

RED-BILLED TEAL
Anas erythrorhyncha

46cm, 570g A fairly small duck with reddish bill, dark crown and pale cheeks; buff speculum visible in flight. A scarce nomad, occurring widely but sparsely on dams and pans. Encountered singly or in small groups. Birds move about widely in southern Africa and are attracted to the park in years of high rainfall when they exploit the productive ephemeral pans. A 'dabbling duck', it feeds by partly submerging the head and bill below water or by 'up-ending'; mainly eats the seeds of grasses and aquatic plants, also small aquatic insects. ROOIBEKEEND

SOUTHERN POCHARD
Netta erythrophthalma

50cm, 820g A medium-sized, mostly dark brown duck. Male has a purplish-brown head and neck, blue bill and red eye; female duller with white crescent from eye to nape, eye dark. In flight, both sexes have a prominent white wingbar extending onto the inner primaries. Scarce and erratic; single birds and small groups recorded on dams and pans from widely scattered localities. A mobile, fast-flying species that may appear when ephemeral pans are productive and leave when they dry up. Entirely aquatic; forages by diving and 'up-ending', feeding on a range of plant seeds and small aquatic insects. BRUINEEND

WHITE-FACED WHISTLING DUCK
Dendrocygna viduata

47cm, 800g After Egyptian Goose, the most commonly encountered duck. A long-legged, dark brown duck with distinctive white face; sexes alike. Resident and local nomad, occurring on dams, pans and any flooded grassy area. Gregarious; usually found in groups of up to 50 birds. Has a distinctive, high-pitched whistling call, used especially in flight; often heard after dark as flocks fly overhead. NONNETJIE-EEND. **Fulvous Whistling Duck** *D. bicolor* (Fluiteend) has a golden-buff body with bold white flank stripes; occasionally recorded on dams and pans.

African Black Ducks

Red-billed Teals

Red-billed Teal

Southern Pochard

Southern Pochard ♂

Southern Pochard ♀

White-faced Whistling Ducks

Fulvous Whistling Duck

VULTURES

Vultures are renowned for their size and formidable appearance, for their keen eyesight and ability to locate, from the air, the carcasses of animals, and for their frenzied feeding behaviour, when a flock can consume an impala-sized animal in a few minutes. Vulture populations are collapsing across much of Africa, and all five species in the park are now globally red-listed as Endangered (2) or Critically Endangered (3), demonstrating the vital role the park plays in providing a safe haven for these iconic, long-lived birds. In addition to the species here, Egyptian, Rüppell's and Palm-nut vultures occasionally visit the park (p204).

WHITE-BACKED VULTURE — *Gyps africanus*

95cm, 5.5kg, wingspan 2.2m Slightly smaller than Cape Vulture; ad has a white back, brown eyes and body slightly darker than ad Cape Vulture; juvs of both species are darker brown with dark eyes and are easily confused. Resident; the most abundant vulture with about 900 pairs in the park, although poisoning by poachers has impacted their numbers. Gregarious; roosts and nests in loose groups and gathers, sometimes in hundreds, to feed at carcasses. Their large stick nests, built on the tops of tall trees, are often clustered along drainage lines and reused annually. WITRUGAASVOËL

CAPE VULTURE — *Gyps coprotheres*

101cm, 8.6kg, wingspan 2.5m Larger than White-backed Vulture; ad has paler biscuit-coloured plumage, yellow eyes and no white back; juv darker than ad, with brown eyes; body becomes progressively paler over 4–5 years. Occurs widely, but sparsely, especially in the central and southern areas. Easily overlooked among the smaller, more abundant species at carcasses. Breeds and roosts on cliffs; closest colony is on the escarpment at Manutsa, 114km west of Satara, where 500–550 pairs breed; the white, guano-streaked rocks make the site visible from kilometres away. KRANSAASVOËL

WHITE-HEADED VULTURE — *Trigonoceps occipitalis*

85cm, 4.0kg, wingspan 2.2m A striking black-and-white vulture with a pinkish-white head, red bill and blue cere. Female has white inner secondaries (absent in male); juv dull brown with duller head and faint white trailing edge to underwing coverts. Resident; about 60 pairs breed in the park. Usually occurs singly or in pairs; sometimes joins other vultures at carcasses, but more usually locates and feeds on carcasses of small animals (hares, reptiles, road casualties) that don't attract other vultures; also occasionally catches and kills such prey. Pairs build a large nest on the top of a tree, often choosing a baobab where these occur. WITKOPAASVOËL

LAPPET-FACED VULTURE — *Torgos tracheliotos*

102cm, 6.7kg, wingspan 2.7m The largest, most formidable-looking vulture, easily identified by its blackish plumage, bare, wrinkled head and powerful beak. Ad has red head and white underwing stripe and leggings; juv all blackish with pinkish head. Resident; about 80 pairs breed throughout the park, with the greatest concentration in the south. Pairs breed solitarily, building a huge nest on the crown of a flat-topped tree. It is unusual to find more than 2–3 birds at a carcass but they invariably dominate other vulture species. SWARTAASVOËL

Lappet-faced, White-backed and Cape vultures

White-headed Vulture

White-backed Vulture

Cape Vulture

White-headed Vulture

Lappet-faced Vulture

HOODED VULTURE
Necrosyrtes monachus

70cm, 2.1kg, wingspan 1.7m Small size, uniformly dark brown plumage and slender bill distinguish this species from other vultures. Its unfeathered face and throat, usually pale pink, may flush scarlet or fade to white, apparently in response to stress. A fairly common resident throughout the park, although most pairs remain fairly close to the larger drainage lines where they breed in tall, densely foliaged trees. Often associates with other vulture species, either soaring alongside them or waiting on the sidelines for an opportunity to feed at a carcass once the larger species are done. MONNIKAASVOËL

KITES

Milvus kites are medium-sized brown raptors with long wings and long, forked tails that give them great buoyancy and manoeuvrability in flight. They often feed on termite emergences. In addition to catching their own prey, they are scavengers and much given to piracy. They are attracted to fires, taking prey fleeing the flames as well as feeding on roasted carcasses of those too slow to escape. In contrast to the migrant *Milvus* kites, the compact Black-shouldered Kite specialises in rodents.

YELLOW-BILLED KITE
Milvus aegyptius

55cm, 640g The most commonly encountered kite in summer. Told from Black Kite by its yellow bill (black in juv), dark eye, brown head and deeply forked tail. A common breeding visitor from tropical Africa, arriving in early August and departing in March. An opportunistic scavenger, usually encountered singly or in pairs, typically on the wing when its long, forked tail is obvious. Often seen circling rest camps or picnic sites, boldly swooping in to steal unattended food off tables, waiting for a feeding opportunity at the fringes of a carcass attended by vultures, or patrolling a road in the early morning for roadkill. GEELBEKWOU

BLACK KITE
Milvus migrans

55cm, 780g Easily overlooked due to its similarity to Yellow-billed Kite, but tail less rufous and not as deeply forked; ad has a pale yellowish eye (not reddish-brown) and greyish (not brown) head; black bill with a yellow cere at all ages. Juv is more heavily streaked yellow below than juv Yellow-billed Kite. A scarce non-breeding visitor from Eurasia, present between October and March. Shares the scavenging behaviour of Yellow-billed Kite and may mix with that species at food sources but, unlike that species, is not a bold food thief around camps. Gregarious at times, especially when the northward migration commences in March. SWARTWOU

BLACK-SHOULDERED KITE
Elanus caeruleus

30cm, 247g A striking little kite with piercing red eyes; juv lightly barred brown with yellow eyes. The abundance of this rodent specialist is determined by the availability of mice. Ringing records show that these birds wander widely across southern Africa in response to changing prey availability. Occurs widely but erratically in open areas, especially on basaltic soils in the east. Hunts solitarily, scanning the ground from a perch or while hovering overhead, then parachutes down onto prey; roosts communally in open trees at night. Perched birds have a distinctive tail-wagging behaviour used to warn other kites not to intrude. BLOUVALK

Hooded Vulture

Hooded Vulture 'blushing'

Hooded Vulture

Yellow-billed Kite

Black Kite

Yellow-billed Kite

Black Kite

Black-shouldered Kite

Black-shouldered Kite

HAWKS, HONEY BUZZARDS AND BUZZARDS

The small to medium-sized hawks that make up this eclectic group are not closely related. Apart from the migrant Steppe Buzzard, which is fairly common in summer, all are scarce and easily overlooked.

BAT HAWK *Macheiramphus alcinus*

45cm, 625g A dark chocolate-coloured hawk showing a varying amount of white on its underparts, with bright yellow eyes and curious white eyelids; in flight, the long, pointed wings resemble those of a falcon or jaeger. A solitary species that preys largely on bats, catching these on the wing during spurts of activity at dusk and dawn. At other times it remains largely inactive, perched high up in a well-foliaged tree. Uncommon resident, mostly encountered in tall trees along larger rivers; probably overlooked to some extent given its crepuscular habits. VLERMUISVALK

EUROPEAN HONEY BUZZARD *Pernis apivorus*

55cm, 748g Superficially resembles a large, floppy Steppe Buzzard but has a distinctly small head, slender bill and pale eyes (ad only). Individuals range from dark brown all over to whitish below; variably barred blackish. Ad tail pattern is diagnostic: two dark bars at the base and a broad dark terminal bar. In flight, soars with wings drooped more than Steppe Buzzard. A scarce non-breeding visitor from Eurasia, present from November to April. Solitary birds may be encountered in well-wooded areas. Preys primarily on wasp larvae, often feeding on the ground. WESPEDIEF

STEPPE (Common) BUZZARD *Buteo (buteo) vulpinus*

48cm, 740g, wingspan 1.2m The most commonly seen brown hawk in summer. Plumage variable; individuals range from dark brown to rufous to grey, and are streaked and barred to varying degrees, hence easily confused with other raptors. Its size and chunky 'buzzard' profile serve to eliminate many look-alikes and a useful feature in many individuals is the presence of a pale chest band. This eastern race of the Common Buzzard breeds on the Russian steppes, visiting southern Africa from November to March; a few overwinter and some now breed in the W Cape. Fairly common throughout; usually encountered singly, perched on an open dead branch surveying the ground below for small mammals and reptiles. BRUINJAKKALSVOËL. **Jackal Buzzard** *B. rufofuscus* (Rooiborsjakkelsvoël) is larger and broader-winged than Steppe Buzzard; ad blackish above with striking white wing panels and rufous breast and tail; imm brown with a longer tail than ad; single birds, mostly imms, occasionally recorded.

LIZARD BUZZARD *Kaupifalco monogrammicus*

36cm, 270g Compact grey hawk, superficially similar to Gabar Goshawk (p38) but more thickset; black tail with two broad white bands and white throat marked by a vertical black stripe are diagnostic. An uncommon resident of woodlands, mainly occurring on the well-wooded granitic soils along the western half of the park, especially in areas of higher rainfall in the southwest. A solitary, still-hunter that watches the ground from a perch, swooping onto prey – usually lizards, but also small snakes, birds or insects – when they are spotted. AKKEDISVALK

Bat Hawk

European Honey Buzzard dark morph

Steppe Buzzard

Steppe Buzzard

Lizard Buzzard

Jackal Buzzard

SPARROWHAWKS, GOSHAWKS AND CHANTING GOSHAWKS

Sparrowhawk and goshawk are common names for the accipiters. Originally, large species were known as goshawks and smaller ones as sparrowhawks, but now the trend is to call the more generalised hunters goshawks, reserving the name sparrowhawk for the specialised bird-hunting species that have especially long legs and toes. Females are larger than males in all species, but the difference is most marked in the sparrowhawks. Accipiters are secretive birds that rely on stealth and ambush to secure their prey. Their rounded wings and long tails allow them to hunt among dense vegetation, with their dashing hunting style making them popular for falconry. Identification is complicated by distinct juvenile plumages, size differences among sexes, and plumage polymorphism in some species. The Ovambo Sparrowhawk also visits the park occasionally (p205).

LITTLE SPARROWHAWK · *Accipiter minullus*

25cm, ♂74g, ♀106g A tiny accipiter, smaller than a dove. Ad and juv are similar in plumage to African Goshawk, but blackish upper tail with two large white spots and narrow white rump are diagnostic. A fairly common resident in all wooded habitats. Easily overlooked, as it spends much of the time perched in concealed positions. A feisty little hawk; preys on small birds, especially waxbills, finches and weavers. KLEINSPERWER

SHIKRA · *Accipiter badius*

29cm, 130g A medium-sized accipiter, most likely to be confused with Gabar Goshawk, especially imms of the two species. Imm and ad distinguished by absence of white rump, ad by cherry-red eyes, yellow (not red) legs and unbarred central tail feathers. A fairly common resident, found in all wooded areas. Usually encountered solitarily, perched unobtrusively on a branch watching the ground below for prey. A still-hunter that feeds mainly on lizards, and frequently changes perches, making it easier to spot than most other accipiters. GEBANDE SPERWER

AFRICAN GOSHAWK · *Accipiter tachiro*

♂38cm, ♀45cm, ♂220g, ♀360g A fairly large accipiter, although male much smaller than female, and more brightly coloured in ad plumage. Larger than Little Sparrowhawk, with dark rump; upper tail usually lacks white spots (but ad male may show two faint spots). A forest-living resident, mainly found along the larger rivers. Like other accipiters, it is a stealth-hunter and therefore easily overlooked, except at dawn, when it gives its distinctive clicking call during a display flight or from an exposed perch. Preys mostly on birds but also takes squirrels and other small mammals, reptiles and, occasionally, termites and other insects. AFRIKAANSE SPERWER

GABAR GOSHAWK · *Micronisus gabar*

32cm, ♂134g, ♀194g A medium-sized hawk with red legs (yellow in juv); readily identified in flight by its broad white rump; central tail banded. Although resembling an accipiter in build and appearance, it is related to the chanting goshawks. A fairly common resident throughout the park; encountered solitarily or in pairs, often at dams and waterholes where it hunts birds coming to drink; also regularly raids nests of weaver birds. Often incorporates pieces of the web-nests of social spiders (*Stegodyphus*) into its own nest, which expand and eventually festoon the entire goshawk nest. KLEINSINGVALK

Little Sparrowhawk

Little Sparrowhawk imm

Shikra

African Goshawk ♀

African Goshawk ♂

Gabar Goshawk

NIGEL DENNIS / IMAGES OF AFRICA

Gabar Goshawk

Gabar Goshawk imm

BLACK SPARROWHAWK
Accipiter melanoleucus

52cm, ♂540g, ♀900g A very large accipiter. Most ads are black above and white below; melanistic ads with mostly black underparts are rare in the park. Juv is dark brown above and rufous below; easily mistaken for imm African Hawk Eagle (p44), but has unfeathered legs. Like other accipiters, it is a secretive bird, hunting by stealth, ambush and hot pursuit, and it is consequently much overlooked. Favours tall, dense woodland and is largely confined to riparian areas along the large rivers. Preys almost entirely on birds, especially on doves and gamebirds. SWARTSPERWER

DARK CHANTING GOSHAWK
Melierax metabates

45cm, 660g, wingspan 1m A very large, long-legged hawk with a distinctive upright stance. Much larger than Gabar Goshawk (p38), with longer legs and no white rump. A fairly common resident, occurring in well-wooded areas. Solitary birds are usually encountered scanning for prey from the top branches of a tree. They are versatile hunters, killing anything they can overpower, from lizards and other reptiles to gamebirds, squirrels and other small mammals. Their common name derives from their habit of calling frequently, especially at dawn: a melodious series of whistles that ascend and descend in scale. DONKERSINGVALK

BAZAS (CUCKOO-HAWKS) AND HARRIER-HAWKS

The cuckoo-hawks are the African representatives of the Asian bazas, whereas the harrier-hawks are unusual raptors confined to the Afrotropics. Both are represented by a single, widespread species in sub-Saharan Africa with a sister species in Madagascar.

AFRICAN CUCKOO-HAWK
Aviceda cuculoides

40cm, 290g Grey back and barred underparts suggest an accipiter or large cuckoo but size, small crest, rufous nape and rufous underwing coverts in flight are diagnostic. At rest, wing tips reach almost to tail tip (tail longer in accipiters). Uncommon resident, largely confined to tall riparian woodland, especially along the Luvuvhu and Sabie rivers. Occurs solitarily or in pairs; usually encountered perched on a dry branch or moving from tree to tree searching the foliage for prey – especially chameleons, other small reptiles and large insects such as mantids, katydids and caterpillars. KOEKOEKVALK

AFRICAN HARRIER-HAWK
Polyboroides typus

63cm, 730g, wingspan 1.4m A large, slender-bodied hawk with a long tail, large, broad, deeply-slotted wings, and a narrow 'beaky' head. Ad distinctive; brown juv could cause confusion with other hawks and eagles. Fairly common resident, mainly in riparian woodland; also ranges over open country. Solitary except when breeding. Its leg joints can bend backwards and forwards, allowing it to extract prey (e.g. bats, reptiles, squirrels, nestling birds) from inside tree and rock crevices; they are often found clinging to tree trunks, wings flailing and a foot inserted into a crack. The alternative common name of Gymnogene refers to the adult's bare facial skin, which can rapidly change from yellow to red or white depending on external stimuli, especially stress. KAALWANGVALK

Black Sparrowhawk ♀

Black Sparrowhawk

Dark Chanting Goshawk

African Cuckoo-Hawk ♀

African Harrier-Hawk

African Harrier-Hawk

HARRIERS

These long-winged and -tailed raptors, related to accipiters, hunt by quartering low over the ground in buoyant flight, alternating bouts of slow wing-beats and glides with wings held in a shallow 'V'. Both species commonly recorded in the park breed in the Palearctic, and are easily confused, especially females and juvs.

MONTAGU'S HARRIER
Circus pygargus

44cm, ♂260g, ♀370g, wingspan 1m Ad male is slightly darker grey than Pallid Harrier with a diagnostic black line across the upperwing and brown-streaked (not plain) flanks and belly. Female and juv are brown-coloured with contrasting white rumps; together with Pallid Harrier females and juvs, they are collectively referred to as 'ringtails'. Identification requires good views; female Montagu's has less striking facial markings than Pallid Harrier; barring on underside of secondaries is well marked, extending to body. Forages singly, mainly in the eastern side of the park where there are open grasslands. BLOUVLEIVALK

PALLID HARRIER
Circus macrourus

44cm, ♂310g, ♀440g, wingspan 1m Ad male is slightly paler grey than Montagu's Harrier with plain white underparts; grey wings have a smaller black tip than male Montagu's. Female and juv have more striking facial markings than Montagu's; juv has diagnostic white margin to the ear coverts. Barring on underside of secondaries becomes faint towards the body. Found mainly over open grasslands in the eastern side of the park where it forages mostly on small birds and rodents. WITBORSVLEIVALK

OSPREYS AND FISH EAGLE

These two raptors mainly feed on fish. Ospreys are a separate family of specialist fish-eating raptors, whereas the African Fish Eagle, with its striking plumage and ringing call, is iconic for the general public.

WESTERN OSPREY
Pandion haliaetus

59cm, 1.5kg, wingspan 1.6m At rest, best identified by its mostly white head with a broad, dark eye-stripe; in flight, the long, narrow wings are mostly pale below with blackish carpal joints. Smaller than imm African Fish Eagle, with more slender wings and white underparts. A scarce, non-breeding visitor from Eurasia to the larger rivers and dams. Juvs remain year-round. Hunts by plunging into the water, talons first; reversible outer toes and strongly curved claws assist in grasping fish. VISVALK

AFRICAN FISH EAGLE
Haliaeetus vocifer

68cm, ♂2.3kg, ♀3.1kg, wingspan 1.9m A striking raptor of the rivers and lakes; ad unmistakable; imm can be mistaken for smaller Osprey but has mostly dark underparts and much broader, darker wings. Common throughout the park wherever habitat is available. Pairs are resident, spaced 5–6km apart along rivers and on the larger dams. Territorial birds typically perch conspicuously in tall trees close to the water, often revealing their presence with their far-carrying, ringing call, which is given in flight or from a perch. Catches fish by plunging talons first into the water but also takes waterbirds and their nestlings, scavenges carrion and often steals prey from other birds. VISAREND

Pallid Harrier ♂

Montagu's Harrier ♂

Montagu's Harrier imm

Pallid Harrier ♀

Western Osprey

Western Osprey

African Fish Eagle

African Fish Eagle imm

SNAKE EAGLES AND SMALL EAGLES

Snake Eagles (*Circaetus*) are a distinctive group of eagle-sized raptors that differ from 'true' eagles (*Aquila*, *Hieraaetus*, etc.) by having short, unfeathered, densely scaled legs and rather small toes. They feed primarily on snakes and have been known to overpower large, highly venomous cobras and adders, their legs well protected against bites. The other two species here are typical eagles, with feathered legs and dashing hunting techniques. In addition to the species here, Ayres's Hawk Eagle and Long-crested Eagle occasionally visit the park (p204).

BLACK-CHESTED SNAKE EAGLE
Circaetus pectoralis

66cm, 1.5kg, wingspan 1.8m Ad distinguished from larger Martial Eagle (p48) by unfeathered legs, unspotted chest and, in flight, white (not all-brown) underwings. Imm distinguished from imm Brown Snake Eagle by pale rufous (not brown) underparts. A fairly common resident throughout the park; numbers probably augmented seasonally by non-breeding visitors when several may be found in close proximity. Usually seen perched on a dead tree or soaring overhead; when homing in on prey it hangs kite-like by flying into the wind, or hovers on gently winnowing wings in calm conditions. SWARTBORSSLANGAREND

BROWN SNAKE EAGLE
Circaetus cinereus

74cm, 2.1kg, wingspan 1.6m A largish, all-brown eagle; distinguished from other eagles by a combination of unfeathered legs, size, broad head and large yellow eye; in flight, all-brown body and largely white underwing are diagnostic. A common species throughout the park, occurring year-round. However, there are very few breeding records, so it seems likely that the bulk of the population is nomadic rather than resident; ringing records show widescale movements in the region. Typically seen perched on a dead branch or other prominent perch from where it scans the ground below for snakes. BRUINSLANGAREND

AFRICAN HAWK EAGLE
Aquila spilogaster

63cm, ♂1.3kg, ♀1.6kg, wingspan 1.45m Ad striking black and white; female larger and more heavily streaked below. Imm easily confused with other brown raptors: combination of its size, feathered legs and warm rufous underparts are diagnostic. A fairly common resident, especially in tall, dense woodland. Pairs defend large territories year-round, and often hunt in unison: one bird distracts the prey while the other sneaks up on the quarry from behind. Gamebirds feature prominently in their diet but they also take other birds and mammals. GROOTJAGAREND

BOOTED EAGLE
Hieraaetus pennatus

50cm, ♂710g, ♀975g, wingspan 1.2m A dashing little eagle, the size of a large buzzard. Pale morph birds are most common; easily identified in flight from below when pale body and underwing coverts contrast with dark brown flight feathers. Dark morph is slightly smaller than Wahlberg's Eagle (p46), with a shorter, broader tail in flight and greater contrast between the pale upperwing coverts and rest of the upperwing. In flight, the white 'landing lights' (at the base of each wing) are diagnostic in both colour morphs. An uncommon non-breeding visitor throughout, occurring year-round, with birds from Eurasia in summer or from the Cape in winter. DWERGAREND

Black-chested Snake Eagle   Black-chested Snake Eagle   Black-chested Snake Eagle imm

Brown Snake Eagle   Brown Snake Eagle   African Hawk Eagle

Booted Eagle   Booted Eagle pale morph

LARGE BROWN EAGLES

These four eagles occur commonly in the park and are easily mistaken for one another, as well as the smaller, dark morph Booted Eagle (p44). However, they can be identified by close attention to plumage detail and structure. Size and associated flight action (large birds flap more slowly) usefully distinguish the large Tawny and Steppe eagles (wingspans about 2m) from the smaller Lesser Spotted and Wahlberg's eagles (wingspans about 1.5m). Tawny and Wahlberg's eagles breed in the park, so birds attending nests can only be one of these. As most brown eagles leave the park in winter, those encountered during this season are typically resident Tawny Eagles.

TAWNY EAGLE
Aquila rapax

71cm, 1.94kg, wingspan 1.9m A large eagle with a powerful bill and often a shaggy appearance; plumage varies among individuals from pale sandy brown through rich rufous to dark brown; female larger and typically darker than male. Common resident throughout; usually the most frequently seen large eagle. Pairs defend territories of about 7,000ha centred on their nest year-round. The nest, built on the crown of a tall tree, is reused annually. A versatile, rapacious hunter; preys on small mammals, reptiles and birds up to the size of guineafowl but also steals prey caught by other raptors, especially Bateleurs, and scavenges on roadkill and alongside vultures at carcasses. ROOFAREND

STEPPE EAGLE
Aquila nipalensis

77cm, ♂2.5kg, ♀3.0kg, wingspan 2.1m Similar in size and shape to Tawny Eagle but has a long gape that extends to the rear of the eye; imm birds, which are most common in the park, have a conspicuous white rump and pale lines along the upper- and underside of their wings due to pale-tipped greater wing coverts. A non-breeding visitor from central Eurasia, present between October and March; numbers vary from year to year. Gregarious; groups often gather to feed on nestlings at quelea colonies or on termite alates as they emerge after rain. STEPPEAREND

LESSER SPOTTED EAGLE
Clanga pomarina

62cm, ♂1.2kg, ♀1.5kg, wingspan 1.5m Resembles a small, weak-billed Steppe Eagle; ad warm brown with slightly darker flight feathers; imm birds, which are prevalent in the park, have pale panels in the outer wing and two narrow whitish bands along the upperwing and one on the underwing. A non-breeding visitor from central Eurasia; individuals from northern Germany tracked to the park. Occurs widely between October and March; more common in some years than others. Gregarious; when migrating, flocks of dozens to hundreds may be seen soaring overhead. GEVLEKTE AREND

WAHLBERG'S EAGLE
Hieraaetus wahlbergi

58cm, ♂1.0kg, ♀1.3kg, wingspan 1.4m This fairly small brown eagle is best identified by its small crest when perched, and in flight by its narrow wings and tail held tightly closed. Coloration varies among individuals; most are light brown with darker flight feathers; dark brown and off-white morphs (so-called 'blondies') are less common; a few have unusually light-coloured heads or crowns. A common summer visitor to the park between August and April; non-breeding range is the northern savanna belt of Africa. Pairs defend territories of about 1,000ha, usually using the same nests each year. Nests built in the upper outer branches of a tree. They are generalists, hunting a wide range of small mammals, reptiles and birds. BRUINAREND

Tawny Eagle

Tawny Eagle

Steppe Eagle

Lesser Spotted Eagle

Wahlberg's Eagle dark morph   Wahlberg's Eagle pale morph   Wahlberg's Eagle

LARGE EAGLES

These eagles are among the most impressive of predatory birds: the Martial Eagle is Africa's largest eagle, the Crowned Eagle is its most powerful, while the Bateleur is a distinctive eagle named for its acrobatic, rolling flight action. The first three species here are 'true' eagles in the sense that they have feathered legs, whereas the Bateleur has bare legs and is allied to the snake eagles.

VERREAUX'S EAGLE
Aquila verreauxii

88cm, ♂3.7kg, ♀4.5kg, wingspan 2m A striking eagle with distinctive, narrow-based wings. Ad unmistakable; juv mottled brown and buff but also shows pale primary bases like ad. The sandstone formations and gorges associated with the Luvuvhu River in the far north provide the only suitable habitat for this splendid eagle, which requires cliffs for breeding and mainly preys on rock hyrax. About seven pairs are resident here, and one is often afforded views of them as they soar effortlessly along the cliffs. Other pairs nest along the escarpment, and it is probably these, or their offspring, that occasionally venture into other areas of the park. WITKRUISAREND

MARTIAL EAGLE
Polemaetus bellicosus

81cm, ♂3.3kg, ♀4.7kg, wingspan 2.2m Ad distinguished from Black-chested Snake Eagle (p44) by larger size, spotted breast and all-dark underwing. Juv has whitish head and underwing coverts; best told from juv Crowned Eagle by its shorter, more finely barred tail and flight feathers, which appear uniform at a distance, and browner upperparts. A powerful and versatile predator that takes a wide range of prey, favouring small antelope, mongooses, monitor lizards and gamebirds. Occurs throughout; ads largely resident. About 170 pairs breed in the park, each defending a territory of 11,000ha; by comparison, leopards have a home range of only 2,000ha. Numbers have declined over much of its range, including in the park, mainly due to imm birds venturing outside the park being persecuted or electrocuted. BREËKOPAREND

CROWNED EAGLE
Stephanoaetus coronatus

85cm, 3.6kg, wingspan 1.7m A forest-living eagle. Ad unmistakable; imm longer tailed than imm Martial Eagle with upperparts and crown buff white (not pale brown). Occurs commonly along the forested escarpment west of the park; within the park it is largely restricted to riparian woodland along the Luvuvhu and Limpopo rivers in the extreme north where a handful of pairs are resident. In most parts of its range it preys on small antelope and monkeys; within the park it mainly subsists on hyrax. KROONAREND

BATELEUR
Terathopius ecaudatus

63cm, 2.2kg, wingspan 1.7m Ad unmistakable; in flight, male has a broader black trailing edge of the wing than female. Juv dull brown with slightly longer tail than ad but flight silhouette is distinctive; takes 5–6 years to acquire ad plumage. Common throughout, with about 400 breeding pairs. They spend much of the day coursing back and forth over their territory, searching for dead or dying animals; also take some live prey. Their rapid gliding flight requires warm, rising air and they remain grounded on rainy days. Imms disperse beyond the park boundaries where they are at risk of being poisoned by bait illegally put out by farmers to deter jackals and other predators. BERGHAAN

Verreaux's Eagle

Verreaux's Eagle

Martial Eagle

Crowned Eagle

Martial Eagle

Crowned Eagle

Bateleur

Bateleur ♀

Bateleur imm

49

FALCONS AND HOBBIES

The falcons, hobbies and kestrels form a distinctive family of raptors. Recent genetic evidence shows they are closely related to parrots and perching birds, rather than other diurnal raptors; their similarity to parrots is apparent in their bill structure. However, many aspects of their ecology and behaviour are similar to those of eagles and hawks, so falcons remain 'birds of prey' in the broad sense. Like the eagles and hawks, females are typically larger than males and do the bulk of the incubation duties while the male forages for the pair. In addition to the species here, five other falcons occasionally visit the park (p205).

LANNER FALCON
Falco biarmicus

42cm, ♂510g, ♀730g A large falcon; distinguished from Peregrine Falcon at all ages by rufous (in ad) or buff (in imm) crown; wings longer and broader; often soars with fanned tail. Scarce throughout park. Solitary individuals are usually encountered in open country, mainly on the eastern basaltic plains. Small numbers may be resident, perhaps breeding in the gorges along the Luvuvhu River, but most birds are probably post-breeding visitors from elsewhere. A more generalised hunter than the Peregrine Falcon; preys mostly on birds but also takes mammals and reptiles. EDELVALK

PEREGRINE FALCON
Falco peregrinus

39cm, ♂530g, ♀770g A large, compact falcon that typically occurs close to cliffs and gorges. Distinguished from similar-sized Lanner Falcon by black (not rufous) crown and black-and-white barred underparts. A few pairs are resident and breed in the gorges along the Luvuvhu and Olifants rivers, but most individuals seen in the park are probably visitors from the escarpment cliffs west of the park or non-breeding migrants from the Palearctic. Scarce; single birds usually encountered perched high up on a dead branch. A supreme hunter; preys exclusively on birds, hunting by swooping on them from a height, when it can attain speeds in excess of 300km/h – a feat unmatched by any other bird. SWERFVALK

EURASIAN HOBBY
Falco subbuteo

32cm, ♂200g, ♀230g A small, dashing falcon, fast and agile in flight, with long, rakish wings. Distinguished from the more kestrel-like female Amur Falcon (p52) by larger size, more slender build, yellow legs and cere, rufous belly (in ad) and elongated chest markings. A non-breeding visitor from Eurasia; most birds arrive in November and depart in March. Occurs widely but sparsely throughout, favouring tall-tree woodland, especially along the large rivers, where it perches on open branches. Catches birds, bats and large insects (e.g. dragonflies, termite alates) in flight; often targets Barn Swallow flocks at reedbed roosts at dusk or dawn. EUROPESE BOOMVALK

SOOTY FALCON
Falco concolor

34cm, 220g Structure similar to Eurasian Hobby but ad is uniform grey; lacks pale head and boldly barred tail of Dickinson's Kestrel (p52) and rufous vent of male Amur Falcon (p52). Juv similar to juv Eurasian Hobby but less heavily streaked below. Rare; single birds occasionally recorded, usually seen perched on a dead branch of a high tree. Mainly hunts at dawn and dusk, taking small birds, bats and large insects in flight. ROETVALK

Lanner Falcon

Lanner Falcon

Peregrine Falcon

Peregrine Falcon

Eurasian Hobby

Sooty Falcon

HUGH CHITTENDEN

KESTRELS

The distinction between falcons and kestrels, if there is one, is slight; both are placed in the same genus. Kestrels typically lack the speed and acceleration in flight that characterise falcons and they hunt mostly from perches or by hovering, rather than by hot pursuit. They do take occasional birds, but they mainly target less mobile prey, with grasshoppers and other insects featuring prominently in their diets. In this context, the Amur Falcon is more like a kestrel as it, too, is a hover-hunter, subsisting largely on grasshoppers, at least in Africa.

AMUR FALCON
Falco amurensis

29cm, 142g Male plain grey with diagnostic rufous vent; female distinguished from larger Eurasian Hobby (p50) by red legs and cere, white belly and flecked rather than streaked chest markings. A common, gregarious, non-breeding visitor, present from November to April. Satellite tracking has revealed details of the extraordinary biennial 22,000km migration undertaken between its breeding grounds in the Amur Basin in China and its winter grounds in South Africa, which includes a 3,000km sea crossing between India and the coast of Somalia that is undertaken in a non-stop 75–80-hour flight. One remarkable bird, assisted by a strong tailwind, travelled 6,000km in five days! OOSTELIKE ROOIPOOTVALK

LESSER KESTREL
Falco naumanni

29cm, 145g Slightly smaller than Rock Kestrel; ad male has plain rufous upperparts, blackish flight feathers and grey greater upperwing coverts. Ad female and juv are rufous-barred dark brown above, and buff below with brown streaks. A scarce non-breeding visitor from Europe from November to April, mostly encountered in open country on the basaltic plains along the eastern side of the park. Regularly forages and roosts with groups of Amur Falcons. Feeds primarily on grasshoppers and other insects, hunting from perches or while hovering. KLEINROOIVALK

ROCK KESTREL
Falco rupicolus

32cm, 220g A rufous-backed kestrel with variable dark brown spotting; female slightly duller with a browner head. Uncommon, but widely recorded in the park. A small resident population probably breeds in the gorges of the Luvuvhu and Olifants rivers, but most individuals probably off-season visitors from highland areas in the interior. An accomplished hoverer and often uses whatever wind is available to leave a perch and take up a position 10–30m above the ground, watching intently below as its steadily beating wings maintain it at a constant position. Any small bird, mammal or reptile that can be overpowered is potential prey and these are taken to a perch to be processed and eaten. KRANSVALK

DICKINSON'S KESTREL
Falco dickinsoni

29cm, 210g A dapper, smoky-grey kestrel with a pale head (ad) and barred tail with a broad subterminal band. A small resident population of this bird breeds in the far north of the park, found mostly in hilly wooded country where there are scattered, large baobabs. Pairs are widely spaced here (at intervals of about 10km), and the occasional birds that are recorded farther south are perhaps post-breeding wanderers. Nests in cavities in trees and its occurrence alongside baobabs in which cavities occur is no coincidence. Like other kestrels, it is a solitary still-hunter, watching the ground below from a perch and changing perches periodically when a site fails to yield prey. DICKINSONGRYSVALK

Amur Falcon ♂

Amur Falcon ♀

Lesser Kestrel ♂

Lesser Kestrel ♀

Rock Kestrel ♂

Dickinson's Kestrel

BUSTARDS AND KORHAANS

The bustards are an Old World family of 26 species in which the smaller species are known as korhaans in South Africa. They are long-legged terrestrial birds that live in open landscapes, especially in grassland and semi-desert. All forage by picking up food on the ground, and their diets (grain, bulbs, berries, insects, spiders, small reptiles, nestling birds and more) vary according to region and species involved. Most bustards are polygynous, with females undertaking all parental care. Males display to attract females during early summer at regularly used sites, sometimes in dispersed leks. Having been hunted historically, they are often wary and unapproachable but sometimes tolerate close approaches by vehicles in the park.

KORI BUSTARD
Ardeotis kori

♂**135cm**, ♀**112cm**, ♂**12.4kg**, ♀**5.7kg** A huge bustard with a black crown and finely grizzled grey neck; male appreciably larger than female. The park is an important refuge for the species, which is among the world's heaviest flying birds. Resident, occurs widely but especially on the basaltic soils along the eastern side of the park where single birds, pairs or groups of up to a dozen are commonly encountered. Breeding males display in leks; when a female approaches, male inflates its neck so that the head virtually disappears, droops its wings, and lifts and fans its tail. He may utter a series of deep-throated booming '*ump-ump, ump-ump ...*' calls while in this pumped-up posture. Competing males sometimes approach each other aggressively, usually resulting in one retreating. The behaviour at these display arenas is absorbing to watch, in contrast to other times when Kori Bustards are seen doing little more than sedately picking their way through the veld. GOMPOU

BLACK-BELLIED BUSTARD
Lissotis melanogaster

62cm, ♂**2.3kg**, ♀**1.3kg** Male distinguished from Red-crested Korhaan by larger size, white cheeks and black extending from belly to throat. Female smaller than male; throat, neck and underparts are buff and white (not black). A fairly common, widespread resident, most regularly encountered in the grasslands on the basaltic soils in the east. Largely solitary but displaying males may consort at dispersed lek sites. The display consists of slowly extending the head and neck upwards and, when at full stretch, uttering a slurred '*quark*'. The head and neck are then rapidly retracted and an explosive sound like a cork being pulled from a bottle is made, sometimes followed by a slow-flapping circular flight when the white primary feathers are conspicuously displayed. LANGBEENKORHAAN

RED-CRESTED KORHAAN
Lophotis ruficrista

50cm, **675g** Small size and absence of black on throat and neck distinguish it from male Black-bellied Bustard; black belly distinguishes it from female. Female lacks male's red crest (although this is barely visible when not displaying). A common, widespread resident species. Often encountered crossing a road or detected by the male's call, which is a series of penetrating whistled notes – '*kyip-kyip-kyip- ...*' – that rise to a near-deafening crescendo. At close range, the 50 or more metallic-sounding tongue clicks that precede each whistle are audible. As a finale to this vocal serenade, the male sometimes flies vertically, above the tree canopy, before pulling in its legs, wings and head and falling to the ground, almost as though it has been shot. The male fans out its shaggy red crest when approached by a female. BOSKORHAAN

Kori Bustard ♂

Black-bellied Bustard ♂

Red-crested Korhaan

GUINEAFOWL AND SPURFOWL

Guineafowl are an all-African family comprising six gamebird species. They are gregarious birds, easily recognised by their large size and bluish-black, finely spotted plumage. African spurfowl form a distinct group of phasianid gamebirds, which typically differ from francolins (p58) in being larger, having red (not yellow) legs, more raucous calls and different behaviour (francolin crouch when disturbed, spurfowl run). Males are larger than females and have leg spurs. In addition to the species here, the Red-necked Spurfowl occasionally visits the park (p205).

HELMETED GUINEAFOWL
Numida meleagris

58cm, 1.48kg Bony casque on crown, blue head and neck and red-tipped wattles distinguish it from Crested Guineafowl. A common resident, especially in the south; mostly encountered in areas that have been heavily trampled or grazed by game and often around waterholes. Gregarious except when breeding, which happens in midsummer. At other times, occurs in flocks which, in midwinter, may number a hundred or more. Forages and breeds on the ground; at night flocks fly into tall trees to roost. The female's monotonous *'buck-wheat'* call, which may continue into the night, is a common sound during the breeding season. GEWONE TARENTAAL

CRESTED GUINEAFOWL
Guttera pucherani

50cm, 1.2kg Differs from Helmeted Guineafowl by its blood-red eyes, crown of curly black feathers, pale blue feather spots and white band of feathers in the wing. Largely restricted to the far north where it is a localised resident, favouring forested riverine areas and *Androstachys* thickets along the Lebombos; most often seen along drives bordering the Luvuvhu River. Rather shy; usually found in parties of 5–20 birds, which give away their presence by the metallic clucking notes uttered at intervals as they scratch among fallen leaves on the forest floor for insects or fruits. KUIFKOPTARENTAAL

NATAL SPURFOWL
Pternistis natalensis

34cm, 446g Easily told from Swainson's Spurfowl by its red (not black) legs, feathered face and throat, and paler belly; the two species occasionally hybridise. A common, widespread resident; favours thickets and is mostly encountered among tangled vegetation along drainage lines and at the base of kopjes. Occurs singly or in groups; can be tame and confiding in rest camps and often comes onto roads at dawn and dusk. At other times, though, its presence is only betrayed by its screeching call (e.g. *'kakkak-kekekekek-kekeek ...'*). NATALSE FISANT

SWAINSON'S SPURFOWL
Pternistis swainsonii

36cm, ♂706g, ♀505g Told from Natal Spurfowl by its black (not red) legs, bare red face and throat and uniform underparts; the two species occasionally hybridise. A common, widespread resident, especially in the grasslands on the basaltic soils in the east. Doesn't venture into rest camps but commonly encountered alongside roads and in open, heavily grazed areas such as around waterholes. Males call from perches on a low branch or termitarium; with head raised, they utter a loud crowing sound, *'kwaaaiii, kwaaaiii ...'*, each note fading as it ends. After a short bout of calling, they hop back to the ground and resume scratching for food, appearing a little embarrassed about the whole episode. BOSVELDFISANT

Helmeted Guineafowl

Crested Guineafowl

Natal Spurfowl

Swainson's Spurfowl

FRANCOLINS AND QUAILS

These ground-living birds belong to a large, widespread gamebird family, the Phasianidae, and have been hunted for food or sport for centuries. At one time the francolins were known as partridges, but that name has since been reserved for several groups of largely Eurasian species. Francolins and quails tend to freeze when alarmed, relying on their cryptic plumage to remain undetected. If approached too closely, they may try to creep away, or flush, flying away on noisily whirring wings.

SHELLEY'S FRANCOLIN
Scleroptila shelleyi

33cm, 468g A handsome francolin with orange-buff sides to the head and neck and a white throat with neat black margins. Resident, occurring widely but sparsely throughout the park, favouring treeless, grassy areas or lightly wooded savanna. Gregarious; lives year-round in coveys of up to eight birds. More often heard than seen; its presence is mostly given away by its characteristic, melodious *'I'll drink y'r beer'*, a common dawn and dusk sound in those areas where it occurs. LAEVELDPATRYS

COQUI FRANCOLIN
Peliperdix coqui

24cm, 244g A tiny francolin with strikingly barred underparts. Male has a plain mustard-coloured head; female duller with black stripes on its face and throat. Resident, occurring widely but sparsely, mostly in broad-leafed woodlands on the granitic soils along the west side of the park. Derives its English and Afrikaans common names (Coqui and *Swempie*) from its distinctive two-syllabled call. Usually occurs in coveys of 4–5 birds. Secretive; more often heard than seen, as it seldom ventures into the open. If disturbed, it crouches to avoid detection. Most often encountered when crossing a road, which they do with slow, deliberate steps and heads kept low. SWEMPIE

CRESTED FRANCOLIN
Dendroperdix sephaena

33cm, 348g The most commonly seen francolin in the park. Unusual in having red legs. Often cocks its tail, resembling a small chicken. Sexes similar, but male has a speckled rump; female's rump is barred. Resident in all wooded areas and in many rest camps. Lives in pairs or, after breeding, in family groups. Often forages alongside roads and frequently scratches for prey among elephant dung. Its call, typically a well-synchronised duet by the male and female (*'tina-turner, tina-turner ...'*), is one of the characteristic sounds of the park. BOSPATRYS

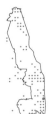

HARLEQUIN QUAIL
Coturnix delegorguei

18cm, 76g Chestnut, brown and black-coloured male unmistakable; female larger than Common Buttonquail (p60), with pale streaked (not scalloped) plumage and dark (not pale) eyes. An erratic summer visitor from tropical Africa that breeds widely and commonly in years of good rainfall but is entirely absent in drought years. Favours areas of open grassland but seldom ventures out of cover; most likely to be seen in the early morning when individuals stand on road verges to escape the dew. Males call day and night when they are present, a penetrating three-syllabled *'wit, wit-wit'*, and in years when they are abundant the area can resonate with their calling. BONTKWARTEL

Shelley's Francolin

Shelley's Francolin

Coqui Francolin ♂

Coqui Francolin ♀

Crested Francolin

Harlequin Quail

FINFOOT, CRAKES AND BUTTONQUAILS

Buttonquails (Turnicidae) are secretive birds that superficially resemble quails, but are more closely related to shorebirds. The Finfoot is one of a family of just three species (Heliornithidae), with representatives in SE Asia, Africa and South and Central America. They are closely related to flufftails, and more distantly to crakes and rails, which are part of a large, widespread family (Rallidae), many of which are secretive and elusive and often only detected by their calls. Only two crakes regularly occur in the park, but several other crakes, rails and flufftails occasionally occur here (p205), typically in years of above-average rainfall.

AFRICAN FINFOOT
Podica senegalensis

55cm, 550g A secretive, river-living species that is resident along parts of the Crocodile, Sabie and Luvuvhu rivers. Distinguished from similar-sized Reed Cormorant (p14) by red legs and bill (blackish in juv). Male head blue-grey; head of female and juv brown with white throat. Toes lobed, like a coot's. Pairs defend territories year-round along sections of the river. Spends much of its time swimming, keeping close to the river margins, often under overhanging vegetation. Feeds on aquatic insects, mainly taken from the fringing vegetation. Easily overlooked, as it seldom ventures into open water; quickly disappears when alarmed. WATERTRAPPER

AFRICAN CRAKE
Crecopsis egregia

22cm, 136g Differs from vagrant Corn Crake (p205) by black-and-white barred underparts and pale brown (not rufous) wings. A breeding migrant from tropical Africa to the savanna regions of South Africa, present November to April. Seldom recorded but this is probably more a consequence of its secretive nature rather than actual rarity. Breeds in seasonally flooded grassy areas, such as those found along the margins of pans, vleis and drainage lines. Its presence is most often revealed by its distinctive and far-carrying, ongoing '*krrk-krrk-krrk-krrk-krrk …*' call, mainly heard at dawn and dusk. AFRIKAANSE RIETHAAN

BLACK CRAKE
Amaurornis flavirostra

21cm, 89g A small, black crake with bright yellow bill and red legs and eyes; juv duller grey with greenish bill and legs. Common and widespread, found along the vegetated margins of streams, rivers, dams and pans. Unlike most other crakes, which are secretive, Black Crakes readily come into the open, walking with an upright cocky stance but darting for cover when alarmed. Remains in pairs year-round, advertising their presence by calling together, producing a bizarre brew of crooning, bubbling, growling and purring. SWARTRIETHAAN

COMMON (Kurrichane) BUTTONQUAIL
Turnix sylvaticus

15cm, ♂37g, ♀50g Smaller size and striking, scalloped plumage distinguish it from female Harlequin Quail (p58). Female larger and more boldly coloured than male; like painted snipes and most jacanas, the female is the dominant sex. Occurs widely and is recorded in all months; probably nomadic, moving about widely in response to rainfall, with numbers fluctuating seasonally and between years. Usually encountered singly or in pairs. Given its secretive nature, it keeps under the cover of grass at all times and is only likely to be seen when crossing a road. Advertising females utter a far-carrying, deep flufftail-like hooting call. Polyandrous; the males incubate the eggs and care for the chicks. BOSVELDKWARTELTJIE

African Finfoot ♂

African Finfoot ♀

African Finfoot ♀

Black Crake

African Crake

Common Buttonquail

COOTS, MOORHENS AND GALLINULES

Together with the crakes, these species belong to the family Rallidae, a diverse group that comprises mostly species dependent on aquatic habitats. The family is surprisingly poorly represented in the park: of the species on this page, only the Common Moorhen is resident; the others come and go erratically in response to changing conditions driven by rainfall. Other occasional vagrants include African Rail and African Swamphen (p205).

RED-KNOBBED COOT
Fulica cristata

39cm, 737g A large, blackish waterbird with a whitish bill and frontal shield; breeding ad has prominent red knobs on top of the shield. Uncommon non-breeding visitor; single birds appear occasionally on the larger dams. Conspicuous and locally abundant on the many farm dams and pans on the highveld west of the park. A highly mobile nomad; ringing results show coots routinely commute hundreds of kilometres between waterbodies, mostly travelling at night. Feeds mainly on submerged aquatic vegetation, which is scarce in the park's wetlands; the occasional visitors probably are en route between the highveld and the wetlands on the Mozambique coastal plain. BLESHOENDER

COMMON MOORHEN
Gallinula chloropus

34cm, 247g Larger size, yellow-tipped red bill, red frontal shield and bright yellow legs with red 'garters' distinguish it from Lesser Moorhen. Juv dull grey-brown with dark bill and grey-green legs. A localised breeding resident, found on larger dams and river pools where there are fringing reeds or other dense vegetation. In seasons of high rainfall its numbers are augmented by visitors when temporary pans become inundated, greatly expanding the size of the habitat available to this species. Unlike the Lesser Moorhen, it is not a shy or reclusive bird and it swims freely into open water. GROOTWATERHOENDER

LESSER MOORHEN
Gallinula angulata

23cm, 132g Smaller than Common Moorhen; ad bill mainly yellow (red confined to the top of the bill); legs pink, brown, grey or dull yellow without red 'garters'. Juv brown with a whitish belly. An erratic migrant from tropical Africa, abundant in years of high rainfall. Arrives in December/January and leaves in April. Breeds in grassy, temporarily flooded pans and depressions, especially on the basaltic plains in the east of the park. Mostly remains hidden within flooded grass; is best detected by its distinctive call, reminiscent of a spluttering engine that would not start. KLEINWATERHOENDER

ALLEN'S GALLINULE
Porphyrio alleni

26cm, 140g Much smaller than African Swamphen (p205), which has an entirely red frontal shield. Breeding male has bright blue frontal shield; female has apple-green shield. Juv pale buff with dark brown feather centres above; bill greyish; legs dull pink. A breeding migrant from tropical Africa from December to April; fairly common in years of high rainfall when pans and depressions become temporarily flooded. Easily overlooked; remains among flooded grass and sedges for much of the time, its presence given away by its loud, rapid 'kek-kek-kek-kek ...' call. KLEINKONINGRIETHAAN

Red-knobbed Coot

Red-knobbed Coot

Common Moorhen

Common Moorhen imm

Lesser Moorhen

Lesser Moorhen imm

Allen's Gallinule

Allen's Gallinule imm

JACANAS, SNIPES AND STILTS

These waterbirds, which belong to four wader families, each require a specific type of habitat. Because the aquatic habitats they favour change seasonally and, depending on rainfall, from year to year, they are to some extent nomadic, moving about widely in response to changing conditions.

AFRICAN JACANA
Actophilornis africanus

28cm, ♂138g, ♀232g A striking chestnut-and-white waterbird; ad has a blue frontal shield; juv duller with white eye-stripe. Common, localised resident at wetlands with water lilies or other floating aquatic plants. Its long toes and nails distribute its weight, allowing it to walk on lily leaves, hence the common name of Lily-trotter. Eats aquatic insects, crustaceans and even small fish. Wanders widely during droughts, and may feed along sandy shorelines. Polyandrous; the larger females defend territories containing multiple males, who undertake all incubation and care for the chicks. When one female displaces another, she systematically destroys any nests to allow 'her' males to breed again. GROOTLANGTOON. **Lesser Jacana** *Microparra capensis* (Dwerglangtoon) is much smaller than African Jacana, with greyish upperwing coverts; white tips to secondaries and black underwings are conspicuous in flight; occasionally recorded on pans and dams.

GREATER PAINTED-SNIPE
Rostratula benghalensis

25cm, ♂116g, ♀133g A rather cryptically patterned shorebird with gold 'braces' along its back and a prominent white eye-stripe; head and neck rich chestnut in ad female, greyish-brown in male, which also has more prominent buff spotting on its wings. Widely but sparsely recorded throughout at dams, pans and edges of rivers and streams where there are shallow, grassy verges. Small numbers are probably resident, supplemented by visitors that arrive to breed in wet years. Polyandrous; the larger and more striking female is the dominant sex, leaving the male to incubate and care for the chicks. GOUDSNIP

AFRICAN SNIPE
Gallinago nigripennis

28cm, 122g A cryptically patterned shorebird with an extremely long, straight bill and rather short legs. Easily overlooked, so the few recent records for the park that suggest it is a vagrant probably don't reflect its true abundance. Its preferred habitat is marshy, muddy, heavily trampled ground with dense, short grass cover and shallow pools of water, and it often forages among emergent vegetation. Such habitats are transient and consequently these birds move about widely in response to changing conditions. Makes a distinctive sucking noise when flushed, flying off rapidly with a jinking flight, before dropping back into cover. AFRIKAANSE SNIP

BLACK-WINGED STILT
Himantopus himantopus

38cm, 167g The extremely long, red legs, needle-like bill and black-and-white plumage are diagnostic. Occurs sporadically, with single birds or small groups found along the shallow, sandy margins of the larger rivers and on some dams. Not known to breed in the park, so they are probably nomads from elsewhere. Forages for aquatic insects and crustaceans while wading in shallow water, its long legs lifted high with each step, darting forward from time to time in pursuit of escaping prey. ROOIPOOTELSIE. **Pied Avocet** *Recurvirostra avosetta* (Bontelsie) has short, blue legs and an upturned bill; occasional visitor.

African Jacana

African Jacana imm

Greater Painted-Snipe ♂

Greater Painted-Snipe ♀

African Snipe

Black-winged Stilt

PLOVERS AND LAPWINGS

Plovers and lapwings are members of a large, widespread shorebird family, the Charadriidae. *Charadrius* plovers are a fairly small, short-legged species, mostly found in aquatic habitats, whereas lapwings (*Vanellus*) are larger, long-legged and mostly a dry-land species. Both groups feed, roost and nest on the ground. They are visual hunters, taking insects and other invertebrates from the ground or at the water's edge. The four here occur year-round in the park but move about locally in response to changing conditions. Several other species of plover visit the park occasionally (p205, p206). Lapwings are further described on p68.

THREE-BANDED PLOVER
Charadrius tricollaris

18cm, 33g The most commonly encountered plover in the park. A wetland plover easily identified by its two black breast bands, white headband and reddish legs. Found along rivers and on most dams and pans with muddy or sandy margins. Occurs year-round but subject to local movements. Territorial pairs defend about 100m of beach, with frequent noisy exchanges between neighbours. Bobs tail up and down and gives a high-pitched '*eeep*' call when alarmed. When foraging along the shoreline, it often uses foot-trembling to attract or disturb prey – standing on one foot, the other is extended forward and its toes are rapidly vibrated while held just above the ground.
DRIEBANDSTRANDKIEWIET

KITTLITZ'S PLOVER
Charadrius pecuarius

13cm, 35g Bold black-and-white head pattern distinguishes it from White-fronted Plover; juv lacks black facial markings and is best distinguished from other plovers by broad, buffy eyebrow and buffy underparts. A nomadic species that breeds locally, mainly in the dry season when receding water levels expose bare ground around the fringes of the larger dams and pans. When incubating birds leave the nest unattended, they have the unusual habit of completely burying the eggs, using their feet to rapidly kick grass or mud pellets over the eggs. Outside the breeding period, it mainly occurs alongside other plovers at pools along the larger rivers.
GEELBORSSTRANDKIEWIET

WHITE-FRONTED PLOVER
Charadrius marginatus

18cm, 46g Rather plain head distinguishes it from Kittlitz's Plover; ad male has broader, darker black band on crown than female and juv. The inland race found in the park is much darker than the more common coastal subspecies. Occurs in small numbers along all the larger rivers in the park, wherever there are extensive sandbanks; breeds mainly in late winter when river levels are lowest. The population is subject to local movements in response to seasonal changes in river flow and may be forced to leave the park entirely during periods of exceptional rainfall that cause all the rivers to flood. VAALSTRANDKIEWIET

SENEGAL LAPWING
Vanellus lugubris

24cm, 122g Distinguished from Crowned Lapwing (p68) by smaller size, black legs and bill, and absence of 'crown'; in flight, white secondaries form a band on the trailing edge of the wing, rather than a white wingbar. Occurs sparsely but widely, especially in the south; favours recently burnt or heavily grazed areas in open woodland. Usually found in small parties. Present year-round but highly nomadic; seldom remains in one area for long. Mainly travels at night, giving away its presence overhead in the dark with its melodious '*chi-wooot*' call. Breeds in spring. KLEINSWARTVLERKKIEWIET

Three-banded Plover

Three-banded Plover chick

Kittlitz's Plover

Kittlitz's Plover imm

White-fronted Plover

Senegal Lapwing

LAPWINGS (cont.)

Lapwings favour areas with minimal groundcover, either recently burnt, heavily grazed areas or sandbanks along river margins. Areas that have been burnt or grazed quickly change after the first rains, so these species seldom stay in the same place for long. Lapwings have carpal spurs, sharp bony projections at the wrist joint covered by a keratinous sheath, which are used in combat; they are capable of inflicting a significant wound on a competitor. White-crowned Lapwings, a particularly aggressive species, have spurs up to 2.5cm long! Lapwings defend their nest and chicks vigorously, dive-bombing any potential predator while giving loud warning calls. The precocious chicks initially freeze when the adults signal danger but larger chicks may run for cover.

CROWNED LAPWING
Vanellus coronatus

31cm, 179g Readily identified by its black-and-white 'crown'; in flight, the white wing coverts form a prominent bar across the upperwing. A fairly common resident and local nomad throughout, wherever there are areas of short-grazed or recently burnt grass. Wanders more widely after breeding, when small flocks form. Pairs breed singly in spring, vigorously defending their nest or offspring from passing animals by swooping on them while uttering strident '*kie-wiet*' alarm calls. KROONKIEWIET

BLACKSMITH LAPWING
Vanellus armatus

30cm, 163g A striking black, grey-and-white lapwing that is named for its metallic '*tink, tink, tink*' call, which is reminiscent of a blacksmith working on an anvil. Common along all rivers and on the margins of most dams and pans. Pairs defend breeding territories during the dry winter months; gregarious at other times, often gathering in groups, a dozen or so usually, and occasionally as many as a hundred together. Occasionally hybridises with White-crowned Lapwing; a hybrid pair near Skukuza has produced some very strangely patterned offspring in recent years. BONTKIEWIET

WHITE-CROWNED LAPWING
Vanellus albiceps

30cm, 187g With its strikingly patterned white-and-black wings and shrill piping call, this species is easily detected. At close range it has long yellow facial wattles but is readily distinguished from African Wattled Lapwing by its white breast and much greater extent of white in the wings. Occurs on rivers throughout, but is most common in the far north along the Luvuvhu and Limpopo rivers. Favours sandy beaches and islands; pairs defend territories 500–1,000m long with much vocal activity and occasional aerial pursuits. May hybridise with Blacksmith Lapwing; a hybrid pair near Skukuza has produced some very strangely patterned offspring in recent years. WITKOPKIEWIET

AFRICAN WATTLED LAPWING
Vanellus senegallus

35cm, 254g The largest lapwing, with yellow and red facial wattles. Most likely to be confused with Crowned Lapwing, but has a white median crown stripe (not white circle around black crown) and yellow (not red) legs. In flight, primary coverts are black (not white). A scarce bird, found mostly in the south along the Crocodile and Sabie rivers where it frequents areas of short grass around wetlands. Found in pairs or small groups after breeding. LELKIEWIET

Crowned Lapwing

Blacksmith Lapwing

White-crowned Lapwing

White-crowned Lapwing

African Wattled Lapwing

African Wattled Lapwing

COMMON MIGRANT WADERS

The scolopacid waders (family Scolopacidae) include sandpipers, stints, godwits, curlews, turnstones, snipes and phalaropes. They differ from plovers and lapwings by having smaller eyes, more slender heads, and slimmer, longer bills that in many species are packed with tactile receptors. These receptors are used to locate prey, primarily by feel. Most species breed in northern Eurasia and North America and migrate south in winter. Those breeding farthest north typically migrate farthest south, and most birds reaching South Africa breed in Siberia or Greenland. All depend on aquatic habitats on their non-breeding grounds, foraging in shallow water or along the water's edge, and are often referred to as waders. The four here are those most likely to be encountered in the park.

WOOD SANDPIPER   *Tringa glareola*
20cm, 60g Distinguished by intermediate size, yellowish legs, long white eyebrow and speckled upperparts; most likely to be confused with the rarer Green Sandpiper (for differences, see p72). The most common scolopacid in the park, arriving in August and leaving in April, although most abundant from September to February. Occurs along rivers and on the fringes of dams and pans where there are exposed shorelines. Feeds solitarily; individuals vigorously chase off others of its kind that approach too closely, but may gather in small groups to roost. Gives a high-pitched '*tiff-iff-iff*' call on flushing. BOSRUITER

COMMON SANDPIPER   *Actitis hypoleucos*
20cm, 47g Similar to Wood Sandpiper but has a diagnostic white 'shoulder' in front of the wing at rest; in flight, has a prominent white wingbar and dark (not white) rump. Shorter legs coupled with hunched gait and tendency to crouch when alarmed make it look dumpier. A common, solitary species found along the margins of rivers, dams and pans, often on rocky shores not frequented by other waders. Often bobs while foraging. When flushed, flies off low over the water, alternating bursts of stiff-winged flaps and glides, while uttering a high-pitched '*ti-ti-ti*' call. GEWONE RUITER

COMMON GREENSHANK   *Tringa nebularia*
32cm, 170g The largest wader regularly recorded in the park. Appears pale grey from a distance; at close range, the long, slightly upturned bill and blue-green legs are diagnostic. In flight, the white back and rump are conspicuous. Most likely to be confused with the rarer Marsh Sandpiper (for differences, see p72). Fairly common throughout on large rivers, pans and dams. A solitary species that forages by wading briskly in shallow water, picking up prey detected by sight; sometimes chases small fish. Typically utters a loud, flute-like, three-syllabled '*tew-tew-tew*' on flushing. GROENPOOTRUITER

RUFF   *Philomachus pugnax*
♂28cm, ♀22cm, ♂170g, ♀100g A fairly large wader, with males being much larger than females. Appears large-bodied due its small head and often raised back feathers; bill only slightly longer than head length, with a decurved tip; brownish-grey upperparts have diagnostic scalloped markings. Legs vary from red through green and yellow to brown. In flight, has narrow dark line down the centre of the white rump. Most males don't migrate as far south as South Africa, and the few that do get this far south don't moult into flamboyant breeding plumage in the region. Some non-breeding males have a white head and neck; white morphs have white heads year-round. Occurs widely throughout at rivers, dams and pans with shallow edges and exposed margins. KEMPHAAN

Wood Sandpiper

Common Sandpiper

Common Greenshank

Ruff

Ruff ♂

Ruff ♀

SCARCE MIGRANT WADERS

Including the African Snipe (p64), 16 scolopacids have been recorded from the park, of which 15 are non-breeding migrants from northern Eurasia. The four here are less common than those on p70, and a further seven species are even more rarely recorded (p206). Wader identification is notoriously difficult, as many species are rather similar in appearance and there is considerable variation in plumage among individuals linked to age and season. Most birds in the park are in non-breeding plumage, which offers fewer clues to their identity, and identification rests largely on size, bill length and leg length. However, some species start to moult into breeding plumage before they leave in autumn.

MARSH SANDPIPER
Tringa stagnatilis

24cm, 69g A long-legged wader; distinguished from Common Greenshank (p70) by appreciably smaller size, more slender body and long, fine, straight black bill. White back and rump in flight similar to that of Common Greenshank. Recorded widely but sparsely throughout at rivers, dams and pans. Mostly solitary, although small groups occur, especially in early and late summer, probably on passage. Forages mainly while wading, sometimes in water up to its belly, picking up invertebrates with its delicate bill like a tiny Black-winged Stilt (p64). Unlike Common Greenshank, seldom calls in flight (a soft '*yup*'). MOERASRUITER

CURLEW SANDPIPER
Calidris ferruginea

19cm, 57g A medium-sized wader with a longish, down-curved bill; white rump visible in flight. Female typically has a longer bill than male. Virtually the entire population breeds in the tundra of Siberia's Taimyr Peninsula. One of the most abundant waders in southern Africa; overwinters mainly on coastal lagoons and estuaries but the W Cape population has fallen dramatically in the last few decades. Small numbers appear regularly in the park between September and May on rivers and dams, probably on passage to or from the coast. Feeds mainly by probing into mud, either on the shore or in shallow water. Often associated with Little Stints. KROMBEKSTRANDLOPER

LITTLE STINT
Calidris minuta

13cm, 23g The smallest wader, with a short, slightly decurved bill that is shorter than its head length. Often forages alongside Curlew Sandpipers, which are almost twice its size. Typically found in small flocks when foraging or roosting; if disturbed, they fly off as a cohesive group. Recorded widely along the shallow edges of rivers, dams and pans. Feeds mainly by probing the surface of the mud, often right along the water's edge; sometimes feeds on dense mats of floating algae or other vegetation. Unlike most other waders, juvs return north in their first year after fledging, so are very seldom recorded in South Africa in winter. KLEINSTRANDLOPER

GREEN SANDPIPER
Tringa ochropus

23cm, 90g Most similar to Wood Sandpiper (p70); distinguished by having darker, less obviously spotted upperparts, shorter and somewhat darker legs, a white eyebrow that doesn't extend behind the eye and black 'armpits' (visible only in flight). A scarce, solitary species that is rather shy and unapproachable. Unlike most scolopacids, it shuns the open shores of rivers and dams, instead favouring streams, pools, ditches and dam backwaters where there is screening vegetation. Its '*tew-a-tew*' flight call is deeper and more melodic than that of Wood Sandpiper. WITGATRUITER

Marsh Sandpiper

Marsh Sandpiper

Curlew Sandpiper

Curlew Sandpiper

Little Stint

Green Sandpiper

COURSERS AND PRATINCOLES

Coursers are long-legged terrestrial birds, similar in appearance to a small lapwing. They run rather than fly if approached and their running is characterised by bursts of speed punctuated by abrupt stops. They favour ground with little or no cover and several species are attracted to recently burnt veld. Pratincoles are in the same family as coursers, but they are shorter-legged and have a more robust down-curved bill, unusually long, pointed wings and a tern-like flight. They fly rather than run if approached. Both groups are insectivorous, coursers foraging on the ground and pratincoles on the wing, especially at dusk. Like plovers and other shorebirds, they breed on the ground, laying their eggs in a shallow scrape. The chicks are precocial, leaving the scrape within hours of hatching, and crouch and freeze when threatened, relying on their camouflage to remain undetected by predators.

TEMMINCK'S COURSER · *Cursorius temminckii*

20cm, 71g A rather plain courser that is active during the day. Occurs widely but sparsely throughout, favouring open areas that are either heavily grazed or have been recently burnt. Nomadic; moves in response to changing veld conditions and often appears on burnt ground within hours of fire. They are alert and unapproachable, and capable of running at great speed. Found in pairs when nesting, otherwise usually in small groups. Pairs sometimes nest on gravel road verges. TREKDRAWWERTJIE

BRONZE-WINGED COURSER · *Rhinoptilus chalcopterus*

27cm, 148g Smaller than a Crowned Lapwing (p68), with characteristic black-and-white head markings, large dark eye and red eye-ring; in flight, lacks bold white wingbar. Primaries tipped iridescent violet. Occurs sparsely in woodland with little or no grass cover; much attracted to recently burnt veld. The small resident breeding population is apparently augmented by non-breeding visitors from the north from December to June. Crepuscular and nocturnal in habits; often seen on roads at night, but spends most of the day standing quietly in the shade. Calls in flight; its loud, weird '*gwaai-wraangg*' call is sometimes heard from rest camps at night. BRONSVLERKDRAWWERTJIE

THREE-BANDED COURSER · *Rhinoptilus cinctus*

26cm, 131g White chest and belly bordered by conspicuous black and chestnut bands distinguish it from other coursers. An uncommon, localised resident in woodland, largely restricted to the far north of the park where most frequently found in mopane between the Luvuvhu and Limpopo rivers. Largely solitary; occurs in pairs when breeding. Like the Bronze-winged Courser, it is nocturnal and crepuscular; stands or sits quietly in shade during the day, when easily overlooked. Best located on night drives. DRIEBANDDRAWWERTJIE

COLLARED PRATINCOLE · *Glareola pratincola*

25cm, 83g The pratincole most typically recorded in the park. Scarce and localised, mostly present in early to midsummer. Occurs singly or in small groups along larger rivers that have extensive sandy or muddy beaches, especially the Letaba, and along the open margins of large dams. May occasionally breed here. Easily overlooked on the ground but conspicuous in flight. ROOIVLERKSPRINKAANVOËL. **Black-winged Pratincole** *G. nordmanni* (Swartvlerkspringkaanvoël) has black (not rufous) underwings; secondaries lack a white trailing edge in flight; vagrant.

Temminck's Courser

Bronze-winged Courser

Three-banded Courser

Collared Pratincole

Black-winged Pratincole

Collared Pratincole imm

THICK-KNEES, TERNS AND SANDGROUSE

Thick-knees, also known as dikkops (meaning 'thick-head'), are large, ground-living birds related to plovers. The large, domed head (hence the local name) has large eyes that reflect the bird's nocturnal lifestyle. Largely inactive by day when they rest up in shade, they become active at dusk and, especially in summer, they make their presence known with loud, mournful, whistling calls. Terns are primarily seabirds, with white plumage, long slender wings and a graceful, bouyant flight. Two so-called 'lake terns' visit the park sporadically, while several other terns – Grey-headed Gulls and African Skimmers – are vagrants (p206). Sandgrouse are short-legged, ground-living birds that most resemble a pigeon. Their diet of seeds contains little water, so they typically visit waterholes every day to drink.

SPOTTED THICK-KNEE
Burhinus capensis

43cm, 483g Distinguished from Water Thick-knee by habitat, larger size and uniformly spotted wings and shoulders. A fairly common, widespread resident, it favours areas with a patchwork of bare or stony ground and grass, either in open woodland or in grassy savanna; often on alluvial soils close to rivers. Easily overlooked during the day, blending with the background when standing quietly or sitting in the shade. Piercing whistled calls, with alternating rapid-fire and slow notes, ending in a crescendo, give its presence away after dark. GEWONE DIKKOP

WATER THICK-KNEE
Burhinus vermiculatus

40cm, 388g Distinguished from Spotted Thick-knee by its broad, pale grey wing panel and narrow black and white lines on the shoulder. A common breeding resident, restricted to the vicinity of water; found along the margins of rivers, streams, dams and pans throughout the park. In pairs while breeding; more gregarious at other times when as many as 20 may roost together. More easily seen than Spotted Thick-knee as it often stands in the open rather than under cover. Enters some rest camps to hunt after dark. WATERDIKKOP

WHITE-WINGED TERN
& WHISKERED TERN
Chlidonias leucopterus
Chlidonias hybrida

21cm, 60g and 24cm, 100g respectively These two lake terns look similar at a glance when in non-breeding plumage, as they mostly are when present in the park. The White-winged Tern is smaller, flapping faster while coursing over wetlands looking for its insect prey. At close range, the black head marks extend below the eye onto the ear coverts but the nape is white, whereas the Whiskered Tern has white cheeks and black down the back of the neck. Both species occur sporadically, singly or in small groups, on the larger dams or pans in the park. The White-winged Tern is a non-breeding migrant from Eurasia, mainly found from November to April. WITVLERKSTERRETJIE & WITBAARDSTERRETJIE

DOUBLE-BANDED SANDGROUSE
Pterocles bicinctus

25cm, 230g Male readily identified by its boldly patterned crown and banded breast; shape of speckled female distinguishes it from a quail or francolin. A breeding resident throughout, most common in the north of the park, especially on sandy granitic soils in the west. Usually encountered alongside roads, either in pairs or small family groups. Easily overlooked; often only detected when they flush. Just before full dark they gather to drink at waterholes, flying in from all directions, calling *'wewe-we-play-volleyball'* as they approach. DUBBELBANDSANDPATRYS

Spotted Thick-knee

Water Thick-knee

Double-banded Sandgrouse ♂

White-winged Tern non-br

Whiskered Tern non-br

Double-banded Sandgrouse ♀

Whiskered Tern br

LARGE DOVES

Doves and pigeons are a large, diverse bird family, well represented in Africa. Ten species have been recorded from the park, but only eight are residents or regular visitors; two other pigeon species occasionally visit the park (p206). The use of the words 'pigeon' or 'dove' is based as much on historical usage as on whether the bird is large (mostly called pigeons) or small (mostly called doves). They are sleek, compact-bodied birds with small heads and short legs and bills. Most species are seed-eaters, obtaining all their food from the ground, but the African Green Pigeon is a fruit-eater that is usually seen in fruiting trees. Flight is swift and direct, but many pigeons and turtle doves have towering aerial displays, rising steeply on noisily flapping wings, before gliding back to earth.

RED-EYED DOVE — *Streptopelia semitorquata*

35cm, 252g Larger than Cape Turtle and African Mourning doves, with a dusky pinkish head and underparts that appear darker than those of the other two species; in flight, tail has broad grey tip, lacking white in outer tail. A fairly common resident throughout, mainly where there are tall trees, especially in woodland along the larger rivers. Much more common in the timber plantations and man-altered landscapes that lie to the south and west of the park. Its diagnostic call is a hooting '*you-chew tobacco-too*' or '*tobacco-too, you chew*'. GROOTRINGDUIF

AFRICAN MOURNING DOVE — *Streptopelia decipiens*

30cm, 156g Distinguished from Cape Turtle and Red-eyed doves by its distinctive call, bluish-grey head, pale yellow (not dark brown) eye and broad red ring of bare skin around the eye; in flight, has whitish tips to outer-tail feathers (less extensive than Cape Turtle Dove). A localised resident, common in riparian woodlands along the Luvuvhu and Limpopo rivers and in several rest camps (e.g. Satara, Letaba, Shingwedzi); scarce or absent elsewhere. Its call starts with a lilting, growling note followed by a series of cooing '*woow-woow-woooo*' notes. ROOIOOGTORTELDUIF

CAPE TURTLE DOVE — *Streptopelia capicola*

27cm, 153g Smaller than Red-eyed and African Mourning doves; told by its distinctive call and absence of a red rim around the dark eye; in flight, has extensive white tips to outer-tail feathers. A very common resident throughout, typically in more open habitats than Red-eyed Dove. Its characteristic call, variously described as '*how's father*', '*work harder*' or '*cas-cara*', is heard year-round and throughout the day. Drinks daily, mostly from 7–10h00; single birds or groups arrive cautiously at dams and reservoirs. Flushes with a clattering of wings at the slightest sign of danger. GEWONE TORTELDUIF

AFRICAN GREEN PIGEON — *Treron calvus*

29cm, 234g A stocky, parrot-like pigeon that can be hard to locate as it is well camouflaged while feeding in tree canopies. Common and widespread resident, found wherever favoured fruiting trees and shrubs occur; figs are especially favoured, but also frequents jackalberry, waterberry, jacketplum and whiteberry-bush. Usually seen in groups of 5–10 birds. Flocks move widely in response to changing fruit availability; flight swift and direct. Call is unlike that of any other dove, starting with several whirly whistled notes that subside into low-pitched growls and end in three or more sharp clicks. PAPEGAAIDUIF. **Speckled Pigeon** *Columba guinea* (Kransduif) is a rare, localised resident, restricted to gorges along the Luvuvhu and Olifants rivers and mountains in the southwest.

Red-eyed Dove

Red-eyed Dove

African Mourning Dove

African Mourning Dove

Cape Turtle Dove

Cape Turtle Dove

African Green Pigeon

Speckled Pigeon

SMALL DOVES

Doves and pigeons are vocal birds, each species distinguishable by its voice; the calls of doves during the heat of the day are among the most characteristic sounds of the bush. Their nests are flimsy platforms of sticks, in which they typically lay two white eggs. They form pairs when breeding, but at other times most species are gregarious, gathering in flocks where food is abundant or at drinking sites when water is scarce. Most species feed mainly on seeds, which contain very little moisture, so they typically drink daily.

LAUGHING DOVE
Streptopelia senegalensis

25cm, 102g Buff-coloured chest with black speckling and absence of a black nape collar are diagnostic. A very common resident throughout, often comes into rest camps. It has been suggested, though not borne out by ringing, that there is an influx in summer resulting from seasonal east–west movements. Ringing has confirmed that these doves often move hundreds of kilometres. Their common name refers to their gentle chuckling '*hu-hoo HA-oo-oo*' call, which rises and falls. They drink daily, often at waterholes alongside Cape Turtle and Emerald-spotted Wood doves. ROOIBORSDUIFIE

EMERALD-SPOTTED WOOD DOVE
Turtur chalcospilos

20cm, 62g A tiny dove; easily told from Namaqua Dove by its short, square-tipped tail. Occurs in drier habitat than Tambourine Dove; lacks that species' striking head pattern and pale breast. A very common resident throughout; its presence usually detected from its characteristic call – a mournful descending series of notes rendered as '*my father's dead, my mother's dead, all my children are dead, and my heart goes du, du, du, du*'. Usually encountered singly or in pairs. Often flushes from the roadside while feeding; regularly visits waterholes to drink. The iridescent green wing spots from which its name comes are only visible at close quarters. GROENVLEKDUIFIE

TAMBOURINE DOVE
Turtur tympanistria

22cm, 71g A small dove, only slightly larger than Emerald-spotted Wood Dove, but easily identified by its striking face pattern, darker upperparts and paler underparts (white in male, off-white in female). Its rich rufous wings contrast with its pale underparts; lacks dark bars on tail of other small doves. An uncommon, localised resident, restricted to areas of riparian forest along the large rivers, especially the Limpopo, Luvuvhu, Sabie and Crocodile. Occurs singly or in pairs. Usually seen when flushed off the forest floor. Call is similar to that of Emerald-spotted Wood Dove, but final '*du*' notes are even-pitched and do not run into each other. WITBORSDUIFIE

NAMAQUA DOVE
Oena capensis

26cm, 40g A small dove, easily told from all other species in the park by its long, pointed tail. Unusually for a dove, the sexes differ markedly: male has black face, throat and chest and red-and-yellow bill; female plain. Resident in small numbers but irrupts in large numbers during dry years. Single birds or small groups may be encountered anywhere in the park, especially in the drier central and northern areas, where it favours bare, open ground around waterholes. Drinks water daily, mainly in the middle of the day. Call is a soft '*huu-hooooo*'. NAMAKWADUIFIE

Laughing Dove

Emerald-spotted Wood Dove

Tambourine Dove ♂

Tambourine Dove ♀

Namaqua Dove ♂; inset: Namaqua Dove ♀

PARROTS

Parrots are a large order of birds that are well known through their long association with humans. They are the closest living relatives to passerines, and are one of only three orders of birds that learn their vocalisations.

BROWN-HEADED PARROT
Poicephalus cryptoxanthus

23cm, 145g Smaller than Grey-headed Parrot, with a light brown head and yellow shoulder; distinguished from Meyer's Parrot by its green (not brown) wings and green (not turquoise) underparts. A widespread resident, occurs throughout the park wherever there are tall trees; common in many rest camps and in riparian woodland. These are noisy birds, found in pairs or small groups, often seen flying at speed overhead, giving their presence away with high-pitched, shrill screeches. Hard to detect when feeding in leafy tree canopies. BRUINKOPPAPEGAAI. **Meyer's Parrot** *P. meyeri* (Bosveldpapegaai) is a rare, localised resident in the far north; may hybridise with Brown-headed Parrot.

GREY-HEADED PARROT
Poicephalus fuscicollis

32cm, 310g Much larger than Brown-headed Parrot; head is grey (not light brown), shoulder is red (not yellow) and its screeching call is much lower-pitched. A scarce, localised breeding nomad, largely confined to the far north but nowhere predictably present as it moves around in response to changing food availability. Occurs in pairs or small groups; usually encountered feeding on fruit or seed pods in large trees where its presence is often given away by its harsh, shrill call. Breeds in holes in baobabs in winter. SAVANNAPAPEGAAI

TURACOS

Turacos, with mousebirds, are the only order of birds confined to Africa. They are large, thickset birds with long tails, short, broad wings and pronounced crests. They live in tree canopies where they subsist on fruit and other plant matter.

GREY GO-AWAY-BIRD
Corythaixoides concolor

49cm, 274g A plain grey turaco. Common, widespread and conspicuous resident throughout. Gregarious, even when breeding; found in groups of up to 10 birds that maintain contact with frequent calling. Their familiar '*go-away*' or '*kwe-er*' call becomes strident if a hawk or other predator is detected; the alarm is picked up by others, which respond similarly, often from a kilometre or more away. They feed on a variety of flowers, leaves, fruits, berries and seeds from trees and bushes; also nectar from aloes and coral trees. KWÊVOËL

PURPLE-CRESTED TURACO
Tauraco porphyreolophus

42cm, 292g A brightly coloured turaco; its vivid red flight feathers are striking in flight. Common west of the park in the wooded foothills of the escarpment. A localised resident within the park itself where it is largely confined to areas of riverine woodland along the larger rivers, especially the Luvuvhu, Sabie and Crocodile; common in Pretoriuskop and Skukuza rest camps. Lives in the canopies of trees, running and hopping through branches with great agility, calling from time to time, a rapid-fire string of harsh, croaking notes. BLOUKUIFLOERIE

Brown-headed Parrot

Meyer's Parrot

Grey-headed Parrot

Grey Go-away-bird

Purple-crested Turaco

Purple-crested Turaco

CUCULUS CUCKOOS

The cuckoos form a large, diverse family, including the roadrunners, couas, malkohas, coucals as well as the cuckoos. Only the Old World cuckoos are brood parasites. The Common Cuckoo, which breeds in Europe and migrates to Africa in winter, is the 'classic' cuckoo and its intriguing parasitic habits and epic migration have been the subject of detailed studies. It is one of the four *Cuculus* species that occurs regularly in the park. These are fairly large, slim-bodied, long-winged and longish-tailed birds with distinctive calls; in flight they are easily mistaken for small accipiters. They are insectivorous, mainly preying on caterpillars, and are easily overlooked when not calling. In addition to the species listed here, a Madagascar Cuckoo *C. rochii* visited the park annually from 2008 to 2013 (p207).

COMMON CUCKOO — *Cuculus canorus*

33cm, 120g Distinguished from very similar African Cuckoo by mostly black bill, yellowish at base only, and undertail indistinctly barred with white. A scarce, solitary, non-breeding migrant from Europe, present throughout from October to April. The name 'cuckoo' is derived from its call, a two-syllabled '*cuck-koo*', a familiar sound during the European spring, but in its winter quarters it is silent. Satellite-tracked birds from Britain mainly winter in the Congo basin; those in the park probably come from farther east in Europe. EUROPESE KOEKOEK

AFRICAN CUCKOO — *Cuculus gularis*

32cm, 103g Distinguished from very similar Common Cuckoo by more extensive yellow base to bill, which typically surrounds the nostril, and broad, distinct white undertail barring. A fairly common breeding visitor from tropical Africa that occurs throughout the park, arriving in late September and leaving in April. Males call frequently in the first few months after arrival; their measured '*coop-coop*' call is usually the first indication of the bird's presence. They parasitise Fork-tailed Drongos, and the presence of agitated drongos may indicate that these cuckoos are in the vicinity. AFRIKAANSE KOEKOEK

RED-CHESTED CUCKOO — *Cuculus solitarius*

29cm, 74g A fairly large grey-backed cuckoo with a rufous breast (less prominent in ad females); juv is blackish above and on the throat and breast. A breeding visitor from tropical Africa, arriving in early October and leaving in March. Most common in the southern half of the park; scarce in mopane woodland where it is largely restricted to riparian woodland. Its presence in early summer is given away by the male's strident, persistent '*piet-my-vrou*' call, often lasting into the night. These are unobtrusive birds and were it not for this vocal activity they'd go largely undetected. Robin-chats, scrub robins and wagtails are their primary hosts. PIET-MY-VROU

BLACK CUCKOO — *Cuculus clamosus*

30cm, 90g A plain, sooty grey-black cuckoo; shows some white in underwing in flight, but lacks white windows in wings of Jacobin and Levaillant's cuckoos (p86). A breeding visitor from tropical Africa, arrives in late October and leaves in March. Occurs throughout the park, mostly in riparian woodland where it is fairly common. The male's presence is usually detected by its 2–3 mournful, drawn-out whistles, often rendered as '*I'm soo sick*', which are repeated monotonously; when excited, its call ends in a rattling '*whurri-whurri-whurri*'. Their primary host in the park is the Southern Boubou. SWARTKOEKOEK

Common Cuckoo

African Cuckoo

Red-chested Cuckoo ♂

Black Cuckoo

LARGE CUCKOOS

'Cuckoo' and 'cuckoldry' are words with strong connotations in the English language and both are tied to the habit of one bird laying its eggs in another bird's nest and leaving the hosts to rear its young. This behaviour is known as brood-parasitism. Hosts and parasites become locked into a complex evolutionary 'arms race' in which the hosts evolve strategies to detect and prevent parasitism and the parasites evolve counter-strategies to overcome host defences. In the species here, Jacobin Cuckoo is an unsophisticated parasite that doesn't lay host-matching eggs and has multiple hosts, while the others are specialised and have complex strategies to outwit their chosen hosts. In addition to these species, the Barred Long-tailed Cuckoo *Cercococcyx montanus* is a very rare vagrant (p207).

GREAT SPOTTED CUCKOO *Clamator glandarius*
39cm, 134g A large, striking cuckoo with white-spotted upperparts and distinctive rufous primaries visible in flight. Ad has grey head; black in juv. A fairly common breeding visitor from tropical Africa, present between October and May; most common in the drier north. Typically encountered in pairs, which are often noisy and conspicuous, drawing attention to themselves with their garrulous chattering call. Parasitises all the larger starling species in the park, especially Meves's and Burchell's starlings; pitched battles between host species and these cuckoos are witnessed on occasion. GEVLEKTE KOEKOEK

JACOBIN CUCKOO *Clamator jacobinus*
34cm, 81g Slightly smaller than Levaillant's Cuckoo. White-fronted morph with plain throat; rare black morph told from Black Cuckoo (p84) or Black Cuckooshrike (p132) and other all-black species by crest, white tail tips and more extensive white wing panels. A common breeding visitor from tropical Africa, arriving in mid-October and leaving in March. Occurs throughout but scarce in the drier mopane country in the north. Unusually for a cuckoo, it lays an unmarked white egg and parasitises a range of species, including bulbuls and greenbuls, bushshrikes and tit-babblers. These species all lay coloured, well-marked eggs but don't eject the cuckoo's eggs, as most hosts do. BONTNUWEJAARSVOËL

LEVAILLANT'S CUCKOO *Clamator levaillantii*
39cm, 122g A large black-and-white cuckoo; best told from pale morph Jacobin Cuckoo by its striped throat and upper breast. A common breeding visitor from tropical Africa, arrives in late October and leaves in May. Occurs throughout the park, parasitising Arrow-marked Babblers. The cuckoo lays a plain dark blue egg that closely matches the colour of the babbler's egg; the cuckoo and babbler nestlings, despite their size difference, are sometimes raised alongside each other. GESTREEPTE NUWEJAARSVOËL

THICK-BILLED CUCKOO *Pachycoccyx audeberti*
36cm, 110g A fairly large cuckoo, blackish above and off-white below; juv has white spots above. Scarce and localised; mostly recorded from tall riparian woodland along the Limpopo, Luvuvhu and Sabie rivers. Breeds in summer, parasitising Retz's Helmetshrike. There are records in winter, so the nature of its seasonal movements, if there are any, is uncertain. Like most cuckoos, it is easily overlooked; usually only detected when calling. In summer males make mid-morning display flights above the canopy, uttering a far-carrying, repetitive *'were-we-wick'* call as they float on slow-flapping wings before disappearing back into the trees. DIKBEKKOEKOEK

Great Spotted Cuckoo

Jacobin Cuckoo pale morph

Jacobin Cuckoo dark morph

Levaillant's Cuckoo

Thick-billed Cuckoo

HUGH CHITTENDEN

GLOSSY CUCKOOS AND COUCALS

The small *Chrysococcyx* cuckoos have iridescent green to bronze upperparts. Both species commonly recorded in the park have white underparts, but the male of the rare African Emerald Cuckoo *C. cupreus* (p207) has a lemon-yellow belly. Females and juvs have uniformly barred underparts. Coucals belong to the same family as cuckoos, but they build their own nests and raise their own chicks. Three species occur in the park, although the Senegal Coucal is restricted to the far north.

DIEDERIK CUCKOO
Chrysococcyx caprius

19cm, 37g Male distinguished from male Klaas's Cuckoo by white wing and tail spots, barred flanks and white eyebrow; female by white wing and tail spots, plain upperparts and thickly barred flanks. Female browner than male and finely barred above and below. A common, widespread breeding visitor from tropical Africa, arriving in October and leaving in March. Males advertise their presence with frequent calling, a rippling '*de-de-e-dee-deederik*'. The most frequent hosts of this cuckoo are weavers, especially Village and Southern Masked weavers. DIEDERIKKIE

KLAAS'S CUCKOO
Chrysococcyx klaas

18cm, 28g Male distinguished from male Diederik Cuckoo by absence of white wing and tail spots and plain white underparts; female by absence of white wing and tail spots and fine barring above and below. Female differs from male by being darker and extensively barred. Occurs widely throughout the park but is less common than Diederik Cuckoo. Seasonal status uncertain: more common in summer but frequently recorded in winter. Males advertise their presence by calling regularly from a perch, a plaintive two-syllabled '*may-chee*'. Parasitises sunbirds, batises and apalises. MEITJIE

BURCHELL'S COUCAL
Centropus burchelli

41cm, 180g Slightly larger than the scarce Senegal Coucal; identity confirmed by its fine black barring on the rump feathers (often not easily seen). A common breeding resident in the southern half of the park, but more localised in the drier mopane country in the north. Sedentary; remaining in pairs year-round and inhabiting thickets and other bushy areas, including reedbeds and areas of tall, rank grass along drainage lines. Calls in summer, frequently at dusk and dawn and sometimes in duet, a rich cascade of deep, bubbling notes that go up and down the scale. Usually calls from inside cover; if one happens to see a bird calling, it will be sitting upright, quivering with its head down and its bill held against its chest. GEWONE VLEILOERIE. **Senegal Coucal** *C. senegalensis* (Senegalvleiloerie) is a rare, localised breeding resident, found in the far north of the park.

BLACK COUCAL
Centropus grillii

35cm, 120g Breeding ad easily recognised by its black underparts; non-breeding and juvs streaky brown above and pale brown below; lacks pale eye-stripe of juv Burchell's Coucal. An erratic summer visitor in years of high rainfall, arriving in December and leaving in April. Largely restricted to the east in areas of rank, temporarily wet grassland on basaltic soils. Polyandrous; males perform all parental duties while females seek new partners. Female calls frequently, perching conspicuously while doing so, uttering a far-carrying double-note '*pop-pop*' at 2-sec intervals. When not calling, these birds remain in dense cover where they are difficult to detect. SWARTVLEILOERIE

Diederik Cuckoo ♂

Diederik Cuckoo ♀

Klaas's Cuckoo ♂

Klaas's Cuckoo juv

Burchell's Coucal

Senegal Coucal

Black Coucal br

LARGE OWLS

Owls are nocturnal birds of prey that have powerful talons and hooked bills similar to those of the diurnal birds of prey (eagles, hawks, buzzards, etc.), but the two families are unrelated. Owls are a large, diverse and cosmopolitan family – two families actually, as barn owls and grass owls (the Tytonidae) are separated from other owls (the Strigidae) at the family level. Eleven of South Africa's 12 owls occur in the park, ranging in size from the very large Verreaux's Eagle-Owl (2kg) to the diminutive African Scops Owl (65g). Despite their size difference, both are potent predators, differing only in the size of prey they hunt.

WESTERN BARN OWL
Tyto alba

32cm, 334g A distinctive pale owl with a whitish, heart-shaped face. A fairly common breeding resident throughout but seldom seen as it is strictly nocturnal. Roosts during the day in a tree hollow, rock cavity, Hamerkop nest or abandoned building. Calls frequently while hunting at night, uttering a rasping, shrill screech that is often heard in rest camps. It is a specialised predator of small rodents, using auditory clues to locate and catch these in the dark. NONNETJIEUIL. **African Grass Owl** *T. capensis* (Grasuil) is much darker above; occurs in rank grass usually near wetlands; rarely recorded, though perhaps overlooked given its nocturnal habits.

SPOTTED EAGLE-OWL
Bubo africanus

45cm, 695g A large, mainly grey owl with yellow eyes. Fairly common breeding resident throughout, but easily overlooked. Roosts during the day among rocks on kopjes or in hollow or densely foliaged trees; emerges at dusk when it frequently forages along roads, hunting a range of creatures from beetles and other insects to small mammals, reptiles and birds. Occurs solitarily or in pairs. In early summer, when these birds breed, the pair calls frequently at dusk, the male uttering a soft double hoot 'huh-hooooo' and the female responding with a lilting triple hoot '*hoo-huh-hooo*'. GEVLEKTE OORUIL

VERREAUX'S EAGLE-OWL
Bubo lacteus

62cm, ♂1.7kg, ♀2.4kg A very large owl; pale grey with black eyes and distinctive pink eyelids. Female distinctly larger than male. A fairly common breeding resident throughout wherever there are tall trees. Usually encountered in pairs; roosting birds are often spotted during the day by carefully scanning for them inside large, well-foliaged trees. They breed in winter, commonly on top of Hamerkop nests – the sight of a pair of long 'ears' projecting above such a nest gives the incubating bird away. Pairs call frequently at dusk and dawn, making a series of deep pig-like grunts, audible at times from several kilometres away. REUSE-OORUIL

PEL'S FISHING OWL
Scotopelia peli

62cm, 2.2kg A very large owl with distinctive ginger plumage. One of the park's iconic bird species, this remarkable owl is, unfortunately, scarce and localised, being restricted to the densely wooded margins of the Luvuvhu, Limpopo and Olifants rivers where, in suitable habitat, pairs are resident at 2–3km intervals. During the day they keep well concealed in densely foliaged trees (especially Natal mahogany), coming out at night to hunt fish from perches overhanging the river. At night, gives a series of wailing and hooting calls. VISUIL

Western Barn Owl

Spotted Eagle-Owl

Verreaux's Eagle-Owl

Pel's Fishing Owl

SMALL OWLS

Owls have numerous adaptations for their nocturnal habits. Their large eyes are packed with sensitive rods that allow them to see in extremely low light. The eyes also face forward (like those of humans), giving enhanced depth perception. They have exceptional hearing, augmented by large facial discs that act as parabolic reflectors. *Tyto* owls (p90) have the added advantage of having asymmetrical ears that allow them to locate prey by sound alone. Another adaptation is their feather structure: the flight feather edges are soft, allowing for silent flight when approaching prey.

AFRICAN SCOPS OWL   *Otus senegalensis*
16cm, 65g The smallest owl in the park, with a pale grey facial disc and yellow eyes. Most birds are grey but some rufous morph birds also occur. A common breeding resident in woodland throughout. Because of their small size and habit of perching frozen against a tree trunk, where their cryptic plumage matches tree bark, it is very difficult to spot these birds from the roads. More easily seen in some rest camps where individuals become habituated to people. Its call is one of the evocative night sounds of the park: a far-carrying, frog-like '*kruup*', uttered at 5–10-sec intervals, which may continue throughout the night in the early summer months. SKOPSUIL

SOUTHERN WHITE-FACED OWL   *Ptilopsis granti*
27cm, 200g A fairly small owl, substantially larger than African Scops Owl, with a white facial disc and red-orange eyes (yellow-orange in juv). A scarce breeding resident, recorded mostly in the drier northern half of the park. Mostly encountered singly, less often in pairs or family groups, typically perched in the mid- or upper branches of a tree, not concealing itself against the trunk as Scops Owls do. Like most nocturnal birds, its presence is mostly given away when it calls at night, a cheerful stuttering '*wh-h-h-Whoo*'. WITWANGUIL

PEARL-SPOTTED OWLET   *Glaucidium perlatum*
19cm, 82g A tiny, compact owlet with a rather long tail and false eye spots on the back of the head. Smaller and more common than African Barred Owlet; told by streaked (not spotted) breast and spotted (not barred) crown and back. A common breeding resident throughout, found in all types of woodland. It is frequently encountered as it is partly diurnal, especially in winter, and often perches conspicuously. Gives away its presence by calling frequently, both in the day and at night. It is a fiery little predator that targets small birds; as a result, such birds often gather to mob it when they find one during the day. Its call is a rising crescendo of piercing whistled notes; those of the female are higher pitched than the male's. WITKOLUIL

AFRICAN BARRED OWLET   *Glaucidium capense*
21cm, 120g Larger than Pearl-spotted Owlet, with a spotted (not streaked) front and barred (not spotted) crown and back; lacks false eye spots on the back of the head. A scarce, localised breeding resident, favouring tall riparian woodland, especially along the Luvuvhu River. Occurs singly or in pairs; roosts inside dense trees by day and comes out at dusk, and sometimes on overcast days, to hunt. Its giveaway call is a steadily repeated, rolling, two-syllabled '*prr-purrr*', sometimes extending into a rapid '*wirow-wirow-wirow ...*'. GEBANDE UIL

African Scops Owl

Southern White-faced Owl

Pearl-spotted Owlet

African Barred Owlet

AFRICAN WOOD OWL
Strix woodfordii

33cm, 300g A dark brown woodland owl, larger than African Barred Owlet (p92), with white spotted and barred plumage, dark eyes and a pale facial disc. A forest-living species, confined to dense riverine woodland. A very localised breeding resident, only common along the forested margins of the Luvuvhu River, where 23 pairs were counted along 15km of river. Very difficult to locate during the day when pairs roost deep inside thick tangles of creepers high up in trees; at night, their presence is given away by their exuberant hooting 'who-hoo, hu-hu-hooo, who-OOOOO', which sometimes ends with a shrill wailing note. BOSUIL

MARSH OWL
Asio capensis

37cm, 313g A dark brown grassland owl with buff bars across its primaries and tail, which are prominent in flight. A scarce breeding resident; probably nomadic as a result of periodic changes to its habitat brought about by fires and grazing. Nests and roosts on the ground in areas of rank grass, not necessarily selecting marshy places as its name would suggest. Hunts over open grassland, flying low over the ground, much as a harrier does, and dropping to the ground when prey, mostly rodents, is detected. In winter, when they breed, hunting often begins long before dark. At night, these owls may come onto roads to hunt. Unlike most other owls, it is not very vocal, typically only giving its short rasping call in flight. VLEIUIL

NIGHTJARS

Nightjars are nocturnal birds that were once considered to be closely related to owls. However, they belong to an entirely different lineage closer to swifts and hummingbirds. They feed mainly on the wing, locating prey with their enormous eyes. They have rather tiny bills but an enormous gape, which is enhanced by long rictal bristles, forming an effective net to scoop up flying insects. Like owls, they have rather soft-edged flight feathers to ensure silent flight. Six species occur in the park, the two below being seasonal visitors from the north. The other four species are described on p96.

EUROPEAN NIGHTJAR
Caprimulgus europaeus

27cm, 68g Large size, very long wing (reaching two-thirds along tail in sitting bird), absence of rufous collar, and dark 'shoulder' patch (the lesser coverts) bordered above by a buff line are diagnostic. Male has small white panels on primaries and tips of outer tail; female lacks these. A fairly common non-breeding migrant from Europe, present between November and March. Solitary and usually roosts during the day on a low tree branch, aligning itself with the branch. May be encountered on roads during night drives. Silent while in southern Africa. EUROPESE NAGUIL

PENNANT-WINGED NIGHTJAR
Caprimulgus vexillarius

27cm, 84g Breeding male unmistakable, even if pennants growing or broken, due to long inner primaries with extensive white bases. Female lacks wing pennants; readily identified by large size, rufous collar, rufous barred wings and absence of white panels on primaries and tips of outer tail. A scarce, localised breeding visitor from tropical Africa, present from late September to March. Occurs mainly in the far north of the park, especially in the broad-leafed woodlands around Punda Maria; migrating birds may overshoot and occur farther south in some years. Males call during display, making a sustained high-pitched cricket-like sound. WIMPELVLERKNAGUIL

African Wood Owl

Marsh Owl

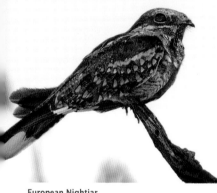

European Nightjar

Pennant-winged Nightjar ♀

Pennant-winged Nightjar ♂

NIGHTJARS (cont.)

Nightjars are a large cosmopolitan family of nocturnal birds. During the day they sit motionless, relying on their cryptic plumage to hide them as they blend into the leaf litter, burnt ground, rock or branch on which they rest. They come alive at dusk and become visible as they waft overhead on broad, silent wings, pursuing aerial insects. They often settle on roads at night, their eyes reflecting vehicle headlights. Night drives provide an opportunity of seeing them close up, but even then they are hard to identify if they are not calling. The name 'nightjar' comes from the jarring calls made by some species, and their vocalisations provide the easiest way of identifying them.

FIERY-NECKED NIGHTJAR
Caprimulgus pectoralis

24cm, 58g The only nightjar with white (not dark) rictal bristles (lining top of gape); distinguished by rufous face, cheeks and nape collar. Male's white spots on outer-tail feathers extend one-third the length of the tail and white spots on outer primaries sit on emargination; female has buff wing and tail panels. A common resident throughout, especially in woodland on granitic soils in the west. Unlikely to be seen except on night drives; after dark, males can be heard calling around every rest camp. Call a melodious, whistled *'good-lord-deliver-us'*. AFRIKAANSE NAGUIL

RUFOUS-CHEEKED NIGHTJAR
Caprimulgus rufigena

24cm, 54g Distinguished by greyish (not rufous) face and cheeks. Male's white tail spots on outer tail extend a quarter the length of the tail and white spots in outer primaries sit above emargination; female has buff wing and tail panels. A scarce breeding visitor from tropical Africa, present between October and March. Occurs commonly in the semi-arid interior of southern Africa and is at the edge of its range in the park, occurring mostly in open areas in the drier central and northern parts. Male call starts with several whoops, then becomes a sustained, evenly pitched churring that may continue unabated for minutes. ROOIWANGNAGUIL

SQUARE-TAILED NIGHTJAR
Caprimulgus fossii

25cm, 58g Distinguished at rest by its broad whitish bar on the folded wing below the shoulder. Male's outer tail entirely white; white spots in outer primaries sit above emargination; female has buff wing and tail panels. A common resident throughout, favouring more open habitats than Fiery-necked Nightjar. Unlikely to be seen except on night drives; after dark, it can be heard calling around every rest camp. Male call is a sustained churring that, at intervals, changes pitch and speed. LAEVELDNAGUIL

FRECKLED NIGHTJAR
Caprimulgus tristigma

28cm, 79g Large size, unusually large head and evenly mottled dark grey plumage are diagnostic, as is its restricted habitat, close to rocky outcrops. Male has white tips to outer-tail feathers and small white spots in outer primaries; female has small buff wing spots and all-dark tail. A localised resident, occurring widely but sparsely in the park. Favours kopjes with large boulders where it roosts in the open on exposed rocks; common, for example, in Mopane rest camp. Male's call is unmistakable, a 2- to 3-syllabled dog-like yapping *'cow-wow'* or *'cow-wowow'*. DONKERNAGUIL

Fiery-necked Nightjar

Rufous-cheeked Nightjar

Square-tailed Nightjar

Freckled Nightjar

SWIFTS

Swifts are among the most aerial of all birds, their cigar-shaped bodies and long, slender wings providing the perfect aerodynamic design for sustained high-speed flight. They are gregarious and spend most of their day on the wing hunting small airborne insects that are scooped up in their wide-held mouths. They have short legs and tiny feet and do not perch like other birds but instead cling to vertical surfaces, typically rock faces or walls of bridges and buildings. They are a large, distinctive family, nine species of which occur in the park, some as residents, others as seasonal migrants.

ALPINE SWIFT
Tachymarptis melba

20cm, 77g The largest swift; easily identified by its white belly and throat, separated by a broad brown neck band. A localised breeding resident in the gorges along the Luvuvhu River in the far north, but mostly encountered in the south and centre of the park where single birds or small flocks, sometimes mixed with other swifts, can be encountered flying overhead. These birds probably commute back and forth daily from their breeding and roosting sites on the high cliffs along the escarpment west of the park. WITPENSWINDSWAEL

AFRICAN BLACK SWIFT
Apus barbatus

19cm, 42g A large, dark-rumped swift; distinguished from the very similar Common Swift by contrast between blackish back and forewing and paler secondaries and greater coverts; appears chunkier with a shallower tail fork and rounded tail tips. A localised breeding resident in the gorges along the Luvuvhu River in the far north, although single birds or small parties, often associated with other swift species, can be encountered anywhere flying overhead. Many birds probably commute daily from the high cliffs along the escarpment west of the park where they breed and roost. SWARTWINDSWAEL

COMMON SWIFT
Apus apus

17cm, 37g A fairly large, dark-rumped swift; distinguished from the very similar African Black Swift by uniform mouse-brown plumage, relieved only by paler throat; appears more slender with a more deeply forked and pointed tail. A non-breeding visitor from Europe that is erratically but sometimes commonly present in the park; any large flock of uniformly brown swifts seen here during summer is likely to be this species. They remain constantly on the wing for the 6–8 months they spend in Africa, moving about widely in response to rain fronts, feeding on airborne insects by day and cruising in a semi-sleep state at night more than 1km above the ground. During migration they can travel as much as 650km/day. EUROPESE WINDSWAEL

AFRICAN PALM SWIFT
Cypsiurus parvus

15cm, 14g A small, slender, pale grey swift with an extremely long, deeply forked tail that is usually held closed, appearing pointed. Juv tail shorter. A common breeding resident mostly found around tall palm trees that have a skirt of dry, down-hanging fronds in which the birds roost and nest, gluing their eggs to the fronds with saliva. In recent years it has taken to nesting under open thatched roofs in some rest camps. Often solitary while foraging; gregarious at nest sites where they circle at high speed, accompanied by shrill screaming, individuals leaving the group to swoop up into the leaf fronds. PALMWINDSWAEL

Alpine Swift

African Black Swift

Common Swift

African Palm Swift

WHITE-RUMPED SWIFT
Apus caffer

16cm, 24g A slender swift with a white throat, narrow C-shaped white rump and fairly long, deeply forked tail, distinguishing it from Little Swift. A common, widespread breeding visitor, present from September to April, with individuals occasionally overwintering. Unlike Little Swift, this species nests solitarily and pairs are commonly encountered in the vicinity of their nesting sites, which typically are inside road culverts and under bridges where the birds commandeer the closed-chamber nests of Lesser Striped and other swallows. WITKRUISWINDSWAEL. **Horus Swift** *A. horus* (Horuswindswael) is intermediate between White-rumped and Little swifts in terms of size of the white rump and depth of tail fork; a scarce visitor, present September to May; probably breeds in holes in sandbanks along large rivers.

LITTLE SWIFT
Apus affinis

13cm, 25g A small, compact swift; distinguished from White-rumped Swift by its short, square tail and much broader white rump; distinguished from Mottled Spinetail by its plain white throat, shorter tail and absence of a white band across its belly. A common, gregarious breeding resident throughout; likely to be encountered anywhere but especially near colonies. Dozens to hundreds of pairs breed together, usually on man-made structures, especially under large bridges and the eaves of buildings. In summer, when the birds breed, they remain close to the colony, whereas in winter they disperse widely during the day, only returning at dusk to roost. KLEINWINDSWAEL

SPINETAILS

Despite their odd-sounding name, spinetails are members of the swift family, differing from typical swifts by having differently shaped wings and stiffened tail feather shafts that extend beyond the rest of the tail. This odd tail structure is probably designed to provide additional support when they cling to vertical surfaces. Both species here are tropical African species at the extreme southern edge of their range in the park and so are of special interest to birders. Both species differ from most *Apus* swifts in having white on their bellies.

MOTTLED SPINETAIL
Telacanthura ussheri

13cm, 33g Easily mistaken for the similar-sized Little Swift and a good view is needed to distinguish it: the white band across its belly is diagnostic and it has a narrower, less obvious white rump and a dark, mottled throat (plain white in Little Swift). A scarce, localised breeding resident in the far north of the park, mostly encountered in the vicinity of large baobab trees. Gregarious; roosts and nests in large hollow tree cavities, gaining access via slits in the trunk which the birds approach at great speed before abruptly disappearing into the hole. GEVLEKTE STEKELSTERT

BÖHM'S SPINETAIL
Neafrapus boehmi

9cm, 20g A tiny swift with an extremely short tail, white belly, distinctive wing shape (bulging in the middle) and bat-like erratic flight action. A scarce, localised breeding resident, restricted to the floodplains of the Limpopo and Luvuvhu rivers. Invariably encountered on the wing, either solitarily or in pairs; often found in the vicinity of large baobab trees inside which it nests. Often hawks aerial insects alongside swallows and swifts, typically keeping within 20–30m of the ground. WITPENSSTEKELSTERT

White-rumped Swift

White-rumped Swift

LIttle Swift

Horus Swift

Mottled Spinetail (left) and Böhm's Spinetail (right)

MOUSEBIRDS, TROGON AND KINGFISHERS

Mousebirds are so different from other birds that they constitute an order of their own, the Coliiformes, with only six species, all found in sub-Saharan Africa. They are small-bodied, fruit-eating birds with small legs and feet, small bills and long, rigid tails, and derive their name from their mouse-like appearance and mouse-like behaviour of creeping about in vegetation. Trogons are a widespread tropical family of brightly coloured birds that are poorly represented in Africa; the sole southern African species is an erratic visitor to the park. Four species of fish-eating kingfishers occur in the park. Kingfishers are further described on p104.

SPECKLED MOUSEBIRD   *Colius striatus*

33cm, 55g Distinguished from Red-faced Mousebird by brownish (not bluish-grey) overall colour and black (not red) facial mask and legs; lower mandible white. A fairly common breeding resident, occurs mainly in bush thickets and riparian vegetation along rivers. Gregarious year-round, in parties of 5–10 birds. Typically encountered flying low from one bush clump to another or, in the early morning, sitting perched on a tree top catching the sun, legs splayed and underpart feathers raised to heat their bellies and thus speed up bacterial fermentation of the plant material they ingested. Its typical call is a harsh '*krrk*'. GEVLEKTE MUISVOËL

RED-FACED MOUSEBIRD   *Urocolius indicus*

32cm, 56g Distinguished from Speckled Mousebird by bluish-grey (not brownish) overall colour and red (not black) facial mask and legs; bill all grey. Flies more strongly than Speckled Mousebird. A common, widespread species in all wooded areas. Resident, but subject to local movements in response to changing food availability. Gregarious; typically encountered in groups of up to a dozen birds, often seen flying rapidly and directly in a tightly bunched group. Its whistled '*swee-woo-woo*' call usually alerts one to its presence. ROOIWANGMUISVOËL

NARINA TROGON   *Apaloderma narina*

32cm, 69g Unmistakable. Female less vividly coloured than male, its face, throat and chest bronze-brown grading to crimson on the belly and vent. This much sought-after bird occurs commonly in forests along the escarpment west of the park but is scarce and nowhere predictably present in the park; the solitary birds encountered along the forested river margins are probably imms or off-season visitors from the escarpment. A perch-hunter, watching for cicadas, mantids, caterpillars and other insects from a perch where it remains motionless in one place for long periods. Despite its vivid colouring, it is easily overlooked, especially if facing away and its green back blends into the background. Best located by the male's grunting call. BOSLOERIE

GIANT KINGFISHER   *Megaceryle maximus*

44cm, 363g A huge kingfisher and the largest in the park; much larger and darker overall than Pied Kingfisher (p104). Male has rufous chest and white belly; female has rufous belly and densely streaked black-and-white chest. Fairly common, occurring throughout on rivers and dams. Territorial pairs are resident along the large perennial rivers, but elsewhere their occurrence is sporadic and dependent on local water conditions. Usually encountered solitarily. Hunts from perches overlooking water, including bridge railings and wires. Often utters a raucous call as it flies between hunting perches. Eats mainly crabs and fish, returning large prey to the perch to be subdued. REUSEVISVANGER

Speckled Mousebird

Red-faced Mousebird

Narina Trogon ♂

Giant Kingfisher ♂

ALBERT FRONEMAN / IMAGES OF AFRICA

KINGFISHERS (cont.)

Kingfishers are a cosmopolitan family distinguished by their long, dagger-like bills, large heads, thickset appearance, upright stance when perched, and short legs and toes. There are three distinct groups: the cerylid kingfishers (represented by the Giant and Pied Kingfishers), the tiny alcedinid kingfishers (represented by the other three species on this page) and the halcyonid kingfishers (p106). They range greatly in size from the 14g African Pygmy Kingfisher to the 363g Giant Kingfisher (p102). The name 'kingfisher' is something of a misnomer as relatively few species prey on fish; most feed on land, mainly taking invertebrates and small reptiles.

PIED KINGFISHER
Ceryle rudis

25cm, 84g A striking, black-and-white kingfisher; smaller and paler than Giant Kingfisher (p102). Male has two breast bands; female only one. A common breeding resident along all the larger rivers and on many dams. Feeds almost exclusively on small fish. Usually forages singly, but often seen in loose groups, with birds giving their excited chittering calls while pursuing one another. Incapable of remaining still for long; frequently changes fishing perches or hunts by hovering. Reputed to be the largest bird capable of hovering in still air; this energetically costly foraging technique enables it to fish in open water away from perches. When there is a breeze to assist hovering, up to 80% of fishing is done this way. Breeds co-operatively; young from previous broods assist with rearing the chicks. BONTVISVANGER

HALF-COLLARED KINGFISHER
Alcedo semitorquata

18cm, 38g The largest alcedinid kingfisher; easily told from the smaller Malachite Kingfisher by its plain blue crown and upperparts and its large, all-black bill. A fish-hunting species that is dependent on perennial rivers, it is an uncommon resident, recorded very sparsely along the Crocodile, Sabie, Letaba and Luvuvhu rivers. Fishes solitarily from low branches overhanging water, often remaining still for long periods and thus is easily overlooked. More conspicuous in flight as it darts low over the water, often announcing that it is on the move with a high-pitched '*tseeep*'. BLOUVISVANGER

AFRICAN PYGMY KINGFISHER
Ispidina picta

15cm, 14g A terrestrial species; distinguished from similar-sized Malachite Kingfisher by its broad orange (not blue) eyebrow and its mauve-coloured (not orange) cheeks. Juvs of both species have black bills. A breeding visitor, arriving in early October and departing in April. Occurs widely but sparsely in wooded areas, especially in riparian woodland. Hunts insects, lizards and geckos from low perches, swooping to catch them in the same manner as a fish-hunting species. Breeds in holes excavated in banks. DWERGVISVANGER

MALACHITE KINGFISHER
Alcedo cristata

14cm, 17g An aquatic species; smaller than Half-collared Kingfisher, with a red bill; blackish in juv. Distinguished from African Pygmy Kingfisher by its orange (not mauve) cheeks and turquoise-and-blue crown. A fairly common resident fish-hunting species, occurs throughout on rivers and dams, especially where there are fringing reeds or sedges. In pairs while breeding, otherwise solitary, typically encountered hunting from a low perch on a plant stem overlooking water. Breeds in holes excavated in banks. Call, usually given in flight, is a high-pitched '*tseeep*'. KUIFKOPVISVANGER

Pied Kingfisher ♀

Pied Kingfisher ♂

Half-collared Kingfisher

African Pygmy Kingfisher

Malachite Kingfisher

Malachite Kingfisher imm

HALCYON KINGFISHERS

Halcyon, a tragic figure in Greek mythology who drowned herself at sea and was transformed into a kingfisher, is the generic name for a group of non-aquatic kingfishers that includes the species listed below. The term 'halcyon days' stems from the mistaken belief that these kingfishers laid their eggs at sea on particularly calm days. All species here have some blue in their plumages, and their calls, preferred habitats and foraging methods are similar. They live in woodland habitats and hunt solitarily from perches, preying mostly on invertebrates and small reptiles caught on the ground. Two are seasonal visitors to the park and two are resident.

WOODLAND KINGFISHER · *Halcyon senegalensis*
23cm, 65g Distinguished by its red-and-black bill and azure-blue back, tail, shoulders and primaries. A common breeding visitor, arriving in the park in early November and leaving in early April; spends the southern winter in the northern savannas of Sudan and Central African Republic. Occurs wherever there are tall trees and potential nest sites. On arrival they quickly form pairs and establish territories around a nest site (a tree cavity, usually made by a woodpecker) and this activity is accompanied by much calling and chasing. Once nesting commences they settle down and become less conspicuous; in the month or two before they leave at the end of summer they are largely silent. Male call is a loud, ringing '*tit tr-r-r-r-r-r-r-r-r-r*'. BOSVELDVISVANGER

BROWN-HOODED KINGFISHER · *Halcyon albiventris*
23cm, 62g Off-white, streaked underparts and streaked brown crown and nape are diagnostic. Male has black shoulders and wing coverts; brown in female. A common resident in all wooded areas. Often found close to drainage lines where there are erosion gullies that provide earth banks for breeding. It excavates a nest tunnel that is used both for breeding and as a night-time roost. Remains in territorial pairs year-round, but hunts solitarily, so is usually encountered singly. Male call is a descending whistled '*tee teu-teu-teu-teu*'. BRUINKOPVISVANGER

GREY-HEADED KINGFISHER · *Halcyon leucocephala*
21cm, 45g Distinguished by its all-red bill, orange belly and underwing coverts, and violet-coloured wings and tail; female has less extensive orange underparts. A scarce breeding visitor from tropical Africa, present between October and April. Mostly encountered, singly or in pairs, in tall woodland along the larger rivers. Similar to Woodland Kingfisher, it is vocally active when pairs and territories are being established; becomes subdued once breeding is under way. Nests in a tunnel that it excavates into an earth bank; the roofs of aardvark holes are a favoured site. Male call is a high-pitched '*chee-chi-chi-chi-chi*' trill. GRYSKOPVISVANGER

STRIPED KINGFISHER · *Halcyon chelicuti*
18cm, 38g The smallest and least colourful *Halcyon* kingfisher, mainly brown above and off-white below with a dark, partially red bill and small areas of blue on the tail, rump and secondaries. A rather scarce resident, occurring throughout the park; most commonly encountered in the southwest. Favours broad-leafed woodland where pairs defend year-round territories. Given its solitary hunting behaviour, single birds are usually encountered. Nests in cavities in trees, especially those excavated by barbets and woodpeckers. Male call is a loud '*tree treuur-r-r-r-r-r*', repeated several times. GESTREEPTE VISVANGER

Woodland Kingfisher

Woodland Kingfisher

Brown-hooded Kingfisher ♂

Brown-hooded Kingfisher ♀

Grey-headed Kingfisher

Striped Kingfisher

BEE-EATERS

Bee-eaters, a mainly African family of colourful and conspicuous birds, are related to kingfishers and rollers. Seven species occur in the park, but only four are commonly encountered (p207). These sleek, long-winged birds use their slender, curved bills to snatch up flying insects. In addition to bees, they eat a range of aerial insects. They nest in holes that they excavate in the ground, usually in earth banks.

EUROPEAN BEE-EATER
Merops apiaster

25cm, 52g Golden brown back, yellow throat and blue underparts are diagnostic. A common, widespread non-breeding visitor from Europe, arriving in late September and leaving in late March. Occurs throughout the park, moving about from place to place in response to rainfall. Gregarious; usually found in flocks of a dozen or more birds. Hunts from perches like other bee-eaters; also spends much time on the wing, giving away its presence high in the air with its liquid '*prrrup*' call-notes. EUROPESE BYVRETER. **Blue-cheeked Bee-eater** *M. persicus* (Blouwangbyvreter) has green upperparts, buffy throat and blue-green belly; rare visitor from the Palearctic from October to April; mostly recorded in small flocks in the far north of the park.

WHITE-FRONTED BEE-EATER
Merops bullockoides

23cm, 35g A striking bee-eater with a red-and-white throat. A common but localised resident, largely restricted to the vicinity of rivers that have eroded, high-walled earth banks, which provide sites for their colonies. Between 10 and 50 pairs excavate nest tunnels that are used both for breeding (in early summer) and as a night-time roost year-round. During the day, birds disperse widely to feed, hawking insects from perches; commonly hawks over water, targeting large dragonflies. Groups maintain regular contact with their nasal, whiny '*queerrr*' call, a note that is very similar to the call of the Greater Blue-eared Starling. ROOIKEELBYVRETER

SOUTHERN CARMINE BEE-EATER
Merops nubicoides

35cm, 62g A mainly reddish-pink bee-eater with a turquoise crown; juv duller. A common non-breeding visitor, arriving in flocks in December and leaving in March/April. Breeds from August in large colonies on the banks of central African rivers; moves south into the park (and elsewhere in northern South Africa) for a few months in midsummer, then heads north into Tanzania, before returning south to its breeding grounds. Gregarious year-round. The flocks in the park invariably include many young birds, some still being fed by their parents. ROOIBORSBYVRETER

LITTLE BEE-EATER
Merops pusillus

16cm, 15g A tiny bee-eater with green upperparts and buffy underparts, washed yellow on its throat. A fairly common, widespread resident; occurs in pairs year-round or, after breeding, in small family groups. These confiding birds are typically encountered perched near one another on neighbouring bushes and trees, each watching intently for passing insects, poised to sally out when prey is spotted. Bees are commonly taken and are brought back to a perch to have the sting removed before being swallowed. The de-venoming is done by delicately rubbing the bee's abdomen against the stem, a process that has probably taken many attempts and several stings to master. KLEINBYVRETER. **Swallow-tailed Bee-eater** *M. hirundineus* (Swaelstertbyvreter) is slightly larger, with an electric blue forked tail; rare visitor, mainly in winter.

European Bee-eater

White-fronted Bee-eater

Southern Carmine Bee-eater

Southern Carmine Bee-eater

Blue-cheeked Bee-eater

Little Bee-eater

Swallow-tailed Bee-eater

ROLLERS

Rollers derive their name from their striking display flight, which is performed during pair formation or when defending a territory. 'Rolling' involves flying high into the air, turning and swooping back down, wings flaying and the body rocking from side to side during the descent while simultaneously calling loudly. Rollers are a mainly African family of 12 species, all colourful, conspicuous and similarly built. They are sturdy-looking birds with short legs and feet and a robust, slightly hooked bill. Most are sit-and-wait predators that watch the ground from a perch, dropping down to take grasshoppers, beetles, scorpions, lizards and other small creatures. Five species occur in the park; the four breeding species all breed in holes in dead trees.

EUROPEAN ROLLER · *Coracias garrulus*

31cm, 122g Uniformly blue head, chest and underparts and square tail distinguish it from other rollers. A common non-breeding visitor from Europe, arriving in early December and departing in March. Occurs throughout, often outnumbering all other rollers in summer. Especially common in the mopane scrub on the basaltic soils in the northeast, where birds are encountered perched every few hundred metres. Unlike the resident rollers, they are essentially silent and undemonstrative during their stay. EUROPESE TROUPANT. **Racket-tailed Roller** *C. spatulatus* (Knopsterttroupant) has a blue face, throat and breast, and brown crown; rare, but probably resident in tall open woodland in the far north of the park; breeds at least occasionally.

LILAC-BREASTED ROLLER · *Coracias caudatus*

32cm, 108g Lilac breast and turquoise crown are diagnostic. A common, conspicuous breeding resident, occuring throughout the park; is unlikely to ever be missed during a visit. In early summer, pairs can be seen 'rolling' – repeatedly climbing high into the air before swooping back towards the ground while rocking from side to side, calling raucously as they descend, their harsh, unpleasant call undoing the beauty of the display. At other times of the year, they occur solitarily, and are typically found, even in the heat of the day, perched on a dead branch or at the top of a bush. GEWONE TROUPANT

PURPLE ROLLER · *Coracias naevius*

35cm, 167g Large size, square tail and purplish-brown underparts heavily streaked with white are diagnostic. A breeding resident, occurring widely throughout the park. Although much outnumbered by the smaller Lilac-breasted Roller, its numbers increase in winter, bolstered by non-breeding visitors from elsewhere. A solitary and largely undemonstrative bird except in the breeding season. Typically encountered perched on top of a tree, watching the ground below for potential prey. Generally less confiding and approachable than the Lilac-breasted Roller. GROOTTROUPANT

BROAD-BILLED ROLLER · *Eurystomus glaucurus*

29cm, 110g Yellow bill and rich mauve, cinnamon and blue plumage are diagnostic. A breeding visitor to the park from tropical Africa, arriving in October and departing in March. Fairly common in the baobab country in the north of the park, especially along the Luvuvhu and Limpopo floodplains; localised elsewhere where it is mainly confined to the margins of larger rivers. On arrival in the park these birds are noisy and conspicuous as they form pairs and establish nesting territories, but they quieten down thereafter. Perches high up in tall trees and catches much of its prey aerially. GEELBEKTROUPANT

European Roller

Racket-tailed Roller

Lilac-breasted Roller

Broad-billed Roller

Purple Roller

111

WOOD-HOOPOES, HOOPOES, SCIMITARBILLS AND HORNBILLS

Three families are included here. The distinctive cinnamon-coloured hoopoes consist of either a single species or four, depending on which authority is consulted. They are closely related to the 8–9 wood-hoopoes and scimitarbills, which are confined to Africa and have glossy blue- or green-black plumage, long graduated tails and specialised foraging habits. Both families are strong smelling thanks to symbiotic bacteria in their preen glands; this is likely to deter predators such as genets from attacking them in their roosts. The hornbills are a larger, more diverse family, which is described in more detail on p114.

GREEN WOOD-HOOPOE · *Phoeniculus purpureus*

33cm, 77g A large, long-tailed, greenish-black wood-hoopoe with white wingbars and tail tips that are prominent in flight. Ad has red bill; juv has blackish bill. Male has appreciably longer bill than female. A common breeding resident wherever there are tall trees, especially in riparian woodland. Gregarious; lives year-round in close-knit groups; only the alpha pair breeds but other members feed the young. Groups maintain permanent territories and noisily advertise their presence with periodic bouts of shrill cackling. They forage for insects on the trunks and branches of trees and nest and roost together in tree cavities. Groups typically contain 5–8 birds; group size is determined by availability of roosting cavities (larger where cavities are scarce). ROOIBEKKAKELAAR

AFRICAN HOOPOE · *Upupa africana*

26cm, 53g Unmistakable. A fairly common, widespread breeding resident. Occurs solitarily or in pairs, frequenting both woodland and open country where there are areas of bare ground or where the grass layer has been shortly cropped or recently burnt. Uses its long bill to probe the ground for invertebrate prey as it walks with a rolling gait; flies to a tree when alarmed. Its flight is dipping and butterfly-like and its extraordinary crest, usually held flat against the head, is fanned open when the bird is excited. The name hoopoe comes from its distinctive call, a soft, deep '*hoop, hoophoop*'. HOEPHOEP

COMMON SCIMITARBILL · *Rhinopomastus cyanomelas*

26cm, 33g Smaller than Green Wood-Hoopoe, with a more strongly curved, black bill, different call and solitary disposition; also shows white wingbars and tail tips in flight. A fairly common breeding resident in all woodland areas. In pairs while breeding, otherwise largely solitary; lone birds often join mixed-species bird parties in winter. Forages for insects on dry branches and tree trunks, using its long, deeply curved bill to probe into crevices. A vocal bird, its presence is often given away by its plaintive whistling call, a series of '*pweep-pweep-pweep ...*' notes. Roosts and nests in tree cavities. SWARTBEKKAKELAAR

CROWNED HORNBILL · *Tockus alboterminatus*

52cm, 225g Red bill, yellow eye and dark brown and white plumage diagnostic. Male has a larger bill casque than female and black facial skin (blue in female). A scarce, localised breeding resident, largely confined to areas of tall riparian woodland along the big rivers, especially the Luvuvhu. In pairs while breeding, otherwise in small parties. Largely insectivorous while breeding; in winter feeds primarily on fruit, moving widely in response to changes in fruit availability. Often seen in flight, when its exaggerated looping flight action is distinctive. Call is a loud '*chleoo chleooo*'. GEKROONDE NEUSHORINGVOËL

Green Wood-Hoopoe

African Hoopoe

Common Scimitarbill ad and juv

Crowned Hornbill

HORNBILLS (cont.)

Hornbills are a family of mainly tropical species from Africa and Asia. Their large, down-curved bills, with a casque in some species, are their most distinctive feature, and are used to offload heat in hot weather. Five species occur in the park, including some of the park's most familiar birds, which come into rest camps and picnic sites to boldly scavenge food from tourists. Their nesting behaviour is unique among birds: the female seals herself inside a tree cavity throughout the incubation and part of the nestling period, during which time she moults all her flight feathers and is entirely dependent on her mate for food.

TRUMPETER HORNBILL — *Bycanistes bucinator*

58cm, 645g A large black-and-white hornbill with red facial skin; female smaller with a reduced casque. A fairly common but localised breeding resident, occurs mostly in tall riparian woodland along the larger rivers, especially those where sycamore figs are well represented. In pairs while breeding, otherwise in parties of up to a dozen birds. Mainly frugivorous; flocks move about widely to find fruiting trees. Easily overlooked when foraging in foliaged trees, but conspicuous in flight, when they often utter their far-carrying, wailing, plaintive *'waaaa-waaaaaa-waaaaa ...'* call. Flight undulating, with bursts of rapid wing-beats interspersed by long glides. GEWONE BOSKRAAI

AFRICAN GREY HORNBILL — *Tockus nasutus*

46cm, 157g A rather drab grey hornbill. Male has a mainly black bill; female's bill mainly red and yellowish-white. A common breeding resident in wooded areas. In pairs while breeding, otherwise solitary or in groups of up to 30 birds. Forages mainly in tree foliage, eating insects such as mantids, beetles, caterpillars, also chameleons, geckos and other small reptiles. Also preys on bird nestlings, and nesting passerines often become agitated at its presence. Has an exaggerated looping flight action; typical call is a piercing series of whistles, *'dee dee dee dee dee deee, de-deu-deu, de-deu-deu ...'*, given with the bill held vertically and accompanied by wing flicks. GRYSNEUSHORINGVOËL

SOUTHERN YELLOW-BILLED HORNBILL — *Tockus leucomelas*

50cm, 190g Yellow bill and larger size distinguish it from otherwise similar Southern Red-billed Hornbill. Male has a larger bill than female. A common, conspicuous breeding resident throughout. Occurs singly, in pairs or in small family groups; doesn't form flocks as other hornbill species do in winter. Forages mostly on the ground and has a diverse diet, from insects and small reptiles to fruit and seeds; has a comical technique of handling such items, picking them up with the tip of the bill, throwing them into the air, then catching and swallowing them. Call is a long series of popping notes, becoming more complex as it reaches a crescendo. GEELBEKNEUSHORINGVOËL

SOUTHERN RED-BILLED HORNBILL — *Tockus rufirostris*

40cm, 139g Red bill distinguishes it from the larger but otherwise similar Southern Yellow-billed Hornbill. Male's bill has blackish base; all red in female. A common, widespread breeding resident, favouring clearings where groundcover is sparse (e.g. heavily grazed or recently burnt areas). Forages mostly on the ground, using its bill to probe and turn over animal dung in search of beetles, centipedes, grasshoppers and other arthropods. Roosts, nests and takes refuge from danger in trees. Call is a series of popping notes, becoming faster and more manic as the call progresses. ROOIBEKNEUSHORINGVOËL

Trumpeter Hornbill ♂

Trumpeter Hornbill ♀

African Grey Hornbill ♂

Southern Yellow-billed Hornbill

Southern Red-billed Hornbill ♂

BARBETS AND TINKERBIRDS

Barbets and tinkerbirds are colourful frugivorous birds that occur in tropical America, Asia and Africa, but recent studies have shown that African barbets differ from those on other continents at the family level. Five species occur in the park. Although they bear little resemblance to each other, all are primarily fruit-eaters and they depend on fruit being available year-round. They excavate nest-holes in soft wood which they use for breeding and as night-time roosts. Closely related to honeyguides, the three larger species are regular hosts to these brood parasitic birds, aggressively chasing any honeyguides that come close to their nests.

CRESTED BARBET
Trachyphonus vaillantii

24cm, 74g The most commonly seen barbet in the park. An unmistakable, large black, yellow, red and white barbet. A widespread breeding resident, found in all woodland areas; common in many rest camps. Territorial year-round, living in pairs. Often forages on the ground; it is less fruit-dependent than other barbets, routinely eating grasshoppers, caterpillars, beetles, termites and other arthropods. The male's call is a loud, sustained dry trill, usually uttered from a tree top; the female often responds with a slower '*puka-puka-puka …*' call. Parasitised by Greater and Lesser honeyguides. KUIFKOPHOUTKAPPER

BLACK-COLLARED BARBET
Lybius torquatus

20cm, 53g The striking red-and-black head is diagnostic; rare individuals have yellow (not red) heads. A fairly common breeding resident, occurring mostly in tall riparian vegetation; common in many rest camps. Territorial; occurs in pairs while breeding but usually in family groups at other times of the year, when they feed and roost together. Diet consists largely of fruit, especially figs, waterberries and jackalberries. Pairs call frequently in well-synchronised melodic duets, usually facing each other and bobbing while doing so, one initiating with the first note, the other responding with the second note: '*two-puddly, two-puddly, two-puddly …*'. Commonly parasitised by Lesser Honeyguide. ROOIKOPHOUTKAPPER

ACACIA PIED BARBET
Tricholaema leucomelas

18cm, 32g Superficially like Yellow-fronted Tinkerbird but larger with bolder face pattern and red (not yellow) forehead. A species of semi-arid savanna, it is a rather scarce breeding resident in the park, found mostly in thornveld, less often in broad-leafed woodland and largely absent from mopane. Occurs solitarily or in widely scattered pairs, its presence usually given away by its low hooting song or nasal trumpet-like call-note that is repeated at intervals. Parasitised by Lesser Honeyguide. BONTHOUTKAPPER

YELLOW-FRONTED TINKERBIRD
Pogoniulus chrysoconus

12cm, 13g Superficially like Acacia Pied Barbet but much smaller; forehead is yellow or occasionally orange (not red). A scarce but widespread breeding resident in any woodland, especially where there are infestations of mistletoe, the fruit of which it depends on for much of the year. Occurs in pairs while breeding, otherwise solitary; given its small size, it is easily overlooked unless calling. Males call throughout summer from tree tops, often in the heat of the day, uttering a monotonous '*pok, pok, pok …*' that may continue unabated for many minutes. GEELBLESTINKER. **Yellow-rumped Tinkerbird** *P. bilineatus* (Swartblestinker) has a boldly striped head and plain black back; rare, localised resident in riparian woodland along the Crocodile River and at Skukuza and Berg-en-Dal rest camps.

Crested Barbet

Black-collared Barbet

Yellow-fronted Tinkerbird

Acacia Pied Barbet

Yellow-rumped Tinkerbird

HONEYGUIDES AND HONEYBIRDS

Despite their drab, sparrow-like plumage, these birds are related to woodpeckers and barbets. Their white outer-tail feathers, conspicuous in flight, are the only distinctive feature of most species. The Greater Honeyguide derives its family name from its habit of leading people to beehives by uttering a distinctive 'guiding call'. Unfortunately, this unique mutualism has died out in most parts of Africa, and only naïve juvs still attempt to guide people. Like the Old World cuckoos, all species parasitise the nests of other birds. Freed of parental responsibilities, males spend much of their time during the breeding season advertising to females from regular call sites.

GREATER HONEYGUIDE
Indicator indicator

20cm, 48g Black throat, white cheeks and pink bill are diagnostic in male; female differs from other honeyguides by uniformly brown upperparts and white underparts; juv is more striking with blackish upperparts and creamy-yellow underparts. A widespread, fairly common breeding resident. Easily overlooked except when calling. The male's advertising call is a far-carrying '*whit-purr*' or '*vic-torr*', uttered from high in a tree, which may continue unabated for long periods. The chattering call it uses to guide honey-hunters is reminiscent of a box of matches being shaken. Reputed to also guide honeybadgers, but this has never been confirmed. Parasitises a wide range of hole-nesting birds: bee-eaters, barbets, woodpeckers, wood-hoopoes, kingfishers and others. GROOTHEUNINGWYSER

SCALY-THROATED HONEYGUIDE
Indicator variegatus

20cm, 48g Larger than Lesser Honeyguide, with a black-streaked throat, face and chest. A scarce, localised resident, mostly restricted to tall woodland along the larger rivers. Unobtrusive and largely undetectable except for the male's distinctive breeding call, a protracted, slurred, insect-like trill that rises in pitch. Does not guide but, like other honeyguides, it is attracted to beehives; eats beeswax, which is presumably digested with the aid of specialised gut bacteria. Parasitises barbets and woodpeckers. GEVLEKTE HEUNINGWYSER

LESSER HONEYGUIDE
Indicator minor

15cm, 28g Distinguished from larger Scaly-throated Honeyguide by its plain head and breast. Superficially resembles a Southern Grey-headed Sparrow (p184), but back is more olive-brown and white outer-tail feathers are obvious in flight. At close range its raised nostril and zygodactylous toes indicate it is not a passerine. A widespread, fairly common breeding resident in woodland, especially along rivers. The male's advertising call, uttered from a regular call site high in a tree, is a repetitive single note, '*frrip*', which is repeated at 1-sec intervals. Black-collared Barbet is its primary host in the park; also parasitises other hole-nesting birds. KLEINHEUNINGWYSER

BROWN-BACKED HONEYBIRD
Prodotiscus regulus

13cm, 14g A tiny grey-brown bird with a slender bill, most likely to be confused with Spotted and African Dusky flycatchers (p160); best told by its white outer-tail feathers and plain head and chest. A solitary species, scarce in the park but probably a breeding resident in woodland areas. Easily overlooked except in early summer when breeding males give their dry, insect-like trills from tree-top perches and perform brief aerial displays. Gleans tree foliage for caterpillars, aphids and scale insects. Parasitises cisticolas and prinias; like honeyguides, the newly hatched chick kills its host's chicks, but sometimes two honeybirds are raised in the same nest. SKERPBEKHEUNINGVOËL

Greater Honeyguide ♂

Greater Honeyguide ♀

Greater Honeyguide juv

Scaly-throated Honeyguide

Lesser Honeyguide

Brown-backed Honeybird

WOODPECKERS

Woodpeckers are well known for their chisel-tipped bills, which they use for excavating wood, two forward-facing and two backward-facing toes that enable them to cling to vertical trunks, stiff tail feathers that provide support for climbing, and a complex 'absorber' system in the head to cope with pounding on hard wood. Their long, barbed tongues extend well beyond the tip of the bill and, in some species, are coated with a sticky secretion to extract invertebrate prey from the holes they create. Some species communicate by 'drumming' loudly and rapidly on dead stems. The closely-related Red-throated Wryneck *Jynx ruficollis* is a rare vagrant to the southwest (p207).

BENNETT'S WOODPECKER — *Campethera bennettii*

23cm, 73g Distinguished from other woodpeckers by finely spotted (not streaked or barred), creamy-white underparts and, in male, by crimson crown and forehead, white cheeks and crimson malar stripe. Female has red nape, black-and-white streaked forehead and crown, and chestnut throat and ear coverts. A scarce to locally common breeding resident in tall woodland; common in some rest camps (e.g. Shingwedzi). Territorial; occurs year-round in pairs or in family groups after breeding. Feeds mainly on ants, often foraging for these on the ground, mopping them up with its sticky tongue as they emerge from their nests. Call is a rolling, whirring trill; does not drum. BENNETTSE SPEG

GOLDEN-TAILED WOODPECKER — *Campethera abingoni*

21cm, 70g Heavily streaked throat and chest and head coloration are diagnostic. Male has red-and-black speckled forehead, crimson crown, nape and malar stripe; female has red nape, black-and-white speckled forehead and crown and no malar stripe. A common, widespread resident throughout in all types of woodland. Usually solitary but often joins mixed-species bird parties. Eats mainly ants, using sticky tongue to lap these up wherever they are concentrated. Hunts for food on decaying tree trunks and branches, and occasionally on the ground. Call is a loud, nasal shriek; occasionally drums softly. GOUDSTERTSPEG

CARDINAL WOODPECKER — *Dendropicos fuscescens*

15cm, 31g Small size and combination of a barred back and heavily streaked underparts are diagnostic. Male has red crown and nape; female has all-black crown and nape; neither have moustachial stripes. A common, widespread resident in all woodland areas. Solitary or in pairs while breeding; often joins mixed-species bird parties. Preys mainly on the larvae of wood-borer beetles, locating them in thin branches and outer twigs by exploratory tapping on decaying wood. Call is a dry trill, '*trr-rrr-rrr*'; both sexes drum softly. KARDINAALSPEG

BEARDED WOODPECKER — *Dendropicos namaquus*

24cm, 83g Large size and combination of black-and-white facial markings and grey underparts finely barred with white are diagnostic. Male has red crown; female black. A common, widespread resident in tall woodland. In pairs while breeding, otherwise solitary. Locates the larvae of wood-borer beetles in decaying wood by exploratory tapping to find their tunnels, then digging them out with its barbed tongue. Call is a loud '*wik-wik-wik*'; both sexes drum loudly, audible from up to a kilometre away. BAARDSPEG. **Olive Woodpecker** *D. griseocephalus* (Gryskopspeg) is a plain olive- and grey-coloured bird; male has red nape; strays from the Drakensberg escarpment occasionally recorded in the southwest of the park.

Bennett's Woodpecker ♀

Bennett's Woodpecker ♂

Golden-tailed Woodpecker ♂

Golden-tailed Woodpecker ♀

Cardinal Woodpecker ♂

Bearded Woodpecker ♂

Olive Woodpecker ♂

Cardinal Woodpecker ♀

Bearded Woodpecker ♀

Olive Woodpecker ♀

COMMON LARKS

Larks, pipits and cisticolas are often called Little Brown Jobs (LBJs): small, ground-living birds that are cryptically marked in shades of brown and not easy to identify without experience. Distinguishing between larks and pipits (p164) can prove difficult too: larks are mostly chunkier than pipits, with proportionately shorter necks, shorter legs and more robust bills, and they stand less upright, don't bob their tails and appear more plodding when they walk. Eight species occur regularly in the park, the four below being those most commonly encountered. Identifying them visually is far less easy than telling them apart from their songs and displays.

SABOTA LARK   *Calendulauda sabota*

15cm, 25g Broad white eyebrow, well-streaked chest, habit of perching on trees and varied song are diagnostic. Common resident; the most frequently encountered lark in much of the park, scarce only in the higher-rainfall southwest. Easily overlooked in winter when silent; in summer males sing conspicuously from the tops of shrubs and trees. Song commences with a few notes of its own, followed by a medley of mimicked phrases from other birds living in the area – bee-eaters, cisticolas, drongos, starlings – developing into a frenzy of mimicry. Not as rich and sustained as the song of robin-chats, but an impressive mimic nonetheless. Sabota is the Tswana name for lark. SABOTALEWERIK

RUFOUS-NAPED LARK   *Mirafra africana*

17cm, 42g Large size, rufous crown (raised as a crest when singing), rufous wing panels and monotonous song are diagnostic. A fairly common resident in areas with adequate grass cover and low tree density; avoids mopane and acacia scrub and largely absent north of Shingwedzi. In summer males sing from termitaria or tops of low bushes, a sweet whistle '*tsee tsee-ooo*'. At intervals, while calling, the male does a small jump and audibly wing-flaps. At dusk males make a short aerial flight, uttering sharp '*preee*' notes as they rise, followed by a string of mimicked notes from other birds' songs. ROOINEKLEWERIK

FLAPPET LARK   *Mirafra rufocinnamomea*

15cm, 26g Smaller than Rufous-naped Lark, with darker and greyer (less rufous) plumage; lacks a crest or rufous wing panels. A fairly common resident, mostly on the basaltic soils in the east and in sour bushveld in the southwest. In summer males perform a characteristic aerial display using their wings to make a distinctive '*frrrrp*' sound while cruising at a height of 50–100 metres. These notes, each lasting ½ sec, are made by rapidly clapping their wings under their bodies (24 beats/second), and are repeated at 3–4-sec intervals. These larks don't perch on trees or bushes and would go largely undetected were it not for this behaviour. LAEVELDKLAPPERTJIE

MONOTONOUS LARK   *Mirafra passerina*

14cm, 24g A small, rather nondescript lark, most likely to be confused with Sabota Lark but lacks that species' pale eyebrow. May appear anywhere in the park, but is especially common in mopane scrub in summers of good rainfall. An enigmatic species of semi-arid savanna; apparently moves about regionally in response to rainfall. Easily overlooked when not singing. Males perch conspicuously on top of trees and shrubs, showing a clearly discernible white throat when singing. Their monotonous, frog-like refrain of '*purple jeep*' or '*syrup is sweet*' often continues late into the night. BOSVELDLEWERIK

Sabota Lark

Sabota Lark

Rufous-naped Lark

Rufous-naped Lark

Flappet Lark

Monotonous Lark

SCARCE LARKS

Larks are a large family of nearly 100 species, most of which are restricted to sub-Saharan Africa. They are mostly birds of open country, from grasslands and steppes to deserts, and as a consequence the park does not support a great lark diversity. The four species here, none very common in the park, provide an interesting cross-section of different genera in the family, from the large, migratory Dusky Lark to the small, sparrow-like Chestnut-backed Sparrow-Lark. In contrast to many larks, species like these are easily recognisable without needing recourse to their displays or songs for positive identification.

FAWN-COLOURED LARK
Calendulauda africanoides

15cm, 24g Most likely confused with Sabota Lark (p122), but less heavily streaked above and below, with warmer, pale ginger-brown upperparts and ear coverts; bill smaller. Although a common species in Kalahari sandveld, it is at the edge of its range in the park. A very localised resident, restricted to the Wambiya sandveld in the far north. This area is closed to the public, so it is unlikely to be encountered by tourists. In summer males sing their chirpy canary-like song from the tops of trees and bushes. VAALBRUINLEWERIK

RED-CAPPED LARK
Calandrella cinerea

15cm, 24g A distinctive lark thanks to its rufous crown (often raised as a crest) and rufous epaulettes; at close range its short, conical bill, plain white underparts and broad white eyebrow are diagnostic. Uncommon and perhaps only erratically present in the park, occurring mostly in open grasslands along the basaltic soils in the east and especially in the drier central areas on bare, recently burnt or heavily trampled ground such as around waterholes. Typically occurs in small flocks; best located by carefully scanning areas of bare ground around dams and pans. When disturbed, flies off giving a dry, sparrow-like call, often moving large distances. ROOIKOPLEWERIK

DUSKY LARK
Pinarocorys nigricans

19cm, 38g Large size, heavily mottled underparts, dark brownish-grey upperparts that have a scaled appearance and black facial markings are diagnostic. Most likely to be confused with the even larger Groundscraper Thrush (p142), but that species has a short tail, uniformly grey upperparts and buff-coloured panels in the wings. This unusual lark visits the park from its Angolan breeding grounds between November and May. Occurs widely but sparsely throughout, but is most common in the drier central areas. Found singly or in small groups. Favours areas of bare ground, often on road verges, and has the odd habit of flicking open one wing from time to time while foraging, apparently to flush small insects. Largely silent on its wintering grounds. DONKERLEWERIK

CHESTNUT-BACKED SPARROW-LARK
Eremopterix leucotis

14cm, 24g Male's rich chestnut back, black underparts and black-and-white head are unmistakable; female lacks black-and-white facial markings but black belly is diagnostic. Resident, occurring widely but sparsely, mostly in the open grasslands on the basaltic soils in the east and especially in the central region of the park. Typically found around waterholes where there is open, bare ground; occurs in small parties. Walks with a shuffling gait, pecking at the ground for seed. As a seed-eater, it visits water daily to drink. ROOIRUGLEWERIK. **Grey-backed Sparrow-lark** *E. verticalis* (Grysruglewerik) is paler, grey-brown above; male has white crown patch; scarce, erratic visitor; irrupts east from its semi-arid home mainly during drought years.

Fawn-coloured Lark

Red-capped Lark

Dusky Lark

Grey-backed Sparrow-Lark ♂

Grey-backed Sparrow-Lark ♀

Chestnut-backed Sparrow-Lark ♂

Chestnut-backed Sparrow-Lark ♀

125

HIRUNDO SWALLOWS AND HOUSE MARTINS

Swallows are among the world's best-known birds as harbingers of summer, for undertaking impressive migrations and for building mud nests. With slender bodies, long wings and bills with broad gapes, they are designed for a life on the wing. Their flight is buoyant and agile with spurts of acceleration, interspersed with banking and twisting, and most of their daylight hours are spent in flight pursuing tiny flying insects. Of the 88 species in this global family, 15 have been recorded in the park. The four here are all similar-looking, with glossy blue upperparts and white underparts.

BARN SWALLOW
Hirundo rustica

15cm, 20g The most commonly seen swallow in summer. Distinguished from other swallows by blackish chest band and chestnut throat and forehead, which make it appear dark-headed in flight. In worn plumage it is brown above and throat and forehead fade to cream; moults into fresh plumage in late summer, with males acquiring long tail streamers. A very common non-breeding visitor from Europe, present throughout from early October to April. Flying during the day and roosting at night, its 10,000km migration is completed in about 30 days. Gregarious; occasionally in flocks of thousands. When not hawking insects on the wing, groups rest in the outer branches of dead trees; roosts communally at night in large flocks, usually in reedbeds. EUROPESE SWAEL

WIRE-TAILED SWALLOW
Hirundo smithii

12cm, 13g Distinguished from other blue-and-white swallows by entirely white underparts and distinctive orange cap (brown in imm). The name refers to the adults' elongated tail streamers, which are only visible at close range. A common but localised resident, restricted to areas near water. Occurs in pairs and remains close to nesting sites year-round. Most nests are under bridges, but also on the underside of partly submerged tree stumps or in the roofs of hides and other structures. Commonly perches on bridge railings. DRAADSTERTSWAEL. **White-throated Swallow** *H. albigularis* (Witkeelswael) is larger, with black breast band and short tail streamers; uncommon visitor, mainly in the south, probably on passage between breeding areas on the highveld and wintering areas on the Mozambique coastal plain.

PEARL-BREASTED SWALLOW
Hirundo dimidiata

13cm, 12g A plain blue-and-white swallow, distinguished by its small size, uniform blue upperparts and plain white underparts (greyish in juv); dark rump differentiates it from Common House Martin and Grey-rumped Swallow (p128). Uncommon and perhaps only seasonally or erratically present, recorded very sparsely in the drier northern half of the park where it favours open grassy areas on the fringes of broad-leafed woodland. Flies close to the ground while hawking and often associates with other swallows at termite alate emergences. Builds its mud nest inside aardvark holes or inside abandoned buildings. PÊRELBORSSWAEL

COMMON HOUSE MARTIN
Delichon urbicum

14cm, 13g Told from other blue-and-white swallows by its short, forked tail and broad white rump (grey in juvs); told from Grey-rumped Swallow (p128) by its much shorter tail, and dark blue (not grey) head. It is unusual in having white-feathered feet and toes, which are visible only at close quarters. Although a few pairs have bred in South Africa, it is a non-breeding visitor from Europe, present between November and April. Erratic in occurrence, but common at times, occasionally in large flocks. Typically forages high in the sky, where it is easily overlooked. Often associated with Barn Swallows. HUISSWAEL

Barn Swallow

Barn Swallow imm

Wire-tailed Swallow

Wire-tailed Swallow imm

Pearl-breasted Swallow

Common House Martin

STRIPED AND OTHER SWALLOWS

Swallows, martins and saw-wings are easily told from swifts by their angled wings and more erratic flight. Breeding strategies vary greatly: some nest solitarily, others in colonies. *Hirundo* swallows (p126) build cup-shaped mud nests, the three *Cecropis* swallows build enclosed mud nests with long entrance tunnels, and other species nest in holes in the ground (Grey-rumped Swallow below) or in tunnels that they excavate in earth banks (martins, saw-wings, p130).

LESSER STRIPED SWALLOW
Cecropis abyssinica

17cm, 18g The most prevalent red-rumped swallow in the park, with boldly striped underparts. Slightly smaller than the rare Greater Striped Swallow; best told by much heavier streaking below and orange (not white) ear coverts. A widespread breeding visitor, mainly found from August to April; some birds remain year-round. Pairs nest solitarily, building a tunnelled mud nest in which they both roost and breed. Distribution is limited by nest-site availability; road bridges, culverts and the eaves of buildings are commonly used nest sites. Their nests are often commandeered by White-rumped Swifts. KLEINSTREEPSWAEL. **Greater Striped Swallow** *C. cucullata* (Grootstreepswael) is an uncommon visitor, sporadically recorded throughout on passage between breeding areas on the highveld and wintering areas on the Mozambique coastal plain.

RED-BREASTED SWALLOW
Cecropis semirufa

22cm, 31g A large, red-rumped swallow; told from Mosque Swallow by its rufous (not white) cheeks and throat and creamy (not white) underwing coverts. A breeding visitor, present from August to March. Found widely but sparsely throughout the park, mainly south of the Olifants River, favouring open, rather than wooded landscapes; often found near dams and other pans. Occurs in pairs or family groups after breeding. Commonly nests in low road culverts or, when these are unavailable, inside aardvark and other holes in the ground. ROOIBORSSWAEL

MOSQUE SWALLOW
Cecropis senegalensis

21cm, 45g A large, red-rumped swallow; told from Red-breasted Swallow by white (not rufous) cheeks and throat and white (not creamy) underwing coverts. Resident year-round, occurring widely but sparsely, especially along the larger rivers; most commonly encountered in the north, especially beyond Shingwedzi, in areas where large baobabs are common. Lives in pairs or family groups after breeding; often seen perching on the uppermost twigs of large trees. Builds a large mud nest which, unusually for a swallow, is sited inside a hole in a tree, usually a baobab. MOSKEESWAEL

GREY-RUMPED SWALLOW
Pseudhirundo griseopyga

14cm, 10g Distinguished from other swallows with all-white underparts by its grey-brown head and broad, pale grey rump. A localised breeding resident, mostly frequenting the flat, open margins of the larger rivers, especially the Olifants and Letaba. Usually encountered in small parties, either perched on the bare twigs of low bushes or hawking insects on the wing, flying close to the ground when doing so. Nests in midwinter, usually in small groups; selects bare, open areas dotted with burrows of gerbils or other rodents. Each pair moves into a burrow and the nest – an open grass cup – is built where the burrow ends, often a metre or more below ground level. GRYSKRUISSWAEL

Lesser Striped Swallow

Greater Striped Swallow

Red-breasted Swallow

Mosque Swallow

Grey-rumped Swallow

Left to right (top): Lesser Striped Swallow, Greater Striped Swallow and Red-breasted Swallow; (bottom): Mosque Swallow and Grey-rumped Swallow

MARTINS AND SAW-WINGS

Most martin species differ from other swallows by being brown-coloured, having a less streamlined build and having shorter, less deeply forked tails that lack streamers. Saw-wings are another distinctive group, unusually slender with long, deeply forked tails. They derive their name from a feature in the male's wing – the outer edge of the first primary feather has a rough outer edge, hence their earlier name of rough-wing. Both groups usually nest in holes in banks. None of the four species below occurs commonly in the park.

ROCK MARTIN   *Ptyonoprogne fuligula*
15cm, 16g Uniformly brown upperparts, paler brown underparts lightening to buff on the throat, and small cream panels near the tips of the outer-tail feathers (visible in flight when the tail is spread) are diagnostic. A scarce, localised resident, largely restricted while breeding to rocky outcrops and gorges such as along the Luvuvhu and Olifants rivers. Unlike most martins, it builds a mud cup nest. Non-breeding birds range more widely, often foraging near dams and rivers; there may be an influx of birds during winter from the high cliffs along the Drakensberg escarpment west of the park. KRANSSWAEL

BROWN-THROATED MARTIN   *Riparia paludicola*
12cm, 12g A small, brown swallow distinguished from similar-looking Sand Martin by its uniformly brown throat and chest. Most individuals have a brown throat and chest grading to white on the belly; in scarce dark morph the underparts are entirely brown. A local migrant in much of southern Africa. Occurs year-round in the park, mostly encountered along the larger rivers where it is usually seen in flight, patrolling over water. Gregarious; seldom seen other than in small parties. Nests colonially in winter in erosion banks overhanging the river; excavates tunnels for breeding or uses unoccupied nest-holes of White-fronted Bee-eater. AFRIKAANSE OEWERSWAEL

SAND MARTIN   *Riparia riparia*
13cm, 13g Distinguished from Brown-throated Martin by white (not brown) throat; much smaller than the rare Banded Martin with brown (not white) underwing coverts and brown crown (lacking a white forehead). An uncommon non-breeding visitor from Europe, present between October and April. Recorded from widely scattered localities; easily overlooked or mistaken for the more common resident Brown-throated Martin. Single birds or small groups often occur among flocks of Barn Swallows; they are best detected by carefully scrutinising perched flocks of Barn Swallows. EUROPESE OEWERSWAEL. The much larger **Banded Martin** *R. cincta* (Gebande Oewerswael) is reported occasionally, mostly in the central part of the park, probably on passage between breeding areas on the highveld and wintering areas on the Mozambique coastal plain.

BLACK SAW-WING   *Psalidoprocne pristoptera*
15cm, 12g A small, slender, glossy-black swallow with a long, deeply forked tail; juv has duller, brown-tinged plumage and a much shallower tail fork. A forest-edge species, commonly seen in summer along the Drakensberg escarpment to the west of the park; scarce and localised within the park, largely restricted to areas of riparian forest along the Sabie, Crocodile and Luvuvhu rivers. Occurs singly, in pairs or in small flocks that spend much time hawking small aerial insects on the wing, flitting back and forth over open ground in wooded areas. Flight extremely erratic as it flits close to the tree canopies. SWARTSAAGVLERKSWAEL

Rock Martin

Rock Martin

Brown-throated Martin

Brown-throated Martin

Sand Martin

Black Saw-wing

CUCKOOSHRIKES, DRONGOS AND FLYCATCHERS

Cuckooshrikes, which are unrelated to cuckoos or shrikes, are a mainly Australasian family of forest and woodland birds. Ten species occur in Africa and two of these, which well reflect the diversity in the family, occur in the park. Drongos are a more homogeneous family of 26 species of glossy, all-black birds best known for their noisy, aggressive behaviour and their aerial skill at catching flying insects on the wing. Four similar-looking species occur in Africa, two of which occur in the park. The unrelated Southern Black Flycatcher is included here because of its similarity to the drongo; see p162 for other *Melaenornis* flycatchers.

BLACK CUCKOOSHRIKE · *Campephaga flava*

21cm, 32g Male distinguished from other all-black species by orange gape and, in some individuals, yellow shoulder patches. Female is mottled yellow and pale brown above white below with indistinct darker barring and yellow underwing coverts; superficially resembles a female Klaas's Cuckoo (p88). A fairly common breeding visitor, present between September and May, with occasional birds overwintering. Found throughout in well-wooded areas, occurring singly or in pairs. Easily overlooked, as it keeps to the leafy canopies of trees and shrubs, only revealing itself when flying from one tree to another. Best detected by its high-pitched, cicada-like trilling call, given by both sexes. SWARTKATAKOEROE

WHITE-BREASTED CUCKOOSHRIKE · *Coracina pectoralis*

27cm, 58g Large size, plain smoky-grey upperparts and white underparts are diagnostic; in flight, blackish primaries and tail contrast with paler grey upperparts. Male has grey throat; female has all-white underparts. Scarce resident or nomad, recorded mainly in areas of tall mopane woodland from Shingwedzi northwards. Found singly or in pairs; usually encountered in the upper branches of trees where it searches for insects in a lethargic manner. Its presence is often given away by its soft, slurred whistled trill. WITBORSKATAKOEROE

FORK-TAILED DRONGO · *Dicrurus adsimilis*

25cm, 46g Distinguished from Black Cuckooshrike and Southern Black Flycatcher by its deeply forked tail and blood-red eye. A common, conspicuous breeding resident throughout. Occurs singly or in pairs, but small flocks may hunt insects fleeing bush fires. These opportunistic birds often accompany large game, catching insects that they disturb. Drongos also join mixed-species bird parties, pirating insects caught by other birds by sounding an alarm, then swooping in and stealing the food during the ensuing panic. Fearlessly pursues passing raptors, even settling on them in flight. MIKSTERTBYVANGER. **Square-tailed Drongo** *D. ludwigii* (Kleinbyvanger) is smaller, with only a weakly notched tail tip; common in the Barberton mountainland fringing the southern border of the park, but only rarely strays into the park along the Crocodile River.

SOUTHERN BLACK FLYCATCHER · *Melaenornis pammelaina*

20cm, 30g Most similar to Fork-tailed Drongo in appearance but smaller; eye is dark brown (not red) and tail is shorter with a shallow notch (not a deep fork). Also more demure in habits. A fairly common breeding resident found throughout the park, but most common in the southwest. Usually in pairs or family parties; frequents woodland with an understorey of short grass and is common in many rest camps. SWARTVLIEËVANGER

Black Cuckooshrike ♀

Black Cuckooshrike ♂

White-breasted Cuckooshrike ♀

Fork-tailed Drongo

Square-tailed Drongo

Southern Black Flycatcher

ORIOLES AND CROWS

Orioles are a mainly Australasian family of woodland and forest birds, which derive their name from the Latin *aureolus*, meaning 'golden'. Males of three species that occur in the park are gold-coloured, although not all orioles are this colour. The males have similar-sounding mellow whistled songs as well as harsh, grating calls. Their diet is varied, ranging from fruit and nectar to insects. Of the three species in the park, two are migratory and one is resident. Crows need little introduction given their large size, black-and-white plumage and close association with humans. There are no common species in the park; the Pied Crow is an uncommon visitor and three others are occasional vagrants (p207).

BLACK-HEADED ORIOLE
Oriolus larvatus

25cm, 71g Vivid yellow underparts and black head and throat are diagnostic. At a glance may be mistaken for breeding male Village Weaver (p186), but is much larger, with a pink bill and different head and back pattern. A common, conspicuous breeding resident in all woodland areas, including in many rest camps. Its liquid whistled call *'qui-op'* or *'quidiloop'* often alerts visitors to its presence. In early summer males extend this simple refrain into a medley of mimicked notes of other birds. Occurs singly or in pairs, although small groups gather at favoured food sources, such as flowering aloes and coral trees, and at fruiting trees (especially figs). SWARTKOPWIELEWAAL

EURASIAN GOLDEN ORIOLE
Oriolus oriolus

23cm, 68g Male told from male African Golden Oriole by having all-black wings, which are especially conspicuous in flight (although underwing coverts yellow). Females vary from duller-coloured versions of male to individuals with greenish-yellow upperparts and yellowish-white underparts, but always have well-streaked underparts, which distinguish them from female African Golden Oriole. A rather scarce but widespread non-breeding visitor from Eurasia, present between November and March. Frequents woodland areas, especially tall mopane. Occurs singly or sometimes in small groups; generally shy and unapproachable. EUROPESE WIELEWAAL

AFRICAN GOLDEN ORIOLE
Oriolus auratus

24cm, 73g Male told from male Eurasian Golden Oriole by having mainly yellow (not black) wings at rest and larger black face mask. Female less vividly yellow than male, lacks black facial mask and has faintly streaked underparts. An uncommon migrant from tropical Africa, erratically present in years of above-average rainfall between October and March. Mostly encountered in tall woodland in the north of the park and especially in the riparian woodlands along the Luvuvhu and Limpopo rivers. AFRIKAANSE WIELEWAAL

PIED CROW
Corvus albus

48cm, 540g Large size and black-and-white plumage are diagnostic. An erratic visitor from adjacent areas to the west and south of the park where it is a very common resident in towns, villages, informal settlements, grain and stock farms, refuse disposal sites and roads, which provide abundant food for this adaptable scavenger. To date it has not established a breeding foothold in the park, which suggests that, in this pristine savanna environment in which it would compete for food against a large suite of scavenging species, it has not been successful. Typical call is a hoarse *'kraai kraai'*. WITBORSKRAAI

Black-headed Oriole

Black-headed Oriole

Eurasian Golden Oriole

African Golden Oriole ♂

Pied Crow

Pied Crow

BULBULS, GREENBULS AND BROWNBULS

Bulbuls are a large Old World bird family, some of which are common and familiar garden birds whereas others are skulking and little known forest dwellers. The name 'bulbul' is used for the species that have crests, these often being called 'toppies' or 'tiptols' locally, while the sombre green- and brown-coloured, non-crested species – mostly forest-living birds – are known as greenbuls and brownbuls, respectively. Fruit features prominently in the diet of all species, supplemented with insects and other arthropods, seeds, nectar and other plant material.

DARK-CAPPED BULBUL · *Pycnonotus tricolor*

21cm, 40g One of the most abundant and familiar birds in the park. Yellow undertail coverts, dark brown crested head and uniformly greyish-brown upperparts and white underparts are diagnostic. A common breeding resident throughout. In pairs while breeding but gregarious at other times of the year. Its call, a cheerful '*chop-chip-kweeko*' or '*sweet-sweet-potato*', is a familiar sound in many rest camps. At dusk groups often gather in a tree and start alarm-calling, the sound building up as more birds join the group, then going silent if they are approached. Commonly parasitised by Jacobin Cuckoo. SWARTOOGTIPTOL

SOMBRE GREENBUL · *Andropadus importunus*

21cm, 36g Plain greenish-olive plumage with startling white eyes and contrasting black pupils are diagnostic; juv has dark eyes. A fairly common, localised breeding resident, frequents dense thickets, particularly those associated with woodland along the larger rivers, especially the Luvuvhu, Sabie and Crocodile. A reclusive bird that does not easily show itself; its presence is usually revealed by its loud '*willie*' call. The full song is a longer string of musical whistled notes rendered as '*willie, come-out-and-fight, sca-r-r-r-ed*', or '*willie, quickly run around the bush and squeeeeeeze-me*'. Occasionally parasitised by Jacobin Cuckoo. GEWONE WILLIE

YELLOW-BELLIED GREENBUL · *Chlorocichla flaviventris*

22cm, 41g Similar to Sombre Greenbul in habits, habitat and looks, but distinguished by larger size, yellow underparts and red eyes with narrow white eye-rings. A common breeding resident in the far north but occurs only sparsely elsewhere, mostly in riparian woodland along the large rivers. Occurs in pairs or small family groups, frequenting riverine and hillside thickets. Typically a shy bird that keeps out of view, although in some rest camps it has become confiding, venturing into the open to pick up food items. Mostly detected by its nagging nasal call – '*yak-yak-yak, yakyakyiek-yak-yak …*' – which can reach a crescendo when several birds call together. GEELBORSWILLIE

TERRESTRIAL BROWNBUL · *Phyllastrephus terrestris*

21cm, 34g Uniformly brown upperparts, paler underparts with a whitish throat and noisy, scolding calls are diagnostic. A breeding resident that occurs widely but sparsely, found commonly in the dense understorey thickets of riparian vegetation along the Luvuvhu and Limpopo rivers. Occurs in small family parties year-round. Forages mostly on the ground in leaf litter, maintaining contact through frequent calling, identified by ongoing low-pitched raspy notes, '*chirrit-chirrt-chit-chit-chirit …*'. Ventures into the understorey when alarmed; often joins other birds to mob owls and other potential predators. Occurs alongside Yellow-bellied Greenbuls in most areas and the calls of the two species are easily confused. BOSKRAPPER

Dark-capped Bulbul

Sombre Greenbul

Yellow-bellied Greenbul

Terrestrial Brownbul

TITS, PENDULINE-TITS, BABBLERS AND NICATORS

Birds from four families are included here. Tits are a worldwide family of insectivorous birds known as titmice or chickadees in parts of their range. Penduline-tits are a small family of tiny, warbler-like species closely related to the tits that occur mainly in Africa and are renowned for their well-woven nests. The babblers are part of a large family of mainly Southeast Asian birds, including the laughing thrushes, which are closely related to the sylvid warblers. The nicators, which resemble a cross between a greenbul and a bushshrike, comprise just three species, all found in Africa.

SOUTHERN BLACK TIT
Parus niger

16cm, 21g White shoulder and wingbar in otherwise all-black plumage is diagnostic. Female similar, but greyish-black. A common breeding resident in all woodland areas; occurs in pairs or small family groups year-round. Active little birds that forage mainly in the leafy canopy of trees, moving from one tree to the next in search of caterpillars, maintaining contact with regular calling, a grating '*twiddy-zeet-zeet-zeet*'. In winter they commonly search for seed pods, pecking them open to extract insect larvae. They are regular members of mixed-species bird parties and are usually the nucleus around which other birds gather. GEWONE SWARTMEES

GREY PENDULINE-TIT
Anthoscopus caroli

8cm, 7g A very small, warbler-like bird with a short, pointed bill and short tail; plain grey-and-white plumage, buff-washed face and belly, and occurrence in groups are the best clues to its identity. A fairly common breeding resident, found mainly in the broad-leafed woodlands on the granitic soils in the east. Usually found in small family groups as it forages for small insects in the leafy outer twigs of trees, often joining mixed-species bird parties, accompanying the group as they move from tree to tree. Nest is a densely woven ball with a false entrance to confuse predators; used year-round for roosting. GRYSKAPOKVOËL

ARROW-MARKED BABBLER
Turdoides jardineii

24cm, 72g A robust, thrush-sized passerine with white 'arrow-mark' streaking on its head and chest and red-rimmed yellow eyes. A common, widespread breeding resident, found in all wooded areas, including rest camps. Gregarious; lives year-round in noisy, territorial groups of 5–10 birds. The group moves cohesively, foraging mostly on the ground, with individuals maintaining contact by regular calling. During territorial disputes they may assemble and call simultaneously in a rousing chorus, very similar to the group chorus performed by the Green Wood-hoopoe. Only the alpha pair in the group breeds, with the other group members assisting to raise the chicks. Commonly parasitised by Levaillant's Cuckoo. PYLVLEKKATLAGTER

EASTERN NICATOR
Nicator gularis

23cm, ♂56g, ♀37g Yellowish-green upperparts, conspicuous pale spotting on wings, hooked, shrike-like bill and yellow eye-ring are diagnostic. Female is one-third smaller than male. A scarce, secretive resident that would go largely unnoticed were it not for the male's rich, far-carrying call in summer, which starts as a stutter then develops into a medley of short liquid, bubbly notes that include snatches of mimicry of other birds. Males call for long spells hidden in the canopy of a forest tree. Most commonly encountered in the far north in thickets associated with river gullies and riparian forest, with scattered records along the eastern and southern fringes of the park. GEELVLEKNIKATOR

Southern Black Tit

Grey Penduline-Tit

Arrow-marked Babbler

Eastern Nicator

CHATS

Chats and thrushes are two morphologically similar groups of birds that, until recently, were considered to belong to a large global family, the Turdidae. Recent genetic studies have shown that the two groups are distinct, with groups such as the rock thrushes, palm thrushes, robin-chats and scrub robins brought into a much-enlarged family of Old World chats and flycatchers, the Muscicapidae. The four species here are typical chats: insectivorous birds that forage mainly on the ground but perch conspicuously to sing or scan their surroundings for prey.

ARNOT'S CHAT
Pentholaea arnotti

18cm, 40g Glossy black plumage and conspicuous white shoulder patches are diagnostic. Male has a whitish crown; female has a white throat and upper breast. A scarce, localised resident confined to tall mopane woodland north of Shingwedzi. Territorial; lives year-round in pairs or, after breeding, in family groups. Lively, active birds that forage on the ground and in the lower branches of trees, seldom going higher than 4–5m up. Moves frequently between perches, and drops to the ground to capture prey. Male sings mainly in early summer, incorporating mimicked notes of other birds in its song. BONTPIEK

FAMILIAR CHAT
Cercomela familiaris

15cm, 22g Uniformly mousy-brown plumage with a buff wash on flanks; told from Pale Flycatcher (p162) by its rufous-orange rump and tail; has the distinctive habit of rapidly flicking its wings half-open after each flight or series of hops. A scarce, localised breeding resident in the park, occurring in areas of open rocky ground such as in the hills around Berg-en-Dal rest camp and on the kopjes near Phalaborwa. Occurs year-round in pairs; typically encountered perched on a rock, a building or pole, dropping to the ground at intervals to forage. The typical call is a dry *'chack'*, sometimes interspersed by whistled notes. GEWONE SPEKVRETER

AFRICAN STONECHAT
Saxicola torquatus

14cm, 15g A small, compact chat with a short tail. Male easily recognised by his chestnut breast, black head and white neck, rump and belly; female duller with upperparts and head streaked buff and dark brown, underparts warm buff. Both sexes show a distinctive white wingbar and white rump in flight. Occurs widely but sparsely throughout, mostly in open grassy areas on basaltic soils in the east. Mainly a winter visitor from the high-lying interior but there may also be a small resident population. Found singly or in pairs; often perches conspicuously on top of weeds and scrubby bushes. Male song is a scratchy series of high-pitched whistles. GEWONE BONTROKKIE

MOCKING CLIFF CHAT
Thamnolaea cinnamomeiventris

22cm, 48g A large, long-tailed chat. Male strikingly coloured; female lead-grey with dark rufous belly, vent and rump. On alighting, it has the distinctive habit of slowly raising and lowering its tail. A fairly common but localised breeding resident, restricted to rocky kopjes, hillsides and ravines, including at some picnic sites and rest camps (e.g. Punda Maria and Olifants) where it has become tame and confiding. Lives in pairs year-round. An active, inquisitive species that calls frequently. Males sing strongly, especially at dawn, mixing rich liquid notes with a jumble of mimicked calls of other birds. DASSIEVOËL

Arnot's Chat ♂

Arnot's Chat ♀

Familiar Chat

African Stonechat ♂

African Stonechat ♀

Mocking Cliff Chat ♂

Mocking Cliff Chat ♀

141

THRUSHES AND ROBIN-CHATS

Thrushes are a well-known family of birds thanks to several species becoming familiar garden birds in many parts of the world: Olive and Karoo thrushes in South Africa, Blackbird in Europe and American Robin in North America. Known for their sweet songs and their fondness for earthworms, these medium-sized passerines have slender bills and sturdy legs and feet. They forage mostly on the ground, feeding on insects and other arthropods but also eat fruit when available. Palm thrushes are a small African genus of three species, typically associated with palms. The robin-chats that occur in the park are more fully described on p144.

KURRICHANE THRUSH
Turdus libonyanus

22cm, 62g Uniformly grey upperparts, paler grey underparts with orange-buff flanks, white belly and throat, orange bill and eye-ring and distinctive black malar stripes are diagnostic. A fairly common breeding resident, occurring throughout the park but mostly in well-wooded broad-leafed woodlands on granitic soils in the west where there is a short-grass ground layer; common in many rest camps. Occurs singly or in pairs, typically encountered foraging on the ground, running and stopping at intervals, cocking its head to listen for prey movement below. Has a sweet song, heard mainly in early summer and briefly at dawn and dusk at other times. ROOIBEKLYSTER

GROUNDSCRAPER THRUSH
Turdus litsitsirupa

21cm, 76g With its boldly spotted underparts it can be mistaken for Dusky Lark (p124); distinguished by its noticeably short tail, longer, more slender bill and uniformly grey-coloured (not scalloped) upperparts. A fairly common, widespread breeding resident that favours open woodland with an understorey of short grass; usually occurs in more open habitats than Kurrichane Thrush. Typically encountered in pairs, which spend much of their time on the ground, flying to trees only when disturbed. Often lifts one wing a few centimetres when pausing between runs. The song is a short, cheerful whistled refrain 'lit-sit-si-rupa'. GEVLEKTE LYSTER

COLLARED PALM THRUSH
Cichladusa arquata

20cm, 35g Rufous wings and tail, grey head, white eye and black line encircling throat and chest are diagnostic. Despite its name, it is not a member of the thrush family but a part of the chat family. This tropical species is rare in the park. A well-known pair bred in Shingwedzi rest camp for several years but they have since disappeared. There have been recent sightings from the southeast of the park, and others may have been overlooked. Closely associated with palms, especially tall *Hyphaene* palm trees. Song is a rich series of melodious, robin-like whistles, including mimicry of other species' calls. PALM MÔRELYSTER

RED-CAPPED ROBIN-CHAT
Cossypha natalensis

18cm, 31g Plain rufous head and underparts contrasting with blue-grey back and wings are diagnostic. A scarce, localised resident, largely confined to the forested margins of the larger rivers. Occurs singly or in pairs; it is unobtrusive, its presence usually given away by its rich song, especially in early summer. A superb mimic; its song incorporates mimicked notes of many other birds from Fish Eagles to camaropteras. At other times, especially at dusk, it makes a gentle 'seee-saw' call, uttered from a hidden position in the undergrowth. NATALJANFREDERIK

Kurrichane Thrush

Kurrichane Thrush

Groundscraper Thrush

Collared Palm Thrush

Red-capped Robin-Chat

Red-capped Robin-Chat

ROBIN-CHATS AND SCRUB ROBINS (cont.)

Robin-chats and scrub robins are ground-living members of the Muscicapidae family, and are found in wooded habitats, especially thickets. They tend to remain in dense cover, where their presence is mostly given away by their pleasing, melodious songs, but they may venture into the open at dawn and dusk. Although these species are shy, retreating to cover if disturbed, some have become tame and confiding in the rest camps. Robin-chats are particularly versatile singers, often dominating the dawn chorus. Some species enrich their songs by mimicking the calls of other birds. The species in the park are frequently parasitised by the Red-chested Cuckoo.

WHITE-BROWED (Heuglin's) ROBIN-CHAT　　　*Cossypha heuglini*

19cm, 35g Warm orange underparts, greyish upperparts and a black hood bisected by a sweeping white eyebrow distinguish it from other robin-chats. A localised resident but common where it occurs, mostly along larger drainage lines where there are thickets under a canopy of tall evergreen trees. Usually shy but tame and confiding in rest camps where it occurs. Its presence is usually given away by its exuberant song, a repeated simple refrain (e.g. *'trickle-chok-weee'*) that starts quietly and gradually builds up to a near-deafening crescendo. Not given to mimicry, but is nevertheless one of the park's star singers. HEUGLINJANFREDERIK

WHITE-THROATED ROBIN-CHAT　　　*Cossypha humeralis*

16cm, 23g Rufous flanks, rump and outer-tail feathers identify it as a robin-chat; white throat and chest and black head cut by a long white eyebrow distinguish it from other robin-chats. A fairly common resident in wooded areas, favouring sites where there is a thick accumulation of leaf litter on the ground below a thicket, often around large termitaria. Mostly encountered on or close to the ground, but males may perch high in trees when singing. Territorial; lives in pairs year-round. Males are most vocal in early summer; their robust whistled song is interspersed with mimicked calls of other birds. WITKEELJANFREDERIK

WHITE-BROWED SCRUB ROBIN　　　*Erythropygia leucophrys*

15cm, 18g Sandy brown upperparts with two white bars on wing coverts, off-white underparts streaked with dark brown, white eyebrow, and warm rufous rump are diagnostic. Frequently cocks its tail when alarmed, displaying its white tail tips and rufous rump. Territorial; lives in pairs year-round. A common, widespread resident, found in wooded country throughout; tantalisingly difficult birds to see. Males sing their somewhat ventriloquial song prolifically from low perches in dense vegetation throughout the day during summer. The sweet, whistled refrain (e.g. *'see-titi-tu-tootoo'*) is repetitive, but varies among males; one of the characteristic sounds of the bush. GESTREEPTE WIPSTERT

BEARDED SCRUB ROBIN　　　*Erythropygia quadrivirgata*

17cm, 26g Slightly larger than White-browed Scrub Robin, with an unstreaked throat and chest and only one white bar on wing coverts. A localised resident, largely restricted to the wooded, creeper-tangled margins of drainage lines, especially common along the floodplain margins of the Luvuvhu and Limpopo rivers. Territorial; found in pairs year-round. Males give their presence away with their sweet melodious song, usually uttered from a hidden perch close to the ground, deep in the undergrowth. BAARDWIPSTERT. **Brown Scrub Robin** *E. signata* (Bruinwipstert) lacks the Bearded Scrub Robin's warm rufous flanks and rump; rare visitor, occasionally recorded along the Crocodile and Luvuvhu rivers.

White-browed Robin-Chat

White-browed Robin-Chat

White-throated Robin-Chat

White-throated Robin-Chat

White-browed Scrub Robin

Bearded Scrub Robin

MIGRANT WARBLERS

'Warbler' is a catch-all name for a diverse array of small insectivorous birds. Despite their similar appearance and habits, the four species here belong to three families: Phylloscopidae, Sylviidae and Hippolaidae. All four are non-breeding migrants from Eurasia. Despite not breeding in Africa, some males sing, especially in late summer before they return north, when their warbling songs give away their presence and provide the easiest means of identifying them. In addition to the species listed here, several other warblers (p207) occasionally visit the park, including the non-migrant Chestnut-vented Tit-babbler *Sylvia subcaerulea*.

WILLOW WARBLER   *Phylloscopus trochilus*
12cm, 8g Small size, uniformly pale brownish-grey upperparts, faintly yellow underparts, prominent pale eyebrow and long undertail coverts distinguish it from other warblers. A common, widespread visitor to all types of woodland, from October to late March. Usually encountered singly, sometimes in loose groups, as it moves through the leafy canopies of trees searching for small insects. Its contact call, a gentle *'who-it'*, is easily missed. A few birds sing soon after their arrival but most only sing in the month before their departure; the song is a sweet, soft, wispy *'si-si-sisi-swee-swee-su-su-sweetsweet-sweetu'*. HOFSANGER

GARDEN WARBLER   *Sylvia borin*
14cm, 19g The plainest warbler in the park. Plump shape, uniform brownish-grey colour, paler below than above, and plain face with large dark eyes surrounded by narrow white eye-rings are diagnostic. A scarce non-breeding visitor from Eurasia between November and late March; skulks in dense thickets and is easily overlooked when not calling. Its song is a sustained jangle of notes skipping up and down the scale, some mellow, others scratchy. TUINSANGER. **Thrush Nightingale** *Luscinia luscinia* (Lysternagtegaal) is a largely nondescript migrant with a rufous-brown rump and tail; forages on the ground under dense thickets; rare visitor, best detected by its rich, varied song, comprising melodious whistles as well as churring notes.

OLIVE-TREE WARBLER   *Hippolais olivetorum*
17cm, 18g Large size, matching Great Reed Warbler (p148) in size; distinctly sloping forehead, long bill, uniformly grey upperparts and uniformly off-white underparts are diagnostic. Occurs widely but sparsely from November to late March, restricted to areas of open thornveld dominated by umbrella thorn or black thorn. Not easily seen as they stay inside the canopies of these trees; usually only detected when heard singing: a loud distinctive song of sustained gruff, low-pitched, ratchet-like *'churr'* and *'tchak'* notes. Song increases in frequency in the month before departure, but some birds sing throughout summer. OLYFBOOMSANGER

ICTERINE WARBLER   *Hippolais icterina*
13cm, 13g Smaller and more brightly coloured than the Olive-tree Warbler; best told by its uniform greyish-green upperparts and pale yellow underparts, distinctly sloping forehead and longish bill. Occurs widely but sparsely from November to late March; more common in the southern half of the park than in the north. A solitary species, best located by its song, which is usually heard coming from the depths of a well-foliaged tree or thicket. The song is a sustained ramble of short, varied phrases, some churrs, others shrill, interspersed with brief snatches of mimicked calls of other birds. Easily overlooked when not singing, but sometimes gives a soft *'chack'* call. SPOTSANGER

Willow Warbler

Garden Warbler

Olive-tree Warbler

Olive-tree Warbler

Icterine Warbler

Icterine Warbler

REED WARBLERS

Reed warblers (Acrocephalidae) are a confusing group of similar-looking warblers characterised by sandy-brown upperparts, buff-white underparts with a darker wash on the flanks, angular heads with flat foreheads and longish bills. The Great Reed Warbler is the largest and is about twice the size of the two smallest species, Marsh and African Reed warblers. The Lesser Swamp and African Reed warblers are breeding residents, whereas the other two species are non-breeding migrants from Eurasia. In addition to the species listed here, two other migrant reed warblers (p207) occasionally visit the park.

AFRICAN REED WARBLER — *Acrocephalus baeticatus*
13cm, 9g A tiny reed warbler that is very similar to the migratory Marsh Warbler but has shorter, rounder wings so that when perched the wing tips do not extend beyond the tail coverts. Occurs sparsely throughout, but is most common along the Crocodile River. Found year-round; largely restricted to aquatic habitats such as reeds or sedges and dense herbaceous growth and adjacent thickets close to water. Its sustained warbling song, with a rapid string of varied churring and whistled notes, is much like that of the Marsh Warbler, but perhaps a little harsher and less varied. KLEINRIETSANGER

MARSH WARBLER — *Acrocephalus palustris*
13cm, 11g Very similar in appearance to African Reed Warbler but longer-winged (wing tips extend beyond the tail coverts). A non-breeding summer visitor, mainly present from November to early April. During migration it travels up to 300km per night. Fairly common, especially in the higher-rainfall southern half of the park, favouring areas of thornveld. Frequents tangled vegetation, especially where rank grass has grown through shrubbery; not restricted to the vicinity of water. Individuals return to the same sites in successive years. Secretive; usually only located by its busy song, given mainly in late summer: a rapid sequence of grates, trills and *'tchak'* notes interspersed with snatches of mimicry of other birds' calls. EUROPESE RIETSANGER

LESSER SWAMP WARBLER — *Acrocephalus gracilirostris*
17cm, 15g A fairly large reed warbler with blackish legs, a distinctive white eyebrow and white, rather than buff-white, underparts. Males give away their presence with their rich, melodious song, a string of bubbling and chortling notes, broken by brief pauses, uttered year-round, but most frequently in summer. A localised resident, restricted to extensive reedbeds growing in standing water. Fairly common along the Crocodile and Sabie rivers, but very localised elsewhere. Ventures out of cover more often than other reed warblers, especially in winter, when it can be seen foraging away from reeds in open grassy patches or along the water's edge. KAAPSE RIETSANGER

GREAT REED WARBLER — *Acrocephalus arundinaceus*
20cm, 30g Large size, plain face lacking a pale eyebrow, long, rather heavy bill and sustained grating song are diagnostic. A scarce but widespread visitor to the park from Eurasia, present from late November to late March. Frequents reedbeds and tangled bush thickets close to water where its presence is mostly detected from its distinctive low-pitched croaking and grating song, rendered as *'karra-karra-krik-krik-krik-gurk-gurk-gurk-tuckle-tuckle …'*. GROOTRIETSANGER

African Reed Warbler

Marsh Warbler

Lesser Swamp Warbler

Lesser Swamp Warbler

Great Reed Warbler

CROMBECS AND EREMOMELAS

These small, insectivorous, warbler-like birds were once considered part of the Sylviidae but are now placed in two separate families. The nine species of crombecs, named for their curved beaks (*krom bek* in Afrikaans), form a small family (Macrosphenidae) with the longbills, grassbirds and Rockrunner, all of which are restricted to sub-Saharan Africa. The 11 species of eremomelas belong to the much larger Cisticolidae family, which, although centred in Africa, has representatives in Eurasia and Australia. Many eremomelas are lusty singers but some have more plaintive calls, possibly giving rise to their unusual name, which means 'desert song' (*eremos* and *melos* being Greek for 'desert' and 'song', respectively). Both groups are arboreal, feeding, nesting and roosting in trees and shrubs.

LONG-BILLED CROMBEC — *Sylvietta rufescens*
11cm, 11g A chubby, unbalanced-looking bird with a longish, curved bill and very short tail, not extending beyond the end of the wings. Common resident in all woodland areas, often encountered in pairs. Active, restless little birds that glean insects from foliage or clamber along branches searching for small insects, sometimes hanging upside down (hence their other common name of Nuthatch-warbler). Often joins mixed-species bird parties in winter. Best detected by its regularly repeated *'tree-cheer'* call-note; also gives a dry trill call. BOSVELDSTOMPSTERT

YELLOW-BELLIED EREMOMELA — *Eremomela icteropygialis*
11cm, 8g Uniformly pale grey above with whitish underparts that grade to lemon-yellow on its belly and undertail coverts; has a narrow dark line through the eye and a short white eyebrow; easily told from Grey Penduline-Tit (p138) by its yellow (not buffy) underparts. Fairly common resident in wooded areas throughout; most common in the southeast. Found singly or in pairs. Usually encountered foraging in the outer twigs of trees and shrubs; active, frequently changing perches. Often joins mixed-species bird parties in winter, foraging alongside crombecs, penduline-tits and other small birds. Song and call-notes are rather subdued and can be confused with those of Long-billed Crombec. GEELPENSBOSSANGER

GREEN-CAPPED EREMOMELA — *Eremomela scotops*
12cm, 9g An attractive eremomela with grey-green upperparts and a pale lemon-yellow chest grading into a white belly; its pale eye, rimmed with red, is distinctive. A scarce resident throughout in areas of dense, tall-tree woodland. Gregarious; usually in groups of 4–5 year-round. Forages in leafy tree canopies; restless, with the group keeping on the move as the birds forage. Often forages with white-eyes and commonly joins mixed-species bird parties in winter. Quite vocal; gives an irritated chatter, often in chorus as all members of the group join in. DONKERWANGBOSSANGER

BURNT-NECKED EREMOMELA — *Eremomela usticollis*
11cm, 9g A tiny warbler with grey upperparts, buffy-yellow underparts and diagnostic pale eyes (see also Grey Penduline-Tit, p138); during the summer breeding season it has an incomplete rusty-coloured chest band ('burnt neck') and a smudge below the eye. Common resident in acacia thornveld, occurring in pairs and family groups; forage in the leafy canopies of umbrella thorns and other acacia trees and shrubs. Often located by their high-pitched, rapid trilling call, started by one in the group, with others frequently joining the chorus. BRUINKEELBOSSANGER

Long-billed Crombec

Long-billed Crombec

Yellow-bellied Eremomela

Green-capped Eremomela

Burnt-necked Eremomela br

Burnt-necked Eremomela non-br

151

APALISES AND WREN-WARBLERS

Apalises are small, distinctively marked warblers in the family Cisticolidae and are characterised by longish tails and lively songs that are often sung in duet. They are restricted to sub-Saharan Africa where they live in the leafy canopies of trees and shrubs, many confined to narrow ranges in forested habitats. Three species occur in the park but only one of them is common. Their name is derived from the Greek word *hapalos*, meaning 'delicate' or 'gentle'. The dark-plumaged wren-warblers are so named for their wren-like habit of cocking their tails – behaviour they share with the closely related camaropteras (p154).

BAR-THROATED APALIS
Apalis thoracica

12cm, 11g Dark olive upperparts, cream underparts, thin black chest band, whitish eyes and white outer-tail feathers are diagnostic. Female has narrower chest band than male. A very common resident in the forested escarpment west of the park; scarce and localised in the park itself where it is confined to thick riverine vegetation along drainage lines. Locally resident, but numbers probably increase in winter due to an influx of birds from the escarpment. Found singly or in pairs. Pairs duet; males give a dry *'krup-krup-krup'*; female responds with a higher-pitched *'trit-trit-trit'*. BANDKEELKLEINJANTJIE

RUDD'S APALIS
Apalis ruddi

13cm, 10g Told from Bar-throated Apalis by its dark (not pale) eyes, thin white eyebrow and absence of white outer-tail feathers. Female has narrower chest band than male. Very localised, restricted to the dense thickets of the Nwambiya sand forest in the far northeast of the park; the area is unfortunately inaccessible to general visitors. Resident and common within this small area; occurs solitarily or in pairs. Its presence is usually revealed by its song, a duet similar to that of the Bar-throated Apalis but more rapid and lower-pitched. RUDDKLEINJANTJIE

YELLOW-BREASTED APALIS
Apalis flavida

12cm, 9g Lemon-yellow chest, reddish eye and eye-ring, and absence of black chest band distinguish it from other apalises. Male has a black bar where yellow meets white underparts (absent in female). A common resident, especially in the southern half of the park, occurring mainly along drainage lines where there are galleries of tall trees; common in many rest camps. Usually in pairs. Typically found high in tree canopies, its presence often given away by the racy call of the male, a rapidly repeated *'chizik'*, to which the female sometimes responds in synchrony with more shrill, quickly repeated *'krit'* notes. Often joins mixed-species bird parties, especially in winter. GEELBORSKLEINJANTJIE

STIERLING'S WREN-WARBLER
Calamonastes stierlingi

14cm, 13g Its uniformly rufous-brown upperparts, white, finely barred underparts, dark red eye and thin red eye-ring are diagnostic. A fairly common resident, especially on the granitic soils in the west, where it occurs in the understorey of mopane, acacia and broad-leafed woodlands. Occurs singly or in pairs. Forages on the ground, but retreats to a bush or low tree if disturbed. Easily overlooked; its presence is mostly given away in summer by its song, a galloping *'biri-rit'* or *'pilly-lip'* repeated steadily and continuously for a minute or more. STIERLINGSANGER.

Bar-throated Apalis

Rudd's Apalis

Yellow-breasted Apalis ♂

Yellow-breasted Apalis ♀

Stierling's Wren-Warbler

Stierling's Wren-Warbler

153

CAMAROPTERAS, RUSH WARBLERS AND PRINIAS

The camaropteras are small, plump, short-tailed warblers in the cisticola family that characteristically cock their rather short tails. Both species occurring in the park have distinctive bleating calls and are found in dense understorey; they probably hybridise where their ranges overlap. The Little Rush Warbler is a member of the Locustellidae warbler family, but is most likely to be confused with the reed warblers (p148), as it skulks among matted reeds and dense vegetation near water. Prinias, like the camaropteras, are cisticolid warblers that frequently cock their tails, especially when alarmed; they are easily recognised by their slender build, and long legs and tails.

GREY-BACKED CAMAROPTERA *Camaroptera brevicaudata*

13cm, 11g Distinguished from Green-backed Camaroptera by grey (not olive-green) back, rump and tail; both species have olive-green wings, grey heads, white underparts and distinctive red eyes. A common breeding resident, occuring mainly in the northern half of the park in thickets and dense woodland understorey; habitat is similar to that occupied by Green-backed Camaroptera. Very vocal, especially in summer when the male's strident *'biddyup-biddyup-biddyup ...'* song is a familiar sound in bush thickets. When alarmed, gives a nasal, wailing call, hence its common name of Bleating Bush Warbler. GRYSRUGKWÊKWÊVOËL

GREEN-BACKED CAMAROPTERA *Camaroptera brachyura*

13cm, 11g Distinguished from Grey-backed Camaroptera by olive-green (not grey) back, rump and tail; both species have olive-green wings, grey heads, white underparts and distinctive red eyes. Found in thickets in woodland throughout the park, but records are concentrated in the southern half, especially along drainage lines and on termitaria. Much less easily seen than heard as it calls from inside dense, leafy tangles. Calls and calling behaviour are similar to those of Grey-backed Camaroptera, considered a subspecies by some authorities. GROENRUGKWÊKWÊVOËL

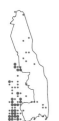

LITTLE RUSH WARBLER *Bradypterus baboecala*

14cm, 15g A marsh-living species, best identified by its distinctive song, uniformly dark coloration and large, broad tail. Scarce and localised in the park, probably resident in places but erratically present in seasonal habitat. Frequents dense sedge beds or stands of bulrush, especially where these are densely matted, mainly along larger rivers. Does not easily show itself except during brief display flights in which, after calling, the male may make a brief flight above the vegetation, wings whirring loudly, before dropping back out of view. Its distinctive song is a series of 20 or more *'krip'* notes that start slowly, then speed up until they run into each other before ending abruptly. KAAPSE VLEISANGER

TAWNY-FLANKED PRINIA *Prinia subflava*

13cm, 9g Long tail, brown upperparts, rufous wing panels, creamy-white underparts with tawny flanks and dark eye-stripe and white eyebrow are diagnostic. Like other prinias, this species' trademark is its behaviour of frequently cocking its long tail while perched. A common, widespread resident, found wherever there is rank grass and scrub, especially along drainage lines. Occurs in pairs or small family groups year-round. A lively, active species; lives within a few metres of the ground. Vocal throughout the year; both sexes make the distinctive, persistent *'pzzzp-pzzzp-pzzzp ...'* call. BRUINSYLANGSTERTJIE

Grey-backed Camaroptera

Green-backed Camaroptera

Little Rush Warbler

Tawny-flanked Prinia

Tawny-flanked Prinia

155

LARGE AND MARSH CISTICOLAS

Cisticolas are small, cryptically coloured warblers that frequent grasslands and shrublands. Most species look similar to one another and are notoriously difficult to identify, especially in winter when males seldom sing. Their identification is further complicated by seasonal changes in plumage and marked sexual size dimorphism in one species, the Croaking Cisticola. The eight species that occur regularly in the park differ in their habitat preferences – open grassland, marshes, rocky slopes, scrub, open woodland – but the males' territorial calls offer the best way to separate the various species. Four of the larger species, two of which are largely confined to marshy habitats, are described here.

RATTLING CISTICOLA
Cisticola chiniana

15cm, 16g The most common cisticola and one of the most abundant birds in the park, found wherever grass cover and scattered trees occur. Found in pairs or family groups after breeding. In winter, best identified by the combination of a longish tail, streaked wings and back, a pale rufous, streaked cap and a noticeably curved bill. Males advertise their presence throughout summer by their strident four-syllable call, *'chew-chew-chew-CHIRRR'*, the last note being the rattle for which the bird is named. Males sing for long spells from the tops of trees and bushes; if alarmed, the call changes to a shriller, grating *'CHER-CHER-CHER ...'*. BOSVELDTINKTINKIE

RED-FACED CISTICOLA
Cisticola erythrops

14cm, 15g A plain-backed cisticola, with light brown upperparts and whitish underparts that are washed rufous on the face and flanks; unusual among cisticolas in lacking a rufous crown. A common but localised resident of rank grass and reeds along the margins of streams and rivers. Typically remains in dense cover, where it is easily overlooked. Males give their presence away in summer by their call, a penetrating series of 10 or more piercing whistles that rise to a crescendo and then fade away: *'tew tew tew tew TEW-TEW-TEW-TEW-tew-tew'*. ROOIWANGTINKTINKIE

RUFOUS-WINGED CISTICOLA
Cisticola galactotes

13cm, 15g A wetland cisticola with a long tail, black back streaked with grey-brown and a rufous crown and wing panels; best told from Rattling Cisticola by its restricted habitat and distinctly brighter plumage. A common vlei-living species on the Mozambique coastal plain; extends inland along low-lying rivers. Only found as a localised resident in marshy areas with sedges or vlei grasses along the main rivers (mainly the Crocodile and Luvuvhu). SWARTRUGTINKTINKIE. **Levaillant's Cisticola** *C. tinniens* (Vleitinktinkie) is another wetland species that is almost as brightly coloured but has a rufous (not grey-brown) tail; rare visitor from the highveld.

CROAKING CISTICOLA
Cisticola natalensis

♂18cm, 25g, ♀15cm, 18g Large size (for a cisticola), fairly short tail, heavy bill and croaking male song are diagnostic. Male appreciably larger than female – could even be mistaken for a female Southern Red Bishop (p190); it has a black bill and mouth in summer; bill pinkish-yellow in winter. A fairly common breeding resident in the far south of the park; scarce in the north where largely restricted to the margins of the larger rivers. Frequents areas of rank open grassland, especially around seasonally flooded ground. Unobtrusive when silent but in summer the male utters a loud, throaty, croaking call, either while perched on top of a bush or while performing a jerky display flight a few metres off the ground. GROOTTINKTINKIE

Rattling Cisticola

Red-faced Cisticola

HUGH CHITTENDEN

Rufous-winged Cisticola

Croaking Cisticola ♀

Croaking Cisticola ♂

SMALL CISTICOLAS

Two small, fairly short-tailed cisticolas occur in grassland areas: Zitting and Desert cisticolas. Their males undertake often-protracted aerial display flights in summer, calling continuously, before diving back to the ground. The two are similar in appearance and occur alongside each other; differences in their aerial displays and calls are the easiest way of distinguishing between them. The two other species here have longer tails and are rather plain-backed with rufous caps. Both occur in woodland, but the Neddicky is more abundant and widespread than the localised Lazy Cisticola.

ZITTING CISTICOLA
Cisticola juncidis

11cm, 9g Typically more richly coloured on the face and flanks than Desert Cisticola; the two live side by side in places, but Zitting Cisticola is more common and is usually associated with denser, taller grass cover, often over damp ground. Easily distinguished from Desert Cisticola when displaying; males cruise 10–30m over their territories in a jerky display flight throughout the summer, uttering, a sharp *'tjik'* (or *'zit'*) note at 1-sec intervals, each note accompanied by a dip in flight. LANDERYKLOPKLOPPIE

DESERT CISTICOLA
Cisticola aridulus

11cm, 9g Typically paler on the face and flanks than Zitting Cisticola; best identified by its different song and display flight. Occurs in grassland, including areas with scattered shrubs, across the park, but most common in the drier north. Male performs a fast, low-level, jerky display flight, uttering a rapid *'si-si-si-si ...'* as he zig-zags a few metres above the ground; he may audibly snap his wings at intervals. The flight is usually performed for the benefit of a female perched below him and he often ends by swooping down, putting her to flight and then pursuing her. WOESTYNKLOPKLOPPIE

NEDDICKY
Cisticola fulvicapilla

11cm, 9g Male territorial call and plain colouring – pale grey-brown upperparts, off-white underparts and a rufous cap – are diagnostic; smaller and shorter-tailed than localised Lazy Cisticola. A common resident throughout, but especially abundant in open broad-leafed woodlands on the granitic soils in the west. Easily overlooked in winter when males are silent; in summer their monotonous *'peep'* song (which explains their alternative common name of Piping Cisticola), or the dry, insect-like ticking call uttered by the male while perched on a bush or tree top, is unlikely to be overlooked. NEDDIKKIE

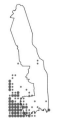

LAZY CISTICOLA
Cisticola aberrans

14cm, 14g A rather plain-backed cisticola with a rich rufous cap; lacks buffy face and flanks of Red-faced Cisticola (p156). Most likely to be confused with the more common and widespread Neddicky, but is larger with a much longer tail and has a finely streaked back and wing coverts. Has the prinia-like habit of frequently cocking its tail as the bird moves about mouse-like, running across rocks. A scarce, localised species in the park, largely restricted to the hilly southwestern corner of the park; prefers rank grassland with thickets and patches of woodland on rocky hillsides. Males reveal their presence in summer with their drawn-out, plaintive *'tshweee'* note. LUITINKTINKIE

Zitting Cisticola

Desert Cisticola

Neddicky

Lazy Cisticola

'OLD WORLD' FLYCATCHERS

The three *Muscicapa* flycatchers are fairly small, rather drab insectivorous birds that mainly hawk flying insects from a perch in a tree or bush, returning to a perch to eat their prey. Larger prey are sometimes taken from the ground. Two species are resident in the park, while the third is a non-breeding migrant from Eurasia. The Grey Tit-Flycatcher is a closely related species that typically remains within the canopy, gleaning insects or briefly chasing those that it flushes as it flits about restlessly, constantly fanning its tail. All are restricted to woodland habitats and tend to be solitary except when breeding.

SPOTTED FLYCATCHER — *Muscicapa striata*

14cm, 16g Larger and more elongate than African Dusky Flycatcher; easily distinguished by its streaked crown and chest and long wings, which, when the bird is seen perched, project halfway down the tail. Has a distinctive habit not shared by the other *Muscicapa* flycatchers of briefly flicking its wings half open on alighting (see also Familiar Chat, p140). A common, widespread non-breeding visitor from Eurasia, present from mid-October to early April. A solitary and largely silent bird, but often quite confiding; likely to be encountered in any wooded area, including those in many rest camps. EUROPESE VLIEËVANGER

AFRICAN DUSKY FLYCATCHER — *Muscicapa adusta*

13cm, 14g Smaller and more compact than Spotted Flycatcher, with an unstreaked crown, only very diffusely streaked chest, thin white eye-ring and shorter wings that only reach the base of the tail; lacks the habit of wing-flicking when it alights. A localised breeding resident, confined to riparian woodland along the larger rivers. Locally common; resident in rest camps along these rivers (e.g. Skukuza and Letaba). Occurs in pairs, which are unobtrusive; easily overlooked and mainly detected when a hawking birds flits out from its perch in pursuit of a small insect. Its call is a rather soft, high-pitched '*trr-r-r-r-rt*'. DONKERVLIEËVANGER

ASHY FLYCATCHER — *Muscicapa caerulescens*

15cm, 17g Slightly larger than Spotted Flycatcher; best identified by its conspicuous white eye-ring and greyish-blue (not brown) plumage with upperparts marginally darker than underparts. Best told from Grey Tit-Flycatcher by its lack of white outer-tail feathers and typically *Muscicapa* foraging behaviour of hawking insects from a low perch. A localised but widespread breeding resident, found patchily throughout in tall riparian woodland. Common in some rest camps (e.g. Skukuza). Song is a lively jumble of high-pitched notes. BLOUGRYSVLIEËVANGER

GREY TIT-FLYCATCHER — *Myioparus plumbeus*

14cm, 13g Marginally smaller and superficially similar to Ashy Flycatcher, but readily distinguished by its white outer-tail feathers that are conspicuously revealed as it pirouettes through the branches while foraging. A fairly common resident, occurring commonly alongside Ashy Flycatcher in the forested margins of rivers, also in drier woodland. Forages inside tree canopies, moving quickly from twig to twig, frequently fanning and closing its tail as it changes position, apparently to disturb small insects. Easily overlooked; its presence is usually given away by its song, a soft, tremulous '*weeed-ildee*'. WAAIERSTERTVLIEËVANGER

Spotted Flycatcher

African Dusky Flycatcher

Ashy Flycatcher

Grey Tit-Flycatcher

Grey Tit-Flycatcher fanning tail

OTHER FLYCATCHERS AND BATISES

The two *Melaenornis* flycatchers here (together with the Southern Black Flycatcher, p132) belong to the Muscicapidae family, but are larger than those described on the previous page (p160), and take most of their prey from the ground. Batises are members of the wattle-eye family, the Platysteiridae (p172), whereas paradise flycatchers are part of the diverse, mainly Australasian monarch family, the Monarchidae. Both hunt small insects among tree canopies, gleaning prey from twigs and foliage or hawking them in the air. Three other flycatchers and one batis visit the park occasionally (p208).

MARICO FLYCATCHER
Melaenornis mariquensis

18cm, 24g Easily told from Pale Flycatcher by its white (not pale buff) underparts, which contrast with its sandy-brown upperparts. This is primarily a species of the dry western half of southern Africa and it reaches its eastern limits in the park. Found mainly in the drier central region between the Satara and the Olifants rivers in areas of thornveld where it is a localised, uncommon resident. Quite conspicuous owing to its white underparts and habit of perching in the open. MARICOVLIEËVANGER

PALE FLYCATCHER
Melaenornis pallidus

16cm, 23g A rather nondescript flycatcher; its alternative name of Mouse-coloured Flycatcher aptly describes its colour. Told from Marico Flycatcher by its pale buff (not white) underparts and from Familiar Chat (p140) by its longer, brown (not rufous) tail and absence of flicking its wings on alighting. A fairly common, widespread resident in tall mopane and broad-leafed woodland throughout; easily overlooked given its unassuming disposition. Occurs singly or in pairs. Typically encountered hunting from a low perch, scanning the ground for prey items which, when spotted, are caught on the ground. MUISKLEURVLIEËVANGER

CHINSPOT BATIS
Batis molitor

13cm, 11g Small, compact black, grey and white birds that are common and conspicuous. Chest band black in male, chestnut in female, which also has a chestnut throat spot (hence the common name). Resident in all wooded areas; these feisty little birds live in territorial pairs year-round. Forages in the mid-strata of trees, hunting small insects on twigs and among foliage; also hawks insects in the air and takes prey from the ground. Regular members of mixed-species bird parties and give away their presence by frequent contact-calling or by the male's distinctive, rather mournful whistled *'three-blind-mice'* song. WITLIESBOSBONTROKKIE

AFRICAN PARADISE FLYCATCHER
Terpsiphone viridis

17cm (excluding male's 20cm tail streamers), 15g A strikingly coloured bird with a short crest and fleshy eye-wattles. Breeding males have larger and brighter blue eye-wattles and most males have long central tail feathers, which are dropped after breeding. Charming, lively little birds; occur commonly throughout the park, especially along rivers but also wherever tall, leafy trees provide a shady understorey. They are breeding visitors, present from October to May, but a few individuals overwinter in some years. Typically encountered flitting from branch to branch inside a tree, hawking insects or gleaning them from twigs and foliage. Usually in pairs; maintain contact with frequent *'skwee-skur'* calls; male song is a musical *'tswee-seee-ur'*. PARADYSVLIEËVANGER

Marico Flycatcher

Pale Flycatcher

Chinspot Batis ♂ and ♀

African Paradise Flycatcher ♂

PIPITS, LONGCLAWS AND WAGTAILS

These birds are all members of the wagtail family, Motacillidae. Pipits are cryptically marked ground-living birds that are notoriously difficult to identify. They are easily confused with larks (p122), but are more slender, with finer bills, longer legs and longer tails (in most species). They have more insipid calls and run more briskly, often ending such runs with a tail-bob. Two other pipits are rare visitors to the park (p208). Longclaws are pipit-like in behaviour, distinguished by their larger size, thickset build and more colourful underparts. Their name derives from their long hind-claws, which assist in walking on thick grass. Wagtails are familiar birds that habitually bob their long tails up and down, and are often tame and confiding.

AFRICAN PIPIT
Anthus cinnamomeus

17cm, 25g A medium-sized pipit with a mottled back and modest streaking largely confined to its upper breast. Distinguished from Plain-backed and Buffy pipits by its mottled back, from Striped Pipit by its smaller size and less streaked underparts, and from Bushveld Pipit by its larger size, longer tail and less streaked underparts. A widespread pipit throughout, but nowhere abundant. Favours open areas with short grass and is often encountered along road verges. Usually occurs singly. In flight, shows white outer-tail feathers; gives a slow, dry *'pli-pli-pli'* during its high-flying, undulating and often protracted display flight. GEWONE KOESTER

BUFFY PIPIT
Anthus vaalensis

17cm, 26g A larger, chunkier pipit than African Pipit with a plain (not mottled) back and buff (not white) outer-tail feathers. A scarce nomad, widely recorded throughout in open, treeless country, especially in heavily grazed or recently burnt areas. Male song is a sparrow-like *'chrrrup-chereeoo'*, given from low perch or in a short, aerial display flight. VAALKOESTER. **Plain-backed Pipit** *A. leucophrys* (Donkerkoester) is another fairly regular nomad found in the same habitat as Buffy Pipit; slightly smaller than that species with a yellow (not pinkish) colour to the base of the bill, longer hind-claw and less pronounced tail-bobbing behaviour.

STRIPED PIPIT
Anthus lineiventris

18cm, 34g A large, well-marked pipit. Readily identified by its heavily striped underparts; back is darker than most other pipits in the park; at close range the narrow yellow fringes to the wing feathers are diagnostic. Uncommon, usually found on wooded, rocky hill slopes. Because of its restricted habitat (at least while breeding), its occurrence is patchy and mostly confined to the southwest. Unusually for a pipit, it has a lusty thrush-like song, mostly uttered in spring when males sing from a tree top. GESTREEPTE KOESTER

BUSHVELD PIPIT
Anthus caffer

13cm, 17g The smallest pipit in the park, with a fairly short tail, heavily streaked plumage and rather plain head; lacks the prominent eye-stripes of the park's other pipits. Occurs widely but sparsely throughout in woodlands; most common in broad-leafed woodlands in the southwest. Usually solitary, but can occur in loose aggregations at times. Easily overlooked; owing to its unobtrusive nature, most records are of birds foraging on road verges; perhaps more likely to be encountered on walking trails. When flushed, it characteristically flies to perch in a tree, alighting with a distinctive *'zweep'* call-note. BOSVELDKOESTER.

African Pipit

Buffy Pipit

Striped Pipit

Plain-backed Pipit

Bushveld Pipit

Bushveld Pipit

165

YELLOW-THROATED LONGCLAW · *Macronyx croceus*

21cm, 49g Easily identified when its chrome-yellow underparts and black collar are visible, but could be confused with a pipit or lark when seen from behind. Locally common, mainly in open broad-leafed woodland in the southern half of the park where it frequents areas with a dense grass cover and scattered trees and shrubs. Found singly or in pairs; usually encountered walking through the grass with a high-stepping gait or perched on the top of a tree or bush from where it utters its rich, fluting call. In flight, alternates rapid flapping bouts with short glides; has prominent white tips to the outer-tail feathers. GEELKEELKALKOENTJIE

AFRICAN PIED WAGTAIL · *Motacilla aguimp*

20cm, 27g Striking black-and-white plumage and typical wagtail profile and behaviour are diagnostic. A common, conspicuous resident throughout, occurring along the margins of all the larger rivers and dams and on the lawns at many rest camps. Usually encountered in pairs, briskly walking along the water's edge, pausing, bobbing their long tails up and down, then walking farther, or perhaps sprinting forwards to catch a small insect. Sometimes forages on backs of hippos. Lively, vocal birds with high-pitched whistled calls. BONTKWIKKIE. Four other wagtails are occasional visitors to the park, with the **Cape Wagtail** *M. capensis* (Gewone Kwikkie) being the most frequent; found at wetlands mainly in winter; told from African Pied Wagtail by its less striking grey-and-white plumage.

BOUBOUS

Boubous are part of the bushshrike family, the Malaconotidae, which is confined to sub-Saharan Africa and is closely related to the helmetshrikes (and more distantly to the wattle-eyes and batises) but unrelated to the 'true' shrikes (Laniidae). Their name is derived from one of their calls: a whistled '*bou-bou*'. All boubous have wide vocal repertoires and are well known for their duetting behaviour in which the female responds, with precise timing, to the male's notes with her own call, the synchronised sound seemingly coming from one bird.

SOUTHERN BOUBOU · *Laniarius ferrugineus*

22cm, 60g Commonly seen in most of the park. Distinguished from Tropical Boubou by its buff-tinged (not pinkish) underparts; male has paler underparts than female. Common in the southern half of the park, but more localised in the north. Resident; found in pairs year-round, mainly in bushy thickets, where they typically remain in dense cover and are more often heard than seen. The male has a wide variety of whistled calls; the female's response in the duet is one or more whistled notes, very different to the harsh, grating response of female Tropical Boubous. Both species give grating alarm calls. SUIDELIKE WATERFISKAAL

TROPICAL BOUBOU · *Laniarius major*

23cm, 50g Very similar to Southern Boubou, but paler below, with only a faint pink wash to the underparts. Resident; confined to the far north, especially in riparian thickets that fringe the Limpopo, Luvuvhu and Mutale rivers. Where its range overlaps with Southern Boubou, it is confined to riverine vegetation. Occurs year-round in pairs, which are easily heard but less easily seen as they tend to skulk inside dense cover; can be lured into the open by pishing or imitating their whistled songs. Duetting pairs can be distinguished from Southern Boubous by the female's harsh, grating call. TROPIESE WATERFISKAAL

Yellow-throated Longclaw

African Pied Wagtail

Cape Wagtail

Southern Boubou ♂

Tropical Boubou

SHRIKES

Five true shrike species (family Laniidae) occur in the park; two are resident, two are non-breeding visitors from the Palearctic, and one is an uncommon nomad. They are conspicuous birds, perching prominently on trees and bushes from which they watch the ground below for prey. Primarily insectivorous, they prey on grasshoppers in particular, but also take mice, small reptiles and whatever other small creatures they can overpower. They are rapacious birds with strongly hooked bills – the family name is from the Latin for butcher and relates to the habit, in some species, of impaling their prey on a thorn before tearing it apart.

MAGPIE SHRIKE
Corvinella melanoleuca

45cm, 82g A large, shaggy-looking black shrike with white wingbars; white flanks in female; all-black in male. Tail varies from long to very long among individuals. A common, conspicuous resident that perches prominently. Gregarious; lives year-round in the park and breeds in co-operative family groups of about 4–12 (or more) individuals. Occurs throughout, especially in thornveld, but also in open areas where there are scattered trees to provide hunting perches. At irregular intervals groups rally together in a tree and call in unison, bowing and half-raising their wings, each uttering loud, mellow whistles (higher pitched in females than males). LANGSTERTLAKSMAN

SOUTHERN WHITE-CROWNED SHRIKE
Eurocephalus anguitimens

24cm, 69g A fairly large, chunky shrike. Its brown-and-white plumage may lead to confusion with White-browed Sparrow-Weaver (p209), but white crown, black facial markings and hooked bill are distinctive. Resident and fairly common, especially in woodlands in the southern and central areas; largely absent from mopane woodland. A co-operative breeding species, occurring year-round in family groups of 3–8 birds, which forage from prominent perches, often on the tops of trees. Individuals maintain contact with periodic calls: a querulous, rather shrill series of *'kwee'* notes. KREMETARTLAKSMAN

LESSER GREY SHRIKE
Lanius minor

21cm, 47g Male easily identified by its grey back, white underparts and broad black mask and forehead; female has a smaller, greyer mask than the male. A fairly common non-breeding visitor from Eurasia, present from November to early April. Single birds may be encountered anywhere in the park, but are most frequently seen in open grasslands in the east. Largely silent while in Africa. GRYSLAKSMAN. **Southern (Common) Fiscal** *L. collaris* (Fiskaallaksman) has black upperparts with a white wingbar and underparts; scarce nomad mainly found in open country along the Sabie River southwards, with a few sightings in the Punda Maria area.

RED-BACKED SHRIKE
Lanius collurio

18cm, 29g Male easily identified by its striking plumage; female is mottled brownish above and faintly scalloped off-white below and can be mistaken for an imm *Melaenornis* flycatcher (p162), but hooked bill and more squat posture when perched are distinctive. A common and at times abundant non-breeding visitor from Eurasia, present from late October to early April. Feeds singly, perching on bushes and low trees. Occurs throughout, but most abundant in open country where there are scattered shrubs and stunted trees to provide hunting perches. Males start to sing a subdued warbling song in the month before leaving for the north. ROOIRUGLAKSMAN

Magpie Shrike

Southern White-crowned Shrike

Lesser Grey Shrike

Red-backed Shrike ♂

Red-backed Shrike ♀

169

PUFFBACKS, BRUBRU AND TCHAGRAS

These members of the bushshrike family (Malaconotidae) are common residents in the park and are found throughout in wooded habitats. They share with 'true' shrikes a hooked bill and a largely insectivorous diet. The Black-backed Puffback and Brubru seek their prey (and build their nests) in the leafy canopies of large trees, whereas the tchagras live lower down in shrubs and bushes, locating much of their food on the ground. They are not particularly shy, but because they live in fairly dense vegetation, they are often not easy to see and are usually first detected by their distinctive calls.

BLACK-BACKED PUFFBACK — *Dryoscopus cubla*

17cm, 27g Black head and upperparts, white underparts and cherry-red eye are diagnostic. Male has an all-black cap; female has duller black upperparts, whitish forehead and short white eyebrows; juv washed buff below. A common resident in woodlands throughout; unlikely to be missed. Lives year-round in pairs, often joining mixed-species bird parties in winter. Its name comes from the male's striking display when courting a female. He raises his white rump and back feathers to create a powder puff-like ball and pursues the female with a bouncy flight, noisy, exaggerated wing-beats and loud bill-clicking. At other times the male's distinctive click-whistle 'chick-weeo' call reveals his presence. SNEEUBAL

BRUBRU — *Nilaus afer*

14cm, 24g Black upperparts, large white eyebrows and wingbars and white underparts with chestnut flanks are diagnostic; female slightly duller coloured. Occurs widely in woodlands throughout the park; less common than Black-backed Puffback but shares the same habitat and habits. Resident; lives in pairs year-round and is a common member of mixed-species bird parties in winter. Its name comes from the male's song, which starts with a chip, followed by a drawn-out, ringing 'brruuuuu'. The female frequently responds in duet with a higher-pitched, shorter 'eeeu'. Curiously, the male's 'brubru' call is mainly heard only in summer; in winter it is replaced by a rather shrill 'pipipipipipi ...' call. BONTROKLAKSMAN

BROWN-CROWNED TCHAGRA — *Tchagra australis*

18cm, 33g Closely similar in appearance to Black-crowned Tchagra but substantially smaller and more slender, with a grey-brown (not black) cap (but care is needed when identifying it, as it has a black line above the white eyebrow and the paler crown can be hard to see from the side). A common resident throughout, but especially in areas of acacia or mopane scrub. Males are often detected by their conspicuous aerial display in summer, flying up with noisy wing-beats to a height of 10–15m, then gliding back to the ground while uttering a series of rolling, descending notes. Both species also have various grating alarm calls. ROOIVLERKTJAGRA

BLACK-CROWNED TCHAGRA — *Tchagra senegalus*

21cm, 54g Similar to, but larger than, Brown-crowned Tchagra, with a heavier bill and a fully black (not grey-brown) crown. Both species have rufous-coloured wings (hence their former name of Redwing Shrike) and white tips to their blackish tail feathers, which are prominent in flight. A common resident throughout, found in broad-leafed woodlands. Encountered singly or in pairs, usually on, or within 2m, of the ground, sometimes alongside Brown-crowned Tchagras. A skulking bird, its presence is usually detected by its lilting, somewhat mournful, descending 5–6-syllabled song, which sounds uncannily like a human whistling. SWARTKROONTJAGRA

Black-backed Puffback br ♂ displaying   Black-backed Puffback ♀

Brubru ♀

Brubru ♂

Brown-crowned Tchagra

Black-crowned Tchagra

BUSHSHRIKES AND WATTLE-EYES

The bushshrikes (Malaconotidae) include boubous (p166), puffbacks and tchagras (p170), but for most people the family is epitomised by the species with olive-green and yellow plumages. Despite their bright coloration, they typically remain in dense cover where their green upperparts blend with the foliage; were it not for their loud, distinctive calls, they would be easily overlooked. All have hooked, shrike-like bills and are primarily insectivorous. Wattle-eyes (Platysteiridae) are in the same family as the batises (p162). Smaller and more demure than bushshrikes, all 11 species are confined to Africa, and most species have black-and-white plumage. Wattle-eyes, too, are insectivores, living in tree canopies.

GORGEOUS BUSHSHRIKE
Chlorophoneus viridis

19cm, 37g Easily identified by its red throat; female has less red on throat, a narrower black chest band and lacks black facial markings. Juv has yellow-orange throat; told from juv Orange-breasted Bushshrike by green (not grey) crown. A localised resident, found mostly in the extreme north and in the southwest of the park where it frequents dense thickets, especially along drainage lines. Pairs are territorial year-round, living in the lower strata of bush clumps, and they are masters at remaining hidden. In summer males call frequently, giving their presence away with their loud, piercing, two- or three-syllabled call, *'kong-koit'* or *'kong-kong-koit'*. KONKOIT

ORANGE-BREASTED BUSHSHRIKE
Chlorophoneus sulfureopectus

19cm, 27g Superficially similar to Grey-headed Bushshrike but is much smaller and has yellow (not grey) forehead and eyebrow and a dark brown (not yellow) eye; female has less orange on chest and lacks the male's black facial mask. A common resident in woodlands through much of the park; least common in the dry central areas. It is encountered singly or in pairs and frequents the mid- to upper strata of trees, foraging by moving quickly through the thinner branches and foliage in search of insects. Less shy than Gorgeous Bushshrike; males call frequently, a series of short, descending whistles sometimes rendered *'coffee, tea, or meeee'* that have a ventriloquial quality. Individuals often join mixed-species bird parties in winter. ORANJEBORSBOSLAKSMAN

GREY-HEADED BUSHSHRIKE
Malaconotus blanchoti

26cm, 77g Much larger than Orange-breasted Bushshrike, with a formidably large hooked bill, an all-grey head with paler grey lores and vivid yellow (not dark) eye. A fairly common breeding resident in woodlands throughout. Occurs solitarily or in pairs while breeding. Hunts inside the canopies of large trees, preying on geckos, lizards, small snakes, mice and bats; also feeds on the usual bushshrike fare of insects. It is a nest-robber of note, taking eggs and nestlings of birds up to the size of a dove. Its presence is usually given away by the male's mournful, drawn-out, rather ghostly *'whooooooo'* whistle, which explains its Afrikaans name (literally 'ghost-bird'). SPOOKVOËL

BLACK-THROATED WATTLE-EYE
Platysteira peltata

13cm, 13g A neat, compact black-and-white bird with fleshy red eye-wattles. Male has white throat and black chest band; female has all-black throat. A rare, localised breeding resident, regularly present only in the riparian woodland along the Luvuvhu and Limpopo rivers, favouring areas where the tall evergreen trees are festooned with trailing tangles of vines. Usually encountered in pairs in the mid- to upper canopy, their presence given away by a soft, rasping *'wichee-wichee-wichee …'*, or their aerial display call, *'ptec ptec ptec'*. Often seen at the Pafuri picnic site. BELOOGBOSBONTROKKIE

Gorgeous Bushshrike ♂

Gorgeous Bushshrike ♀

Orange-breasted Bushshrike

Orange-breasted Bushshrike

Grey-headed Bushshrike

Black-throated Wattle-eye ♂

HELMETSHRIKES, MYNAS AND STARLINGS

Closely related to bushshrikes, helmetshrikes (Prionopidae) are distinguished by, and named for, the small bristle of feathers on their foreheads. All eight species, of which two occur in the park, are restricted to the Afrotropics. They are gregarious, living year-round in closely knit family groups. Starlings and mynas (Sturnidae) are a large, diverse Old World family, with nine species recorded from the park.

RETZ'S HELMETSHRIKE
Prionops retzii

20cm, 42g Larger than White-crested Helmetshrike; easily identified by its jet-black head and underparts and white vent; at close range the tuft of forehead feathers, coral-red bill and eye-ring are diagnostic. Juv duller with brown bill, eye and legs. Resident, occurring widely but sparsely throughout the park, mainly in areas of tall woodland such as those found along the larger rivers. Groups mostly forage for insects in the canopies of larger trees, moving from tree to tree as a cohesive unit, occasionally (especially in winter) joining up with groups of White-crested Helmetshrikes. Parasitised by Thick-billed Cuckoo. SWARTHELMLAKSMAN

WHITE-CRESTED HELMETSHRIKE
Prionops plumatus

18cm, 34g Easily recognised by their striking black-and-white plumage with white wingbars prominent in flight; at close range the tuft of forehead feathers, bright yellow eyes and eye-wattles, and reddish legs are diagnostic. Juv has short crest, dark eyes, no eye-wattles and yellow legs. A common resident, especially in mopane, *Combretum* and other broad-leafed woodlands on the sandy granitic soils in the west. Groups of 5–8 birds (rarely 4–15) move as a cohesive unit through the woodland as they forage for insects, usually keeping within a few metres of the ground and maintaining contact with their peculiar ratchety call-notes. WITHELMLAKSMAN

COMMON MYNA
Acridotheres tristis

23cm, 101g A large, brown, starling-like bird with yellow bill, face and legs; white wing panels are striking in flight. Native to India, this species was introduced to Durban in 1888 and to Johannesburg in the 1930s. It has spread widely from these areas and now occurs across most of northern South Africa and more locally in Zimbabwe and eastern Botswana, and has recently reached Zambia. It is regarded as a pest and efforts to control its numbers have not been successful. Common in the towns, villages and settlements adjacent to the park; occurs only sporadically in the park, usually at rest camps where new arrivals are discouraged from becoming established. INDIESE SPREEU

WATTLED STARLING
Creatophora cinerea

21cm, 75g The only pale grey-brown starling; male in breeding condition is almost white with bright yellow skin on the back of the head and loose-hanging black skin on the crown and throat. At other times male resembles the pale grey female, whose main distinguishing features are the dark grey flight feathers and whitish rump, prominent in flight. Occurs widely but erratically in the park, found on the eastern basaltic plains. Often in flocks, sometimes numbering thousands of birds; its presence is apparently dictated by rainfall and locust abundance. Breeds in large numbers in the park when locusts are plentiful. Colonies sometimes cover many hectares, with every available knob thorn used to support the birds' bulky, football-sized nests. Nests remain intact long after the birds have left the area and are often used by other species. LELSPREEU

Retz's Helmetshrike

Retz's Helmetshrike

White-crested Helmetshrike

Wattled Starling ♂ br

Common Myna

Wattled Starling non-br

GLOSSY STARLINGS

With their iridescent, all-blue plumage, the 'glossy starlings' are among the park's best-known birds, as they have become tame and confiding in rest camps and at picnic sites. The genus name *Lamprotornis* means 'radiant bird'. They are resident in the park and, although they separate into pairs while nesting, they are gregarious for most of the year, feeding together and roosting at night in large, noisy flocks. The sexes are alike, but juvs are duller. They have a varied diet, eating fruit and nectar when available, or insects, and they spend much of their time foraging on the ground. All nest in holes in trees and are parasitised on occasion by Greater Honeyguides and Great Spotted Cuckoos.

BURCHELL'S STARLING
Lamprotornis australis

32cm, 120g A long-tailed glossy starling that is appreciably larger than Meves's Starling but with a relatively shorter tail; the ranges of the two do not overlap in the park. Occurs widely and commonly throughout the southern half of the park; becomes progressively more scarce in the mopane country north of the Olifants River and is largely absent north of the Shingwedzi River. Usually encountered foraging on the ground in pairs or small groups; favours parkland with scattered tall trees and a sparse or shortly grazed grass understorey. The typical call is a throaty *'chreeow'*. GROOTGLANSSPREEU

MEVES'S STARLING
Lamprotornis mevesii

34cm, 79g Smaller-bodied but longer-tailed than Burchell's Starling; their ranges do not overlap in the park. Meves's Starling is restricted to the hot, low-lying floodplain areas of the Limpopo and Luvuvhu rivers in the far north. Common within this restricted range and unlikely to be missed if this area is visited. Occurs in pairs or small groups; usually encountered foraging on the ground in bare open areas in the woodland, flying up with shrill calls and taking cover in a tree if disturbed. LANGSTERTGLANSSPREEU

CAPE GLOSSY STARLING
Lamprotornis nitens

23cm, 83g The most commonly seen glossy starling in the park. Closely similar in size and appearance to the less common Greater Blue-eared Starling, with which it often occurs in mixed flocks. Cape Glossy Starling is more uniformly glossy blue-green in colour, with a fairly plain head, little contrast between its upperparts and underparts, and less prominent blackish tips to its greater coverts. Both species often assemble inside leafy trees in the heat of the day and utter similar rambling warbled songs, but their contact calls are quite different: Cape Glossy Starlings give a rolling *'whurra-whurra-whurra ...'* call. KLEINGLANSSPREEU.

GREATER BLUE-EARED STARLING
Lamprotornis chalybaeus

22cm, 85g Closely similar to Cape Glossy Starling in size and appearance; often joins it in mixed-species flocks. Distinguished by its rich blue underparts, which contrast with its green-tinged upperparts, more prominent blackish greater covert tips and its whining *'wheeea'* contact call, which is similar to the call of the White-fronted Bee-eater. Occurs throughout the park, although sparse in the drier central areas; favours riparian woodland, especially along the larger rivers. GROOT-BLOUOORGLANSSPREEU. **Black-bellied Starling** *Notopholia corrusca* (Swartpensglansspreeu) is smaller and less glossy than other species; rare, localised resident in riparian woodland along the Crocodile River between Crocodile Bridge and Malelane.

Burchell's Starling

Meves's Starling

Cape Glossy Starling

Cape Glossy Starling imm

Greater Blue-eared Starling

Black-bellied Starling

177

STARLINGS AND OXPECKERS

The two starlings on this page are distinctive species without close relatives among the other starlings in the park. Oxpeckers (Buphagidae) are closely related to starlings, and are confined to African savannas, where they have co-evolved an extraordinary symbiotic relationship with large mammals. They spend most of their day perched on their hosts, obtaining all their food (ticks and other parasites, but also blood) from them, mating and interacting socially with each other while astride them, and they even collect body hair from them to line their nests. Many hosts display irritation at the birds' presence, especially when the oxpeckers extend their foraging to wounds and facial areas. There are only two species, both of which occur in the park. They leave their hosts at night, roosting communally in tree holes.

VIOLET-BACKED STARLING   *Cinnyricinclus leucogaster*

18cm, 45g Male iridescent purple with white belly; female has yellow-brown upperparts streaked with black, and white underparts streaked with brown; at a glance resembles a small Groundscraper Thrush (p142), but seldom ventures onto the ground. A common breeding summer visitor from tropical Africa, arriving in mid-October and leaving in April or May, by which time the iridescent violet plumage of the male has faded to brown. In pairs while breeding, otherwise in groups or in flocks before migration. Their diet is mainly fruit, although like many birds they favour termite alates when these emerge after rain. Song is a series of buzzy whistles. WITBORSSPREEU

RED-WINGED STARLING   *Onychognathus morio*

30cm, 135g A large starling, easily recognised by its blackish plumage and brick-red outer wing panels; adult female has a grey head; juv and male have black heads. A localised resident, occurring mainly where rock faces provide nest and roost sites (e.g. in gorges along the Luvuvhu and Olifants rivers); also breeds under the eaves of buildings in some rest camps. Usually in pairs; forms flocks outside the breeding season, when it ranges widely to feed on fruiting trees and shrubs. Song is a sweet, whistled *'teoo'* or *'whu-tleoo'*; also gives harsh, grating calls. ROOIVLERKSPREEU

RED-BILLED OXPECKER   *Buphagus erythrorhynchus*

20cm, 51g Distinguished from Yellow-billed Oxpecker by its more slender, all-red bill, yellow eye-ring and uniformly dark back and rump; juv has blackish bill and no eye-ring. A common breeding resident throughout. Feeds on a wide spectrum of hosts, from warthogs to giraffe, and can occur alongside Yellow-billed Oxpeckers, especially on large herds of buffalo. Appears sleek and long-tailed in flight, when it often gives high-pitched *'zit'* or *'tsi'* calls. ROOIBEKRENOSTERVOËL

YELLOW-BILLED OXPECKER   *Buphagus africanus*

20cm, 59g Marginally larger than Red-billed Oxpecker; distinguished by its heavy, yellow-based bill, lack of a yellow eye-ring and a pale rump that contrasts with the darker back and tail. Juv has blackish bill – best told from juv Red-billed Oxpecker by its heavier bill. Yellow-billed Oxpeckers disappeared from the park early in the 20th century following extensive use of toxic dips on cattle, but recolonised the far north of the park in 1980. They have gradually extended southwards to the Crocodile River, but are scarce south of the Olifants River. Large animals – rhino, giraffe and, especially, buffalo – are favoured hosts; at the buffalo herds in the north Yellow-billed Oxpeckers usually outnumber their red-billed counterparts. GEELBEKRENOSTERVOËL

Violet-backed Starling ♂

Violet-backed Starling ♀

Red-winged Starling ♂

Red-billed Oxpecker

Yellow-billed Oxpeckers

Yellow-billed Oxpecker

SUNBIRDS

Sunbirds are small, active nectar-feeding birds from the Old World that have long, decurved bills for probing deep into flowers and long, slender tubular tongues for sucking nectar from plants. They share this diet, and some of the adaptations they have for extracting and digesting nectar, with the New World hummingbirds. Unlike hummingbirds, sunbirds seldom hover while extracting nectar. They are best observed on flowering trees and shrubs in rest camps. Six species occur regularly in the park, with two others recorded occasionally (p208). Most are sexually dimorphic; adult males are colourful with iridescent plumage, whereas females are rather drab and their identification can be tricky. They are favoured hosts of Klaas's Cuckoo.

MARICO SUNBIRD
Cinnyris mariquensis

14cm, 12g The most prevalent 'purple-banded' sunbird in the park. Roughly one-third larger than Purple-banded Sunbird with a substantially longer, more deeply curved bill. Male has a broader purple breast band than Purple-banded Sunbird with greenish (not blue) rump; female is more heavily mottled on the breast and has narrow white edges to the outer-tail feathers. A common resident that occurs widely in the park; however, because it favours thornveld, it is more frequently encountered in the southern half than in the mopane-dominated north. Males perch and sing conspicuously from tree tops, often basing themselves on mistletoe-infested trees where they have assured supplies of nectar. MARICOSUIKERBEKKIE

PURPLE-BANDED SUNBIRD
Cinnyris bifasciatus

11cm, 8g Smaller than Marico Sunbird, with a shorter, less deeply curved bill. Male has a narrower purple breast band than Marico Sunbird and a blue (not greenish) rump; female has only faint streaking on the breast and lacks white edges to outer tail. Common along the coastal plain to the east but scarce in the park and perhaps only seasonally present; largely restricted to the low-lying riparian fringes of the Crocodile and Luvuvhu rivers. Given its similarity to the Marico, all sightings in the park should be carefully verified. PURPERBANDSUIKERBEKKIE

SCARLET-CHESTED SUNBIRD
Chalcomitra senegalensis

14cm, 14g Male easily recognised by his scarlet chest; female distinguished from Amethyst and Marico sunbirds by dark, heavily mottled underparts and small, pale eyebrow that only starts above the eye. Resident but generally rather scarce, occurring most commonly in the far south – it is common, for example, in Pretoriuskop and Lower Sabie rest camps, especially in spring when coral trees are in flower, and one can find the brightly coloured males noisily and vigorously defending their chosen tree from incursions by other males. ROOIBORSSUIKERBEKKIE

AMETHYST SUNBIRD
Chalcomitra amethystina

15cm, 15g Male easily mistaken at a glance for male Scarlet-chested Sunbird but chest is black, not scarlet; female paler below and has a more prominent pale eyebrow than female Scarlet-chested Sunbird. A common species along the escarpment to the west; scarce across most of the park and only regular in the southwestern corner. It is known to move widely elsewhere in its range – perhaps most occurrences in the park are seasonal or irregular visitors coming east from the escarpment. SWARTSUIKERBEKKIE

Marico Sunbird ♂

Marico Sunbird ♀

Purple-banded Sunbird ♂

Purple-banded Sunbird ♀

Scarlet-chested Sunbird ♂

Scarlet-chested Sunbird ♀

Amethyst Sunbird ♂

Amethyst Sunbird ♀

WHITE-BELLIED SUNBIRD
Cinnyris talatala

11cm, 8g A small sunbird, told from other species by its whitish underparts; ad male has a plain white belly; female has off-white underparts. A common, widespread resident present in all wooded areas, especially thornveld; probably the most numerous sunbird in the park. Not a conspicuous bird except around aloes and other nectar sources where this and other sunbird species noisily and actively jostle to feed. During the breeding season the male spends much time singing lustily from the top branches of trees while the female attends the nest, which is always slung in a low shrub close to the ground. WITPENSSUIKERBEKKIE

COLLARED SUNBIRD
Hedydipna collaris

11cm, 8g A small, short-billed sunbird with yellow underparts; male has an iridescent green throat and upper breast; female has entire underparts yellow. Easily confused with Plain-backed Sunbird *Anthreptes reichenowi*, which occurs along the coastal plain of Mozambique and may perhaps venture into the low-lying eastern fringes of the park from time to time. A forest-living species, occurring commonly along the escarpment to the west; generally scarce and localised in the park, where it is largely restricted to riparian vegetation such as that fringing the Luvuvhu, Sabie and Crocodile rivers; common in Skukuza rest camp. Its presence is often given away by the male's excited, tripping little song. KORTBEKSUIKERBEKKIE

WHITE-EYES

Although common and familiar garden birds across much of southern Africa, white-eyes are only rather infrequently encountered in the park. They are small, greenish-yellow warbler-like birds distinguished by a broad white eye-ring after which they are named. They feed on fruit, small insects and nectar, often stealing nectar from long-tubed flowers by using their short, sharp bills to pierce flower bases and thus avoid being dusted with pollen. When not breeding they are gregarious, living in small parties which often join other insectivorous species. Groups maintain contact with soft call-notes as they move through the leafy canopies of trees and creepers in pursuit of food.

CAPE WHITE-EYE
Zosterops virens

12cm, 11g Distinguished from the very similar African Yellow White-eye by the greenish wash to its upperparts, chest and belly. Given its abundance elsewhere, it is a surprisingly uncommon bird in the park, found mostly in riparian woodland along the larger rivers. Typically found in small parties that move cohesively through the leafy canopies of trees in search of food, maintaining contact with soft chittering calls; also frequently joins mixed-species flocks of insectivorous birds, especially in winter. Its loud, sweet, warbling song is usually heard at dawn, mainly in summer. KAAPSE GLASOGIE

AFRICAN YELLOW WHITE-EYE
Zosterops senegalensis

12cm, 10g A bright yellow white-eye, distinguished from Cape White-eye by the absence of a greenish wash on the underparts and yellower upperparts. A common species in tropical Africa, its range extends south along the Mozambique coastal plain, narrowly entering the extreme north of the park where it is confined to the dense riparian woodlands associated with the floodplains of the Limpopo and Luvuvhu rivers. Typically white-eye in behaviour and feeding habits, and care must be taken in this area in distinguishing it from the Cape White-eye. GEELGLASOGIE

White-bellied Sunbird ♂

White-bellied Sunbird ♀

Collared Sunbird ♂

Collared Sunbird ♀

Cape White-eye

African Yellow White-eye

BUFFALO WEAVERS, SPARROWS AND PETRONIAS

Buffalo weavers are the giants of the weaver-bishop-widowbird family, the Ploceidae, while sparrows and petronias belong to a closely related family, the Passeridae. Both families are confined to Old World, with most species found in sub-Saharan Africa. They are primarily granivorous in their diet and are mostly gregarious in disposition. The four species below are all common residents in the park, although the House Sparrow is essentially confined to the vicinity of rest camps and staff accommodation.

RED-BILLED BUFFALO WEAVER
Bubalornis niger

23cm, ♂84g, ♀71g More like a starling than a weaver in appearance and demeanour. Male is readily identified by his blackish plumage and red bill and legs; female is smaller and duller with a rather scaly appearance. A common resident, occurring wherever tall trees (especially baobabs) or structures (powerlines, windmills) provide nest sites and areas of bare ground for foraging. Its name stems from a perceived (but erroneous) association with buffalo, which has brought it membership of the park's 'little five' species. Gregarious; its large communal stick nests built in the outer branches of trees are a conspicuous feature in the landscape. During summer, when the birds breed, these colonies are a hive of activity, whereas in winter buffalo weavers are nomadic and become far less conspicuous. BUFFELWEWER

SOUTHERN GREY-HEADED SPARROW
Passer diffusus

15cm, 25g The most commonly seen sparrow in the park. A rather drab bird with a plain grey head and chestnut back and wings, with a sliver of white on the wing coverts. Breeding male has a black bill; female has a dull yellow bill all year. An abundant resident, found throughout in woodland and savanna. Gregarious, except when breeding; for much of the year small flocks are commonly encountered along the roads, foraging on the verges and taking cover in nearby bushes when disturbed. Also frequents rest camps and picnic sites, taking food scraps alongside starlings, House Sparrows and waxbills. Its call is a series of typical sparrow chirps. GRYSKOPMOSSIE

HOUSE SPARROW
Passer domesticus

15cm, 24g Male distinguished from Southern Grey-headed Sparrow by its black throat, mottled back and grey rump; female is paler and duller, but also has a streaked back and a buffy eyebrow. A common but undistinguished resident in most rest camps in the park, nesting in the eaves of buildings and foraging for food scraps on the ground. Introduced to Durban, East London and other port cities in South Africa more than a century ago, this essentially European species has used urban and rural human settlements to extend its range northwards across Africa. HUISMOSSIE

YELLOW-THROATED PETRONIA
Gymnoris superciliaris

16cm, 27g A fairly large, pale grey-brown sparrow; named for a small, bright yellow spot on its throat, although this is seldom visible; its most distinctive features are the broad white stripe eyebrows and two pale bars on the folded wing. A fairly common resident, occurring widely in all the well-wooded areas. Unlike other sparrows, it is mainly arboreal and is frequently seen walking along the larger branches of trees, although it also feeds on the ground. Often joins mixed-species bird parties in winter. Usually encountered in pairs; its presence is often given away by the sparrow-like but more robust two- or three-syllabled 'chip-chip ...' call, uttered from the upper branches of a tree. GEELVLEKMOSSIE

Red-billed Buffalo Weaver ♂

Red-billed Buffalo Weaver ♀

Red-billed Buffalo Weaver nests

Southern Grey-headed Sparrow

House Sparrow ♂

Yellow-throated Petronia

PLOCEUS WEAVERS

Weavers are an Old World family renowned for their intricately woven nests made from shreds of grass, reed or palm leaf, or other plant material. Each species has its own favoured building material, nest design and preferred breeding sites. Most species are polygynous, with males being more brightly coloured when breeding than females; like sunbirds, care is required to identify females and non-breeding males. They are mainly granivorous, and often form large flocks in winter that range widely in search of food. The four yellow-plumaged species here are typical members of this master-builder clan and their handiwork can be seen throughout the park during summer when nesting occurs. They are the main hosts of the Diederik Cuckoo. The ranges of three other yellow-plumaged *Ploceus* weavers just extend into the extreme south of the park (p209).

VILLAGE WEAVER
Ploceus cucullatus

16cm, 40g Male distinguished from other black-faced weavers by large size, spotted back, red eye and all-yellow forehead; female by size, reddish eye and a marked contrast between yellowish head and pale grey underparts. Resident throughout, mostly encountered along the larger rivers. Conspicuous at the large breeding colonies it establishes during summer in tall trees in some rest camps (e.g. Skukuza); easily overlooked when not breeding. Colonies can number hundreds of nests, which are built by multiple males, mostly suspended from the branches of tall trees, but sometimes in reedbeds. BONTRUGWEWER

SOUTHERN MASKED WEAVER
Ploceus velatus

15cm, 37g The most widely encountered of the yellow weavers in the park. Male distinguished from other black-faced weavers by lightly streaked back, red eye and black forehead; female by brown eye and uniformly pale underparts. A common resident, occurring especially along drainage lines. Breeds colonially, but seldom in multi-male colonies. In most instances a single male builds a series of nests at a site, usually in a tree overhanging water. Successful males may attract two or more females to breed in their nests. SWARTKEELGEELVINK

LESSER MASKED WEAVER
Ploceus intermedius

13cm, 24g Both sexes distinguished from other black-faced weavers by small size, slender bills and white eye; the male's black face extends over the forehead to the centre of the crown. A common, widespread resident; breeds in summer in large, conspicuous multi-male colonies located either in large trees or in reedbeds, and often together with Village Weavers. Unlike other weavers, this species may also build its nests beneath the eaves of thatch-roofed buildings (e.g. in Shingwedzi rest camp). After breeding, it joins nomadic mixed-species flocks of weavers, when it is easily overlooked. KLEINGEELVINK

AFRICAN GOLDEN WEAVER
Ploceus xanthops

17cm, 44g A large, pale-eyed, yellow weaver that lacks a black mask; bill much heavier than Spectacled Weaver (p188) and lacks that species' black lores. Male retains its bright yellow plumage year-round; female only slightly duller than male, with an olive wash on the crown. An uncommon, localised resident, occurs patchily in the southeast and far north, mostly in riparian vegetation along the larger rivers. An unobtrusive breeder; single males build a handful of nests either on branches overhanging water or in reeds, and may attract one or two females. GOUDWEWER

Village Weaver ♂ br   Village Weaver ♀

Southern Masked Weaver ♂ br   Southern Masked Weaver ♀

Lesser Masked Weaver ♂ br   African Golden Weaver ♂ br

WEAVERS AND QUELEAS

These four weavers and queleas demonstrate the diversity in both appearance and breeding habits found in the Ploceidae. Thick-billed Weavers lack yellow plumage and are polygamous, breeding in small colonies. Spectacled Weavers resemble many other *Ploceus* weavers, but are monogamous, solitary breeders that remain in pairs year-round. Red-headed Weavers are also usually monogamous, but can be polygamous, breeding singly or in small colonies. Red-billed Queleas are an iconic savanna species, breeding in vast colonies that can contain more than a million birds.

THICK-BILLED WEAVER *Amblyospiza albifrons*
18cm, ♂51g, ♀41g A heavy-billed weaver; male is deep chocolate brown with white frons and wing panels conspicuous in flight; female smaller than male with a yellowish bill and white underparts heavily streaked dark brown. A scarce resident largely restricted to the south, especially close to the extensive reedbeds along the Sabie and Crocodile rivers. Lives in small groups year-round, feeding in trees and on the ground, taking a range of seeds from trees and grasses. Roosts and breeds colonially in reedbeds; weaves a large, neat and distinctively shaped nest from finely shredded reeds, which is attached to multiple reeds and has a side-opening entrance. DIKBEKWEWER

SPECTACLED WEAVER *Ploceus ocularis*
16cm, 30g A bright yellow weaver with pale eyes, black lores and a chestnut wash on the head, which is less intense in the female, who also lacks a black throat. A mainly forest-living weaver that is a widespread but scarce resident, found mostly in riparian woodlands. Insectivorous and monogamous; pairs mainly forage in well-foliaged trees. Easily overlooked; best located by its call, a descending series of short whistles *'dee-dee-dee-dee-dee …'*. In summer pairs build a finely woven nest with a long entrance tunnel that extends for 50cm or more. BRILWEWER

RED-HEADED WEAVER *Anaplectes rubriceps*
15cm, 23g A distinctive weaver with a plain grey back, white belly and slender, pink bill; breeding male has a striking red head, breast and nape; yellow in non-breeding male and female. Resident in well-wooded areas throughout the park, but scarce in the south; most commonly encountered north of the Olifants River, especially where large baobabs provide favoured nesting sites. Insectivorous and solitary for much of the year; often joins mixed-species bird parties in winter. Breeds in summer, mostly in single-male colonies, building a distinctive shaggy-looking nest with a long entrance tunnel from long shreds of bark. ROOIKOPWEWER

RED-BILLED QUELEA *Quelea quelea*
12cm, 20g Non-breeding male and female are dull brown birds, distinguished from winter-plumage bishops by their red bill; breeding male has a black (rarely white) facial mask fringed by a pink or buff crown and neck. A nomadic, wide-ranging savanna species, often referred to as 'Africa's feathered locust' on account of its vast numbers and propensity to destroy crops. In wet years, millions move into the park to feed on grass seeds on the rich basaltic soils in the east. They rapidly initiate breeding, forming colonies that extend over 10–50 hectares, filling every thorn tree with dozens of nests. Colonies attract many raptors, storks and other carnivores, but the short (30-day) breeding cycle is completed before predators can greatly impact their numbers. Small numbers of queleas usually remain in savanna habitats year-round. ROOIBEKKWELEA

Thick-billed Weaver ♂ displaying

Thick-billed Weaver ♀

Spectacled Weaver ♂

Red-billed Quelea ♂

Red-headed Weaver ♂ br

Red-billed Quelea br ♀

BISHOPS AND WIDOWBIRDS

Members of the weaver family, bishops and widowbirds are classic representatives of polygynous mating systems. Males build nests and display extravagantly to attract and mate with multiple partners, while females undertake all parental care. Sexual selection has resulted in males acquiring striking breeding plumage, which is shown to maximum effect during aerial displays. In contrast to this visual splendour, their vocalisations are limited to dry, buzzy calls. Males moult into drab, female-like eclipse plumages in winter, but retain some wing feathers that aid in their identification. They join weavers, sparrows and other granivores in nomadic mixed-species flocks. Two other bishops are occasional visitors to the park (p209).

SOUTHERN RED BISHOP
Euplectes orix

13cm, ♂25g, ♀21g Breeding male easily identified by its red-and-black plumage and short tail; non-breeding male and female nondescript with a yellowish eye-stripe and less heavily streaked upperparts than other widowbirds. An uncommon, localised species, occurring widely but sparsely along the larger rivers in marshy areas where reeds and bulrushes provide nesting sites. Breeds in colonies; males establish display territories within a few metres of the colony, from where they call excitedly and display by raising their crimson crown and rump feathers and engaging in short, buzzy flights. After breeding the birds gather into large, nomadic flocks, often mixing with other seed-eating birds. Often parasitised by Diederik Cuckoo. ROOIVINK

FAN-TAILED WIDOWBIRD
Euplectes axillaris

15cm, ♂29g, ♀22g Breeding male easily identified by its mainly black plumage, red shoulders and rufous-edged wing coverts; non-breeding male retains red shoulder and blackish flight feathers. Female has reddish-brown wing coverts and broad, buffy eye-stripe. A localised resident, restricted to the southern half of the park where it occurs patchily in seasonally damp areas of rank grass, mostly on the basaltic soils in the east. When breeding, males defend widely dispersed territories, perching conspicuously on prominent plant stems from which they periodically make short display flights with slow, exaggerated wing-beats. KORTSTERTFLAP

WHITE-WINGED WIDOWBIRD
Euplectes albonotatus

15cm, ♂23g, ♀17g Breeding male easily identified by its mainly black plumage, yellow shoulders and white-edged wing coverts; non-breeding male retains yellow shoulder and white primary coverts. Female has whitish belly and yellow edges to wing coverts. A common, gregarious resident throughout, in areas of rank grass. Breeding males are conspicuous as they fly back and forth with exaggerated wing-beats over breeding territories, frequently in pursuit of neighbouring males and arriving females. In winter the birds form nomadic flocks, often numbering hundreds of individuals, which are easily identified from the males' yellow and white wing panels. WITVLERKFLAP

RED-COLLARED WIDOWBIRD
Euplectes ardens

12cm (plus 20cm tail in br ♂), ♂23g, ♀20g Breeding male easily identified by its black plumage, red collar and very long tail; non-breeding male retains blackish flight feathers. Female has broad, buffy eye-stripe; best identified by small size and association with males. A localised resident, largely restricted to the far south, especially in hilly, higher-rainfall areas in the southwest. Breeding birds favour areas of rank grass, often on open hillsides where territorial males perch prominently and make periodic flights after other males or arriving females, their long black tails streaming behind them. ROOIKEELFLAP

Southern Red Bishop ♂ br   Southern Red Bishop ♀   Fan-tailed Widowbird ♂ br

White-winged Widowbird ♂ br

Red-collared Widowbird ♀   Red-collared Widowbird ♂ br

191

PYTILIAS AND FIREFINCHES

Together with the waxbills and mannikins, these small seed-eating birds are often collectively referred to as estrildid finches (family Estrildidae). Pytilias are easily identified, but firefinches are all rather uniformly reddish-brown in colour. They have similar behaviours and habits, but their high-pitched trilling call-notes are useful in detecting the different species. All species do most of their foraging on the ground, subsisting primarily on grass seeds, but seldom venture far from cover, retreating to the shelter of bushes or trees when threatened. The nests of all four here are parasitised by host-specific indigobirds and whydahs (Viduidae).

GREEN-WINGED PYTILIA
Pytilia melba

13cm,15g A strikingly coloured finch; male has red frons, throat and rump; female lacks red facial markings and greenish breast band. Common, widespread resident in all types of woodland, but especially thornveld. Occurs in pairs year-round, typically encountered feeding on the ground, flying into the lower branches of a tree or bush when disturbed and usually pausing there, allowing one to scrutinise them at leisure. Parasitised by Long-tailed Paradise Whydah; where the one occurs the other is likely to be found in the same area. GEWONE MELBA. **Orange-winged Pytilia** *P. afra* (Oranjevlerkmelba) has orange (not green) wing panels and mottled (not barred) underparts; rare visitor recently recorded near Pafuri, Letaba, Phabeni, Berg-en-Dal and Shingwedzi.

RED-BILLED FIREFINCH
Lagonosticta senegala

10cm, 9g The most commonly encountered firefinch in the park. A tiny species, distinguished from Jameson's and African firefinches by its conspicuous yellow eye-ring and pink (not blue) bill and legs. Resident in all wooded areas where bare ground and thickets provide habitat. Occurs in pairs while breeding (late summer); found in family groups or flocks of 20 or more at other times of the year. Like most seedeaters, all firefinches are dependent on water and so bird baths in rest camps are often good places to find them in the heat of the day. Parasitised by Village Indigobird. ROOIBEKVUURVINKIE

JAMESON'S FIREFINCH
Lagonosticta rhodopareia

11cm, 9g Male told from male African Firefinch by its rather uniformly ruddy-coloured head (lacking a grey crown); female paler than male with vent feathers tipped buff, appearing barred. Distinguished from Red-billed Firefinch by its blue bill and legs, and dark vent. A fairly common, widespread resident, favours wooded areas with thickets. Usually encountered in small family groups, which often feed on grassy road verges, flying into cover in nearby undergrowth when disturbed. Parasitised by Purple Indigobird. JAMESONSE VUURVINKIE

AFRICAN FIREFINCH
Lagonosticta rubricata

11cm, 11g Male told from male Jameson's Firefinch by its grey (not ruddy-coloured) crown, ear coverts and nape; female paler, more orange-pink below; easily confused with female Jameson's Firefinch but averages darker. Distinguished from Red-billed Firefinch by its blue bill and legs and dark vent. Occurs commonly along the forested escarpment west of the park, entering the park mainly in the higher-rainfall southeast and northeast. Found in small family groups in areas of dense thicket along drainage lines. Because it is easily misidentified for Jameson's Firefinch, the widespread occurrence of this species in atlas records (see map) may be a consequence of it being mistaken in places for the more common species. Parasitised by Dusky Indigobird. KAAPSE VUURVINKIE

Green-winged Pytilia ♂

Green-winged Pytilia ♀

Red-billed Firefinch ♂

Red-billed Firefinch ♀

Jameson's Firefinch ♂

African Firefinch ♂

WAXBILLS

These small, colourful, easily identified seed-eating birds, together with the pytilias, firefinches and mannikins, form part of the mainly African and Australian Estrildidae family. Males are more colourful than females. They are typically gregarious, living in groups or flocks when not breeding. All have simple, melodious, high-pitched songs that often prove useful for detecting and identifying them. Their diet of mainly seeds contains very little water, so estrildids typically drink daily; bird baths in rest camps are often good places to see at least some species. Most estrildids breed in late summer when grass seed production peaks. Two other waxbills are occasionally recorded from the park (p209).

BLUE WAXBILL
Uraeginthus angolensis

12cm, 10g The only small, pale blue and brown bird in the park; female and juv have less extensive blue underparts. A very common, widespread resident, likely to occur wherever there are trees or shrubs, although numbers decrease in drought years. Common in rest camps and often encountered in flocks in heavily trampled areas where it forages on the ground, flying up to take cover in the nearest shrubbery when disturbed. Often consorts with firefinches and other waxbill species while foraging. Breeding pairs often select a nest site on a branch alongside an active wasp nest, presumably to reduce the risk of predation. Song is a high-pitched *'swee-swee-eer'*; contact call is a dry *'trrt'* or *'trrt-trrt-trrt'*. GEWONE BLOUSYSIE

VIOLET-EARED WAXBILL
Uraeginthus granatinus

14cm, 12g A fairly large, long-tailed waxbill, readily identified by its striking violet face, electric blue rump and frons and red bill. Male's body is warm chestnut; female is pale buff below. Primarily a species of dry savanna, it is a scarce resident throughout the wooded areas of the park. Mostly encountered in pairs. Forages mainly on the ground, often in association with Blue Waxbills. Its lilting *'tiu-woo-weee'* call often gives away its presence; contact call is dry *'swee'* or *'swit-it-it-it'*. Parasitised by Shaft-tailed Whydah. KONINGBLOUSYSIE

COMMON WAXBILL
Estrilda astrild

12cm, 8g Easily identified by its red bill and facial mask and pink-washed belly, but these features may be missed if seen at a distance, when it could be dismissed as a featureless 'little brown job'. Juv has black bill. Resident; occurs widely but sparsely throughout, favouring open areas with rank grass, forbs or sedges, typically over moist or seasonally flooded ground. Gregarious when not breeding; occurs in flocks of 10–100 birds, usually seen in flight as they move from one feeding spot to another, uttering their dry *'zrt zrt'* contact call; once settled they frustratingly keep out of view. Song is a whirring *'zwee-zwee-zwerrrrr'*. Primary host of Pin-tailed Whydah; post-breeding flocks often include juvenile whydahs. ROOIBEKSYSIE

ORANGE-BREASTED WAXBILL
Amandava subflava

9cm, 7g A tiny waxbill with orange-red eyebrow and rump and mostly yellow underparts, washed orange on the central belly; female duller than male; juv plain brown with a rufous rump and dark bill. Uncommon and perhaps not resident in the park, only occurring in years of high rainfall. When present, found mainly in seasonally flooded areas of rank grass on basaltic soils in the east. Easily overlooked as it forages low down on sedge and grass seed-heads. Usually in family groups or small flocks. Call is a very high-pitched *'zink zink zink'*. ROOIASSIE

Blue Waxbill ♂

Blue Waxbill ♀

Violet-eared Waxbill ♂

Violet-eared Waxbill ♀

Common Waxbill

Orange-breasted Waxbill ♂

MANNIKINS AND FINCHES

These estrildid finches represent three distinctive genera: mannikins (*Lonchura*), the Quailfinch, the sole member of the monotypic genus (*Ortygospiza*), and the two closely related *Amadina* finches. Like all estrildids, these are seed-eating birds. None is particularly common in the park, and none is a brood host to the parasitic whydahs and indigobirds. In addition to these species, two twinspots are occasionally recorded from the park (p209).

BRONZE MANNIKIN
Lonchura cucullata

9cm, 10g Adults alike, with blackish head and throat and two-tone bill; plain brown juv can be mistaken for juv indigobirds or whydahs. Its name refers to the adults' iridescent bronze wing coverts. An abundant resident along the escarpment to the west; generally scarce and localised within the park, occurring most predictably in the southeast or in riparian habitat along the larger rivers. Gregarious; lives year-round in flocks of 10–30 birds. Usually encountered when disturbed while foraging on the ground and the group flies to the safety of a tree. Frequently visits bird baths in some rest camps. GEWONE FRET. **Red-backed Mannikin** *L. nigriceps* (Rooirugfret) is larger and more richly coloured, with a black head and breast, rich chestnut back and whitish bill; scarce visitor, recorded from riparian thickets along the Luvuvhu, Sabie and Crocodile rivers.

AFRICAN QUAILFINCH
Ortygospiza atricollis

10cm, 12g A tiny, ground-living finch of open grassland. Seen at close range, male has a striking face pattern and barred flanks; female duller. Occurs throughout the park in areas of uninterrupted open grassland, such as those found on the basaltic soils in the east. Seldom seen except in flight when it gives its distinctive squeaky '*djink*' or '*djink-jink*' calls. Most often encountered as they commute to and from drinking sites, and the best chances of seeing them on the ground are usually as they drink at the edges of dams, pans and even road puddles. GEWONE KWARTELVINKIE

CUT-THROAT FINCH
Amadina fasciata

12cm, 18g A fairly large, heavily barred finch with white wing spots; male has diagnostic red 'cut throat', which is absent in female. Female best told from female Red-headed Finch by its barred (not plain) head. Occasionally hybridises with Red-headed Finch. A fairly common resident in open tree savanna, mainly in the drier northern half of the park; often encountered close to waterholes. Ringing has shown that these birds are nomadic, moving about widely. Gregarious year-round; flocks often mix with other seed-eating species. Breeds in late summer in disused weaver nests. BANDKEELVINK

RED-HEADED FINCH
Amadina erythrocephala

14cm, 23g A large, chunky, pale-coloured finch; male could possibly be mistaken for Red-headed Weaver (p188), but heavy white (not pink) bill, scalloped underparts and white wing spots are diagnostic; female has pale grey-brown head and barred underparts. Hybrids with Cut-throat Finch have underparts intermediate between the two species, red throat collars and some red on the forehead. An arid-country species that makes periodic drought-driven incursions into the park, at times remaining for some years before disappearing until the next incursion. Occurs in heavily grazed, open grassy areas, which are more open than those favoured by Cut-throat Finches. ROOIKOPVINK

Bronze Mannikin

African Quailfinch ♂

Cut-throat Finch ♂

Cut-throat Finch ♀

Red-headed Finch ♂

Red-headed Finch ♀

WHYDAHS AND INDIGOBIRDS

Whydahs and indigobirds belong to an exclusively Afrotropical family, the Viduidae. The Latin name *Vidua*, meaning 'widowed' or 'bereaved', alludes to the black plumage of indigobirds. All species are obligate brood parasites, with complex co-evolutionary relationships with their host species. They are polygamous and strongly sexually dimorphic, with males acquiring striking seasonal breeding plumages. In summer males establish call/display territories. Females are promiscuous, and after mating they seek out host nests where they lay one or more eggs. However, unlike cuckoos and honeyguides, the parasites can be raised with one or more host chicks. The Viduidae family is further described on p200.

LONG-TAILED PARADISE WHYDAH
Vidua paradisaea

15cm (plus 20cm tail in br ♂), 20g Breeding male unmistakable; transitional male has speckled head and buff collar. Female has very boldly striped head, but best identified by association with male; juv plain brown above and pale grey below. A common resident throughout in all wooded habitats, especially in thornveld, which is favoured by its host, the Green-winged Pytilia. Males conspicuous in summer when they establish call sites on tree tops and defend them from other males; also perform elaborate aerial displays, singing as they fly above the tree canopy with jerky wing-beats, their long tails trailing beneath them. GEWONE PARADYSVINK

SHAFT-TAILED WHYDAH
Vidua regia

11cm (plus 18cm tail in br ♂), 15g Breeding male unmistakable; female has a red bill and a rather plain head compared to other female whydahs; juv mottled brown above and buff below. An arid-savanna species, associated with its host, the Violet-eared Waxbill, so mainly restricted to open woodland in the drier northern half of the park. Rather scarce and localised, probably a year-round resident. In summer males defend areas with seeded grasses from other males, singing at intervals from one or more tree tops to attract females. PYLSTERTROOIBEKKIE

PIN-TAILED WHYDAH
Vidua macroura

13cm (plus 18cm tail in br ♂), 16g Breeding male unmistakable; female has striped head and black bill when breeding, dull red when not breeding; non-breeding male has red bill; juv plain brown above and off-white below. A fairly common resident but, like other *Viduas*, easily overlooked when male not in breeding plumage. Frequents open, shrubby habitats, especially near water or patches of favoured grasses in seed where males establish display areas from which they chase away other birds; they attract females by singing and perform a bouncing flight when females appear. Their primary host is the Common Waxbill; also parasitises other estrildids on occasion. KONINGROOIBEKKIE

DUSKY INDIGOBIRD
Vidua funerea

13cm, 15g The least common of the indigobirds in the park. Male and female distinguished from respective sexes of other indigobirds by the combination of a white bill and pink feet. A forest-edge species, common in the escarpment region west of the park where its host, the African Firefinch, is found; localised in the park, occurring mostly along wooded drainage lines. Care is needed when distinguishing this species from the Purple Indigobird (p200). Parasitises African Firefinch. GEWONE BLOUVINKIE

Long-tailed Paradise Whydah ♂ br

Shaft-tailed Whydah ♂ br

Dusky Indigobird ♂

Pin-tailed Whydah ♂ br

Dusky Indigobird ♀

INDIGOBIRDS (cont.)

The eggs and chicks of *Vidua* finches match those of their hosts, with the chicks having evolved the same begging calls and mouth spot patterns as their hosts. Indigobird nestlings learn their host's calls, and males include phrases of their host's calls in their own to attract females, ensuring each species remains specific to its host. Hybrids (e.g. indigobirds with central tail streamers) indicate mismatches. The Cuckoo Finch, occasionally found in the park, is another member of this family (p209).

VILLAGE INDIGOBIRD *Vidua chalybeata*

11cm, 13g The most prevalent indigobird in the park, as its host, the Red-billed Firefinch, is the most common firefinch. Male and female distinguished from respective sexes of other indigobirds by the combination of pink bill and pink feet. Like its host, the Village Indigobird occurs in most woodland habitats where there are areas of bare ground and thickets. Assumed to be resident, but seldom recorded in winter when males are not in breeding plumage. STAALBLOUVINKIE

PURPLE INDIGOBIRD *Vidua purpurascens*

11cm, 13g Male and female distinguished from respective sexes of other indigobirds by the combination of white bill and white feet; care is needed when distinguishing this species from Dusky Indigobird (p198) as feet can appear pale pink. Occurs widely throughout where there are thickets, especially along drainage lines. Fairly common; probably resident, but status in winter unclear. Parasitises Jameson's Firefinch. WITPOOTBLOUVINKIE

CANARIES AND SEEDEATERS

Canaries are small granivorous birds known for their melodious songs and colourful (typically yellow) plumage in the canaries, or often more drab plumage in seedeaters. Two other canaries occasionally visit the park (p209).

YELLOW-FRONTED CANARY *Crithagra mozambica*

12cm, 12g A small canary with yellow underparts and eyebrows, prominent moustachial streaks and white tail tips; female paler than male. A common resident, especially in broad-leafed woodlands on granitic and sandy soils. Gregarious except when breeding; groups often mix with other seed-eating species. Mainly feeds on seeds of grasses and forbs. Often detected by its sweet, lilting song uttered from a tree top. GEELOOGKANARIE. **Brimstone Canary** *C. sulphurata* (Dikbekkanarie) is larger, with heavier bill and olive (not grey) crown; lacks white tail tips; occasionally visits the southwest of the park.

LEMON-BREASTED CANARY *Crithagra citrinipectus*

12cm, 11g Resembles a dull Yellow-fronted Canary, but has a grey back, white belly, white wingbars and short, white eye-stripe in front of its eye; female has pale buff wash on breast. Could be mistaken for a female *Vidua*, bishop or widowbird but yellow rump and white tail tips are diagnostic. Confined to the coastal plain of northern KwaZulu-Natal and southern Mozambique; extends inland along larger rivers and is fairly common among thickets of *Hyphaene* palms on the floodplain of the Limpopo and Luvuvhu rivers. Occurs in pairs or small groups; sometimes mixes with Yellow-fronted Canaries. GEELBORSKANARIE

Village Indigobird ♂

Village Indigobird ♀

Purple Indigobird ♂

Purple Indigobird ♀

Yellow-fronted Canary

Yellow-fronted Canary

Lemon-breasted Canary ♂

Lemon-breasted Canary ♀

STREAKY-HEADED SEEDEATER — *Crithagra gularis*

15cm, 20g A drab canary with a diagnostic long, white eyebrow contrasting with the plain grey face and grizzled crown; Yellow-throated Petronia (p184) also has a white eyebrow but cheeks are paler and it has white wingbars. Resident; occurs widely but sparsely throughout wooded areas; most common in broad-leafed woodlands in the high-rainfall southwest. Found in pairs year-round. Unobtrusive and easily overlooked; its presence is usually given away by its melodious, canary-type song. Forages on leaf and flower buds in trees and shrubs as well as on the ground. STREEPKOPKANARIE

BUNTINGS

Buntings are sparrow-sized, seed-eating birds that form part of the New World sparrows (Emberizidae). All three species have striped heads, hence their Afrikaans name *Streepkoppie* (meaning 'striped head'), although the pattern is very subtle in the Lark-like Bunting. They mainly feed on the ground, although Golden-breasted Buntings fly up into trees when alarmed. Males sing from elevated perches on the ground, shrubs or trees.

GOLDEN-BREASTED BUNTING — *Emberiza flaviventris*

16cm, 19g The boldly striped head, white wingbars and bright yellow underparts are diagnostic. Male has brighter underparts than female, with breast suffused orange-yellow. A common resident, found in all woodlands throughout the park. Usually found in pairs, occasionally in small parties. Forages on the ground and is typically seen when birds are disturbed while feeding on the roadside, showing distinctive white outer-tail feathers as they fly off to take cover in a nearby tree. Song is a cheerful, loud series of whistles '*weechee, weechee, weechee*'. ROOIRUGSTREEPKOPPIE

CINNAMON-BREASTED BUNTING — *Emberiza tahapisi*

15cm, 15g The boldly striped head and chestnut underparts are diagnostic; female has less distinct head markings and paler underparts than male. Mainly summer visitors in the park, from November to April, although a few individuals remain year-round. Ringing indicates that they regularly undertake long-distance movements. Occurs throughout the park, mostly on rocky or stony ground, especially in rock-strewn hillsides. The male's short, repetitive refrain is given from exposed branches on top of trees and bushes. KLIPSTREEPKOPPIE

LARK-LIKE BUNTING — *Emberiza impetuani*

15cm, 15g A nondescript, sparrow-like bird with rufous wing coverts, faint buff eye- and moustachial stripes and buffy underparts. Mainly a bird of the arid western parts of southern Africa, it periodically irrupts eastward, perhaps linked to drought in its core range. In such years (e.g. 2003, 2007 and 2013), it can be fairly common in the park, occurring widely in the drier central and northern areas. Drinks regularly and is often found in small groups in the vicinity of windmills and dams. Song is a repetitive '*chiriri chippy-chirpy-chirip*'. VAALSTREEPKOPPIE

Streaky-headed Seedeater

Streaky-headed Seedeater

Golden-breasted Bunting ♂

Golden-breasted Bunting ♀

Cinnamon-breasted Bunting ♂

Lark-like Bunting

Tropical Shearwater *Puffinus bailloni*
One recovered near Shingwedzi, in Sep 1988, following a tropical cyclone in the Mozambique Channel. Identity remains somewhat controversial, but almost certainly this species. TROPIESE KLEINPYLSTORMVOËL

Great White Pelican *Pelecanus onocrotalus*
Single birds or small groups occasionally recorded on dams and pans. WITPELIKAAN

Pink-backed Pelican *Pelecanus rufescens*
Single birds or small groups occasionally recorded on dams and pans, most recently on Sunset Dam in Nov 2013. KLEINPELIKAAN

Slaty Egret *Egretta vinaceigula*
One recent record of a bird at Crocodile Bridge. ROOIKEELREIER

Rufous-bellied Heron *Ardeola rufiventris*
Occasional summer visitor, mainly in wet years; most recent record at Komatidraai in Nov 2010. ROOIPENSREIER

Lesser Flamingo *Phoeniconaias minor*
Single birds or small groups occasionally recorded on dams and pans, most recently at Crocodile Bridge in Aug–Sep 2013. KLEINFLAMINK

Greater Flamingo *Phoenicopterus roseus*
Single birds or small groups occasionally recorded on dams and pans, most recently three birds near Satara in June 2013. GROOTFLAMINK

Cape Teal *Anas capensis*
Single birds occasionally recorded on dams and pans, most recently one east of Mopani rest camp in Apr 2013. TEELEEND

Blue-billed Teal *Anas hottentota*
Single birds occasionally recorded on dams and pans, most recently on Mazithi Dam near Tshokwane in Dec 2009. GEVLEKTE EEND

Cape Shoveler *Anas smithii*
Single birds occasionally recorded on dams and pans, most recently one on Transport Dam near Pretoriuskop in Nov 2009. KAAPSE SLOPEEND

Maccoa Duck *Oxyura maccoa*
Single birds recorded twice on dams in the 1970s; no subsequent records. BLOUBEKEEND

Egyptian Vulture *Neophron percnopterus*
Single birds occasionally recorded, mostly in the south, most recently a single bird at Nhlanganzwani Dam in May 2013. EGIPTIESE AASVOËL

Rüppell's Vulture *Gyps rueppelli*
One observed just west of the park at Thornybush Nature Reserve in Jan 2012, but not yet recorded in the park. RÜPPELLAASVOËL

Palm-nut Vulture *Gypohierax angolensis*
Single birds, mostly imms, occasionally recorded in the park, most recently at Pafuri in Oct 2013. WITAASVOËL

Ayres's Hawk Eagle *Hieraaetus ayresii*
Single birds, mostly imms, occasionally recorded in the park Jan–May, most recently at Pafuri in Feb 2011. KLEINJAGAREND

Long-crested Eagle *Lophaetus occipitalis*
Single birds occasionally recorded in the park, most recently in 2010. LANGKUIFAREND

Greater Flamingo

African Marsh Harrier

Ovambo Sparrowhawk *Accipiter ovampensis*
Rare resident; infrequently recorded throughout the park in areas of tall woodland, most recently at Pafuri in Nov 2012. OVAMBOSPERWER

African Marsh Harrier *Circus ranivorus*
One recent record from reedbeds along the Crocodile River. AFRIKAANSE VLEIVALK

African Hobby *Falco cuvierii*
Occasionally recorded in the northern half of the park, most recently at Pafuri in Feb 2012. AFRIKAANSE BOOMVALK

Eleonora's Falcon *Falco eleonorae*
Palearctic vagrant; one record of a bird photographed near Berg-en-Dal in Feb 2005. ELEONORAVALK

Red-necked Falcon *Falco chicquera*
One record of a bird photographed near Satara in Apr 2015. ROOINEKVALK

Red-footed Falcon *Falco vespertinus*
Palearctic migrant; single birds occasionally recorded together with Amur Falcons, with two recent records from the south. WESTELIKE ROOIPOOTVALK

Greater Kestrel *Falco rupicoloides*
Rare visitor from farther west; no recent records. GROOTROOIVALK

Red-necked Spurfowl *Pternistis afer*
Occasionally reported in the southwest, most recently from Nwatimhiri waterhole in June 2011. ROOIKEELFISANT

Blue Crane *Anthropoides paradiseus*
Two birds present at intervals on Shithlave Dam near Pretoriuskop between Feb 2009 and Dec 2010. BLOUKRAANVOËL

Grey Crowned Crane *Balearica regulorum*
Twice recorded – 8 birds near Letaba in Feb 1972 and one bird at Nsemani Pan near Satara in May 2013. MAHEM

African Rail *Rallus caerulescens*
Occasionally recorded in seasonal wetlands along the margins of the Limpopo, Sabie and Crocodile rivers. GROOTRIETHAAN

Corn Crake *Crex crex*
Palearctic migrant; occasional birds recorded, most in the southwest, in years of above-average rainfall, most recently at Jocks Safari Lodge in Mar 2011. KWARTELKONING

Baillon's Crake *Porzana pusilla*
Occasionally recorded in the park in years of above-average rainfall, most recently on Engelhard Dam in July 2009. KLEINRIETHAAN

Striped Crake *Aenigmatolimnas marginalis*
From tropical Africa; occasionally visits seasonally flooded marshy areas in the park, most recently (breeding) at Renosterkoppies in Feb–Mar 2011. GESTREEPTE RIETHAAN

Red-chested Flufftail *Sarothrura rufa*
Occasionally recorded in the park in years of above-average rainfall, most recently near Pretoriuskop in Mar 2009. ROOIBORSVLEIKUIKEN

Buff-spotted Flufftail *Sarothrura elegans*
One undated record of a bird at the Skukuza nursery. GEVLEKTE VLEIKUIKEN

African Swamphen
Porphyrio madagascariensis
Occasionally recorded in seasonal wetlands in years of above-average rainfall, most recently at Leeupan in Jan 2000. GROOTKONINGRIETHAAN

Common Ringed Plover *Charadrius hiaticula*
Palearctic migrant; single birds occasionally recorded on pans and dams throughout the park. RINGNEKSTRANDKIEWIET

Chestnut-banded Plover *Charadrius pallidus*
Single birds very occasionally recorded on pans and dams in the park, most recently on Makwadzi Pan, Pafuri area, in Nov 2010. ROOIBANDSTRANDKIEWIET

Grey-headed Gull

Caspian Plover *Charadrius asiaticus*
Palearctic migrant; single birds or groups occasionally recorded in open bare areas around dams, most recently east of Mopani rest camp in Dec 2012. ASIATIESE STRANDKIEWIET

Black-winged Lapwing
Vanellus melanopterus
A single record from Skukuza in Jan 1997. Easily mistaken for Senegal Lapwing and careful verification of future records is needed. GROOTSWARTVLERKKIEWIET

Long-toed Lapwing *Vanellus crassirostris*
One record of a single bird photographed on the Crocodile River in Aug 2015. WITVLERKKIEWIET

Ruddy Turnstone *Arenaria interpres*
Palearctic migrant; single birds occasionally recorded on pans and dams in the park, the most recent being one at Kanniedood Dam in Oct 2013. STEENLOPER

Pectoral Sandpiper *Calidris melanotos*
Holarctic vagrant; single birds occasionally recorded on pans and dams in the park, the most recent being from Makwadzi Pan in the far north in Dec 2014. GEELPOOTSTRANDLOPER

Sanderling *Calidris alba*
Palearctic migrant; occasionally recorded on pans and dams in the south of the park, the most recent being three birds at Pioneer Dam in Feb 2003. DRIETOONSTRANDLOPER

Black-tailed Godwit *Limosa limosa*
Palearctic migrant; one record of a single bird on the Sabie River below Lower Sabie rest camp in Oct 2010. SWARTSTERTGRIET

Common Whimbrel *Numenius phaeopus*
Palearctic migrant; single birds occasionally recorded on pans and dams in the park, the most recent being one at Engelhard Dam in Nov 2012. KLEINWULP

Great Snipe *Gallinago media*
One record of a solitary bird at Sweni River in Dec 2014. DUBBELSNIP

Red Phalarope *Phalaropus fulicarius*
Palearctic migrant; single birds recorded twice in the park, most recently photographed at Boyela waterhole near Shingwedzi in Jan 2009. GRYSFRAIINGPOOT

Red-necked Phalarope *Phalaropus lobatus*
Palearctic migrant; one record of a single bird on Nkaya Pan near Satara in Nov 2005. ROOIHALSFRAIINGPOOT

Grey-headed Gull
Chroicocephalus cirrocephalus
Single birds occasionally recorded on large dams throughout the park. GRYSKOPMEEU

Caspian Tern *Sterna caspia*
One record of a single bird on Lake Panic in 2007. REUSESTERRETJIE

Sooty Tern *Onychoprion fuscatus*
Occasional birds have been found exhausted in the park following tropical cyclones in the Mozambique Channel, the most recent being one in Feb 2000, which was rehabilitated and released. ROETSTERRETJIE

African Skimmer *Rhynchops flavirostris*
One recent record of a bird on a pan on the Limpopo floodplain. WATERPLOEËR

Rock Dove *Columba livia*
Single birds occasionally recorded in the park – all these so far have worn colour rings, indicating that they are off-course racing pigeons rather than feral Rock Doves. TUINDUIF

African Olive Pigeon *Columba arquatrix*
One recent record from near Pretoriuskop. GEELBEKBOSDUIF

Rose-ringed Parakeet *Psittacula krameri*
Escapee; a single bird recorded at Shimuwini rest camp in Aug 2009. RINGNEKPARKIET

Madagascar Cuckoo *Cuculus rochii*
A male recorded in successive years
between 2008 and 2013 near Byamithi,
calling from Oct–Dec. MADAGASKARKOEKOEK

Barred Long-tailed Cuckoo
Cercococcyx montanus
One record of a single bird in riparian
woodland on the Luvuvhu River in
Jan 2001. LANGSTERTKOEKOEK

African Emerald Cuckoo
Chrysococcyx cupreus
Strays from the Drakensberg escarpment
occasionally recorded in riparian woodlands
in the southwest of the park and along the
Luvuvhu River. MOOIMEISIE

White-throated Bee-eater *Merops albicollis*
Rare vagrant from East Africa; single
birds or small groups recorded very
occasionally in summer, from Nov–Feb, with
records scattered throughout the park.
WITKEELBYVRETER

Red-throated Wryneck *Jynx ruficollis*
Occasionally recorded in the southwestern
corner of the park. DRAAIHALS

Grey Cuckooshrike *Coracina caesia*
Strays from the Drakensberg escarpment;
occasionally recorded in winter in
riparian woodlands, most recently a bird
photographed in the Skukuza nursery in
Sep 2012. BLOUKATAKOEROE

Cape Crow *Corvus capensis*
Occasional birds wander into the western
fringes of the park; no recent records.
SWARTKRAAI

House Crow *Corvus splendens*
One record of a single bird in Satara rest camp
in Feb 1988, perhaps a stray from Maputo,
Mozambique, the nearest population. An
invasive species from Asia; records should be
reported to park personnel. HUISKRAAI

White-necked Raven *Corvus albicollis*
One record of a bird in Skukuza rest camp
in Aug 1991. WITHALSKRAAI

Capped Wheatear *Oenanthe pileata*
Single birds occasionally recorded
from central and northern areas.
HOËVELDSKAAPWAGTER

Cape Robin-Chat *Cossypha caffra*
Strays from the Drakensberg escarpment
occasionally recorded in winter in riparian
woodlands, most recently in 2010. GEWONE
JANFREDERIK

White-starred Robin *Pogonocichla stellata*
Strays from Drakensberg escarpment
occasionally recorded during Jul–Oct in
riparian woodlands (Skukuza, Pretoriuskop,
Letaba, Malelane), most recently a bird
photographed in the Skukuza nursery in
Sep 2012. WITKOLJANFREDERIK

Kalahari Scrub Robin *Cercotrichas paena*
One record of a bird photographed on
the Nyalaland Trail in the far north in Aug
2012. KALAHARIWIPSTERT

Common Whitethroat *Sylvia communis*
Palearctic migrant, mainly to arid savanna;
a few recent records from around Satara.
WITKEELSANGER

Chestnut-vented Tit-babbler
Sylvia subcaerulea
Rare, but perhaps a breeding resident; a
few records from the drier central areas of
the park between Balule and the Limpopo
River. BOSVELDTJERIKTIK

Eurasian Blackcap *Sylvia atricapilla*
Palearctic vagrant; one record from Pafuri
in Oct 2009. SWARTKROONSANGER

Southern Hyliota *Hyliota australis*
Rare, localised resident in broad-
leafed woodlands northwest of Pafuri.
MASHONAHYLIOTA

River Warbler *Locustella fluviatilis*
Scarce Palearctic migrant; a few recent
records from the north, centre and south
of the park, most recently from Skukuza in
Mar 2012. SPRINGKAANSANGER

Basra Reed Warbler *Acrocephalus griseldis*
Rare Palearctic migrant; one record from
Pafuri in Feb 1993. Possibly overlooked.
BASRARIETSANGER

Sedge Warbler *Acrocephalus schoenobaenus*
Palearctic migrant; occasionally recorded
in summer, most recently from Shingwedzi,
Pretoriuskop and the Limpopo floodplain.
EUROPESE VLEISANGER

Dark-capped Yellow Warbler *Iduna natalensis*
Strays from Drakensberg escarpment occasionally recorded from the margins of the Crocodile, Sabie and Letaba rivers. GEELSANGER

Broad-tailed Warbler *Schoenicola brevirostris*
Occasionally present along southwestern edge of the park in wet summers, with males singing near Pretoriuskop in Mar–Apr 2009. BREËSTERTSANGER

Cape Grassbird *Sphenoeacus afer*
One recent record from southwestern edge of park near Pretoriuskop, probably straying from the Drakensberg escarpment where it is a common resident. GRASVOËL

Fiscal Flycatcher *Sigelus silens*
Occasional birds recorded in winter in the southern and central areas, most recently at Balule in June 2011. FISKAALVLIEËVANGER

Cape Batis *Batis capensis*
Strays from Drakensberg escarpment occasionally recorded in the winter months in the south, most recently at Berg-en-Dal and Pretoriuskop in Sep 2007. KAAPSE BOSBONTROKKIE

Fairy Flycatcher *Stenostira scita*
Occasional birds recorded in winter in the southwest, most recently at Pretoriuskop in Aug 2007. FEEVLIEËVANGER

Blue-mantled Crested Flycatcher *Trochocercus cyanomelas*
Strays from the Drakensberg escarpment occasionally recorded in the southwest of the park, most recently at Pretoriuskop in Sep 2007. BLOUKUIFVLIEËVANGER

Long-billed Pipit

Mountain Wagtail *Motacilla clara*
Strays from the Drakensberg escarpment occasionally recorded along the Crocodile and Sabie rivers. BERGKWIKKIE

Western Yellow Wagtail *Motacilla flava*
Palearctic migrant; occasional birds recorded around dams in summer, most recently near Komatipoort in Nov 2011 and Pafuri in Dec 2011. GEELKWIKKIE

Grey Wagtail *Motacilla cinerea*
Palearctic vagrant; one record of a bird at Boulders rest camp in Feb 2011. GRYSKWIKKIE

Long-billed Pipit *Anthus similis*
A few recent records from the Letaba area. NICHOLSONKOESTER

Golden Pipit *Tmetothylacus tenellus*
Vagrant from East Africa; eight records, mostly from drier central areas of the park, most recently a bird photographed at Byamiti weir in Feb 2012. GOUDKOESTER

Crimson-breasted Shrike *Laniarius atrococcineus*
A few recent records from the Limpopo–Luvuvhu floodplains and from along the Satara–Orpen road. ROOIBOSLAKSMAN

Olive Bushshrike *Chlorophoneus olivaceus*
A few recent records from Punda Maria area and from the Crocodile and Limpopo rivers, probably occasional winter visitors from forests along the Drakensberg escarpment west of the park. OLYFBOSLAKSMAN

Gurney's Sugarbird *Promerops gurneyi*
One record of a male at Berg-en-Dal rest camp in southern section of the park in Sep 2009. ROOIBORSSUIKERVOËL

Olive Sunbird *Cyanomitra olivacea*
A common resident in the Barberton mountainland fringing the southern border of the park, occasionally visiting the park here along the Crocodile River. OLYFSUIKERBEKKIE

Variable Sunbird *Cinnyris venustus*
Occasionally reported from the Pafuri area in the far north of the park, most recently in Oct 2011. Is easily mistaken for

Collared Sunbird or male White-bellied
Sunbird in transitional plumage and
future records need careful verification.
GEELPENSSUIKERBEKKIE

White-browed Sparrow-Weaver
Plocepasser mahali
A few recent records from Tshokwane north
to the floodplain of the Luvuvhu River.
KORINGVOËL

Cape Sparrow *Passer melanurus*
A few recent records from the dry central
area, from Shawu Dam south to Satara,
where nesting was recorded in Dec 2010.
GEWONE MOSSIE

Scaly-feathered Finch
Sporopipes squamifrons
A few recent records from the Limpopo
valley in the far north of the park.
BAARDMANNETJIE

Cape Weaver *Ploceus capensis*
Common along Drakensberg escarpment
west of the park with one recent record
from Pretoriuskop area. KAAPSE WEWER

Yellow Weaver *Ploceus subaureus*
Rare, localised resident; a small population
occurs along the Crocodile River around
Crocodile Bridge, breeding here alongside
Southern Brown-throated Weaver.
GEELWEWER

Southern Brown-throated Weaver
Ploceus xanthopterus
Rare, localised resident; a small population
occurs along the Crocodile River around
Crocodile Bridge. BRUINKEELWEWER

Yellow-crowned Bishop *Euplectes afer*
Rare visitor; erratically present in summers
of above-average rainfall when it may
occur anywhere in the park. GOUDGEELVINK

Yellow Bishop *Euplectes capensis*
Recently recorded in Punda Maria area.
KAAPSE FLAP

Cape Weaver

Green Twinspot *Mandingoa nitidula*
Recent records from Punda Maria area and
Skukuza (pair with two fledged young in
Oct 2010). GROENKOLPENSIE

Pink-throated Twinspot
Hypargos margaritatus
Rare resident; restricted to Nwambiya sand-
forest in the far north. Historical records
of Red-throated Twinspot almost certainly
refer to this species. ROOSKEELKOLPENSIE

Grey Waxbill *Estrilda perreini*
One recent record of a bird photographed
at Lake Panic in Aug 2009. GRYSSYSIE

Swee Waxbill *Coccopygia melanotis*
A few recent records from Punda Maria and
near Skukuza. SUIDELIKE SWIE

Cuckoo Finch *Anomalospiza imberbis*
Rare visitor, present from Oct–Feb; recent
records are mostly from the southwestern
corner of the park. KOEKOEKVINK

Black-throated Canary *Crithagra atrogularis*
One recent record from Letaba area.
BERGKANARIE

Cape Canary *Serinus canicollis*
One recent record from Manungu Loop,
Pretoriuskop area, in Oct 2010. KAAPSE
KANARIE

UNSUBSTANTIATED RECORDS

Eurasian Bittern
Botaurus stellaris
GROOTRIETREIER

Southern Banded Snake Eagle
Circaetus fasciolatus
DUBBELBANDSLANGAREND

Western Marsh Harrier
Circus aeruginosus
EUROPESE VLEIVALK

Black-rumped Buttonquail
Turnix nanus
SWARTRUGKWARTELTJIE

Common Quail
Coturnix coturnix
AFRIKAANSE KWARTEL

Grey Plover
Pluvialis squatarola
GRYSSTRANDKIEWIET

Common Redshank
Tringa totanus
ROOIPOOTRUITER

Dunlin
Calidris alpina
BONTSTRANDLOPER

Burchell's Courser
Cursorius rufus
BLOUKOPDRAWWERTJIE

Parasitic Jaeger
Stercorarius parasiticus
ARKTIESE ROOFMEEU

Lesser Black-backed Gull
Larus fuscus
KLEINSWARTRUGMEEU

European Turtle Dove
Streptopelia turtur
EUROPESE TORTELDUIF

Blue-spotted Wood Dove
Turtur afer
BLOUVLEKDUIFIE

Lemon Dove
Columba larvata
KANEELDUIFIE

African Pitta
Pitta angolensis
ANGOLAPITTA

Northern Wheatear
Oenanthe oenanthe
EUROPESE SKAAPWAGTER

Yellow-streaked Greenbul
Phyllastrephus flavostriatus
GEELSTREEPBOSKRUIPER

Common Redstart
Phoenicurus phoenicurus
EUROPESE ROOISTERT

Mountain Wheatear
Oenanthe monticola
BERGWAGTER

Cloud Cisticola
Cisticola textrix
GEVLEKTE KLOPKLOPPIE

Wing-snapping Cisticola
Cisticola ayresii
KLEINSTE KLOPKLOPPIE

Black-chested Prinia
Prinia flavicans
SWARTBANDLANGSTERTJIE

Black-fronted Bushshrike
Chlorophoneus nigrifrons
SWARTOOGBOSLAKSMAN

Miombo Blue-eared Starling
Lamprotornis elisabeth
KLEIN-BLOUOORGLANSSPREEU

READING LIST

Chittenden, H. & Whyte, I. 2008. *Roberts bird guide: Kruger National Park and adjacent lowveld.* Cape Town: John Voelcker Bird Book Fund.

Hilton-Barber, B. & Arthur, L. 2008. *Guide to best birding in Kruger.* Cape Town: Prime Origins.

Hockey P.A.R., Dean, W.R.J. & Ryan, P.G. 2005. *Roberts birds of southern Africa.* Cape Town: John Voelcker Bird Book Fund.

Joubert, S. 2007. *The Kruger National Park. A history.* Vols 1–3. Johannesburg: High Branching.

Kemp, A.C. 1974. *The distribution and status of birds of the Kruger National Park.* Koedoe monograph No. 2. Pretoria: National Parks Board of Trustees.

GLOSSARY

Arboreal Tree dwelling

Cere A fleshy covering at the base of the upper mandible in some birds (e.g. raptors, parrots, pigeons)

Colonial Associating in close proximity while roosting or nesting

Crepuscular Active at dawn and dusk

Cryptic Well camouflaged

Dimorphic Species that show two distinct morphotypes (in plumage, size or both), usually linked to sexual differences

Diurnal Active during daylight hours

Eclipse plumage Dull plumage attained by some male birds during a transitional moult after the breeding season, before they acquire brighter plumage (e.g. some ducks, sunbirds, bishops)

Feral Describes species that have escaped from captivity and now live in the wild

Flight feathers The longest feathers on the wings and tail

Fulvous Reddish-yellow or tawny

Gape The angle of the jaw where the upper and lower mandibles meet; characterised by fleshy, yellow flanges in chicks and recently fledged juveniles of many bird species

Immature A bird that has undergone its first moult from juvenile plumage but has not attained adult plumage

Irruption A rapid expansion of a species' normal range

Juvenile The first fully feathered plumage of a young bird

Melanistic Describes a dark morph of a particular species, the colour resulting from high levels of the pigment melanin; in southern Africa, most frequently encountered among raptors, especially hawks

Migrant A species that undertakes (often) long-distance flights between its breeding and non-breeding areas

Morph A colour variant within a species; the colour variation may or may not be linked to sub-specific status

Moult The replacement of old, worn feathers with new ones

Nocturnal Active at night

Overwintering A bird that remains in the subregion instead of migrating to its breeding grounds

Palearctic North Africa, Europe, Asia north of the Himalayas, and southern China

Passerine A member of the largest order of birds (Passeriformes), comprising mostly small, perching songbirds, but also some larger species such as crows and ravens

Race A geographical population of a species; a subspecies

Range A bird's distribution

Raptor A bird of prey

Resident A species not prone to migration, remaining in the same area year-round

Speculum A panel of distinctive colour on a bird's wing, most often applied to ducks

Supercilium A stripe above the eye of a bird

Territory The area a bird establishes and then defends against others for breeding, feeding, or both

Vagrant Rare visitor to the region that has wandered outside its normal range

INDEX TO SCIENTIFIC NAMES

INDEX TO AFRIKAANS NAMES

INDEX TO COMMON NAMES

KRUGER NATIONAL PARK

KRUGER VISITOR SITES

1 Pafuri Picnic Site
2 Crooks' Corner
3 Dzundzwini Lookout
4 Babalala Picnic Site
5 Kanniedood Hide
6 Tshanga Lookout
7 Nyawutsi Hide
8 Shibavantsengele Lookout
9 Pioneer Hide
10 Stapelkop Dam
11 Mooiplaas Picnic Site
12 Makhadzi Picnic Site
13 Mingerhout Dam & Lookout
14 Engelhard Lookout
15 Matambeni Hide
16 Sable Hide
17 Masorini Picnic Site
18 Olifants Lookout
19 Ratelpan Hide
20 Timbavati Picnic Site
21 Sweni Hide
22 N'wanetsi Dam & Picnic Site
23 Muzandzeni Picnic Site
24 Mondzweni Lookout
25 Nhlanguleni Picnic Site
26 Tshokwane Picnic Site
27 Orpen Dam
28 Shilolweni Dam
29 Lake Panic Hide
30 Nkuhlu Picnic Site
31 Mlondozi Dam & Picnic Site
32 Matekenyane Lookout
33 Stevenson-Hamilton Memorial
34 Transport Dam
35 Ntandanyathi Hide
36 Nhlanganzwane Dam
37 Afsaal Picnic Site
38 Renosterpan
39 Gardenia Hide

MAP KEY

——— Main park road
——— Minor park road
■ Town/main camp
▪ Small camp
· Park gate

0 ▭▭▭▭▭ 50km

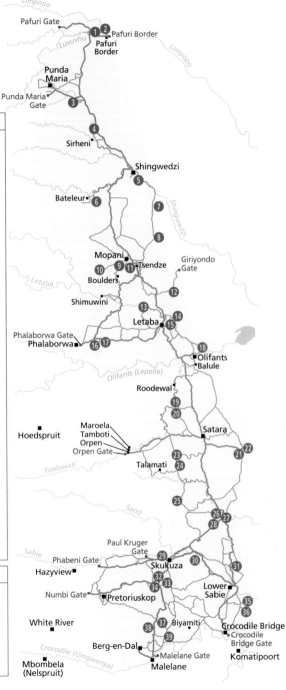